——THE NEW——
ILLUSTRATED
DICTIONARY
—OF—
TROUT
FLIES

THE NEW ILLUSTRATED DICTIONARY OF
OF
TROUT FLIES

JOHN ROBERTS

London
GEORGE ALLEN & UNWIN
Boston   Wellington   Sydney

**George Allen & Unwin (Publishers) Ltd,
40 Museum Street, London WC1A 1LU, UK**

George Allen & Unwin (Publishers) Ltd,
Park Lane, Hemel Hempstead, Herts HP2 4TE, UK

Allen & Unwin Inc.,
8 Winchester Place, Winchester, Mass 01890, USA

George Allen & Unwin Australia Pty Ltd,
8 Napier Street, North Sydney, NSW 2060, Australia

George Allen & Unwin with the Port Nicholson Press,
PO Box 11-838 Wellington, New Zealand

First published in 1986

British Library Cataloguing in Publication Data

Roberts, John, *1953–*
 New illustrated dictionary of trout flies.
 1. Flies, Artificial   2. Salmon-fishing
 3. Trout fishing
 I. Title
 799.1'755   SH451

 ISBN 0–04–799035–X

Set in 10 on 11 point Palatino by Nene Phototypesetters Ltd
and printed in Great Britain by
Anchor Brendon Ltd, Tiptree

Contents

Foreword

FINDLATER'S DRY FLY SHERRY is delighted to be associated with the production of this new dictionary of fishing flies.

DRY FLY sherry has been associated with fly fishing since the 1930s; an association that has continued to this day. The DRY FLY name originated from a chance remark from a fellow sherry shipper who commented that Findlater's new medium dry amontillado sherry was as 'light on the palate as a fishing fly on the brook'; thence the new sherry was christened DRY FLY.

Today DRY FLY's association with fishing continues on a world wide basis, being the official sponsor in 1985 of the Federation of Fly Fishers in the USA as well as being associated with fishing activities from New Zealand to Scotland.

DRY FLY – the best sherry in fifty years.

For my friends David Howden, Richard I'Anson,
Nick Bradley and David Burnett

Introduction

In compiling this book I have concerned myself with patterns of trout and grayling flies that are in use to a greater or lesser extent in the United Kingdom. A few of these patterns have been introduced only recently, and the extent of their success has yet to be judged. Others have been in use for a century or more; they have survived that most critical of tests, time, and have proved reliable takers of trout.

I have researched more than a hundred fly-fishing books and have had correspondence with fly-fishers as far afield as Devon and the Orkney Islands, on the Continent and in the United States. Scores of different dressings have been devised to represent some of the natural flies; I provisionally listed more than fifty Mayfly dressings and, emphasising the recent boom in stillwater fly-fishing, more than twenty corixa patterns. I have little doubt that far more trout-fly patterns exist than there are trout-fishers, for all of us have developed our own patterns with which, from time to time, we catch fish.

But the line had to be drawn as to which flies should be included in this list, and I therefore sought to limit it to the proven and reliable patterns in contemporary use for brown trout, rainbow trout and grayling. My aim: to produce a modern reference work that is more comprehensive than any other, and to include flies for both stillwater and river fishermen, covering the widest possible range – natural flies and their imitations, general, traditional and fancy patterns, and lures.

I include illustrations of artificials tied by their creators, so giving an accurate picture of what the tyers' intentions were in devising each pattern. Not only are these illustrations an invaluable guide to the tying of each dressing, but they are a unique collection of modern patterns from some of our most inventive and thoughtful fly-tyers.

I have credited the reader with a certain amount of fly-tying knowledge, but if you are a beginner, you should learn the basics from a more specialised book, although I do detail in the glossary the materials and styles used. The methods are straightforward and only in particular circumstances do I elaborate on them.

No one angler will need all the patterns described, and the cynics will say just that. Indeed, no hospital patient needs all the drugs in the pharmacy, nor does the concert violinist have to perform all the classics, but they are there to be drawn on if need be.

Our trout flies are works of art, craft and science, the culmination of centuries of angling theory and practice, and an inheritance to be used, enjoyed and developed further.

John Roberts
1985

Acknowledgements

Just as fly-dressers draw upon all that has gone before, so, inevitably, do angling writers. Izaak Walton was not the first to do this, nor shall I be the last. I owe a great debt to all those fly-fishing writers, past and present, whose patterns I have included within these pages. The authors to whom I have referred are listed in the bibliography. Credit must go to them, too.

However, I have not simply compiled a list of previously-published flies selected for their present relevance, but I have carefully drawn upon the help of a number of contemporary fly-creators and fly-dressers for their comments on their own well-known and widely-used patterns. I am indebited to all those listed below who have provided examples of their flies for the illustrations. Some responded beyond all expectation and offered advice on the best method of fishing the pattern, or gave background information as to how and why a fly was developed. I am pleased to acknowledge the help of:

Geoffrey Bucknall	Bob Carnill
Bob Church	Brian Clarke
Roger Fogg	Gordon Fraser
John Goddard	Brian Harris
Stan Headley	Preben Torp Jacobsen
Chris Kendall	Peter Lapsley
Sid Knight	Peter Mackenzie-Philps
Gordon Mackie	Steve Parton
Donald Overfield	Alan Pearson
Neil Patterson	Freddie Rice
S. D. (Taff) Price	Pat Russell
Reg Righyni	Dave Tait
Tom Saville	Conrad Voss Bark
Peter Thomas	Richard Walker
Tony Waites	Harry Whitmore
Barrie Welham	Lee Wulff

The Royal Entomological Society, the Freshwater Biological Association and Professor H. B. N. Hynes of University of Waterloo, Canada have all generously allowed me to reproduce line drawings of aquatic insects in this book.

I am grateful, too, to my good friend and fishing companion, Nick Bradley, who, with me, tied the remainder of the flies for illustration. My final thanks go to David Burnett, who encouraged me in my task, to Merlin Unwin for expressing faith in the earliest draft of this book, and to Roy Eaton who edited my final manuscript. Les Shipsides has produced some superb photographs of the flies and I am also grateful to him.

Reader's Note

The natural and artificial flies listed in this book have been arranged for the most part in alphabetical sequence. The exception to this rule is when there is an overriding logic in listing flies of a particular species, family or series together rather than in disparate, unrelated positions throughout the book. In such instances flies have been listed in the order of nymph, dun and spinner. If you have any difficulty in finding a particular fly you should refer to the index on page 218.

NEW ILLUSTRATED DICTIONARY
OF
TROUT FLIES

ACE OF SPADES Plate 7

This matuka-style lure was devised by Dave Collyer. It is an excellent pattern that has received much praise. It is best fished deep during the early part of the season and retrieved slowly with pauses. The brown version is known as the BROWN BOMBER (*see page 27*).

Hook: Longshank 6–10
Tying silk: Black
Body: Black chenille
Rib: Oval silver tinsel
Beard hackle: Guinea-fowl fibres
Wing: Two hackles dyed black and tied back-to-back with the rounded tip extending beyond the hook. The underside fibres are stripped so that the feather quill rests on the body. The rib is taken through the wing fibres. For fuller details of the winging style, see in the section headed MATUKAS (*see page 107*).
Overwing: Dark bronze mallard or goat-hair dyed ginger

ADAMS Plate 23

In 1932, a North American, Ray Bergman, wrote a book, *Trout*, which was to become a standard work on trout-fishing on that continent. Not only could Bergman fish and write well, but he also knew what made a good trout fly. This dry fly is one of Bergman's creations which is still extensively used in his homeland and has found its way into English fly-boxes. It is a useful general pattern and a passable Iron Blue copy.

Hook: 14–16
Tying silk: Grey
Tail: Grizzle hackle fibres
Body: Blue-grey dubbed wool or fur
Wings: Two grizzle hackles tied upright
Hackle: Red grizzle cock

AIRY-FAIRY Plate 18

This is a pattern passed on to me by Orkney fisherman, Stan Headley, who ties it as a variation of his own Worm Fly. It works well on difficult bright days, and as a bob fly in windy conditions. It is also a good representation of fish-fry and has a reputation for catching better-than-average fish. Blue mountain hare's ear fur is difficult to obtain unless you know a gamekeeper on a grouse-moor. It is greyer than brown hare's ear and a good substitute is rabbit's ear fur, although the fibres are shorter.

Hook: Longshank 10–12
Tying silk: Black
Tail: Three fibres of yellow golden-pheasant rump feather
Abdomen: Lightly-dubbed blue mountain hare's ear fur (white phase)
Rib: Oval silver tinsel
Mid-hackle: Greyish honey-dun hen tied between the abdomen and thorax
Thorax: As for the abdomen, but more heavily dubbed
Rib: Fine silver wire
Hackle: Two greyish honey-dun hen hackles slightly longer-fibred than the mid-hackle

ALDER (*Sialis lutaria, S. fuliginosa*)

These are two common species which can be considered together. The adults are commonest during May and June on rivers and stillwaters. The head and legs are nearly black, and the wings are hard, shiny and roof-shaped, like those of a sedge. The wings lack the hairs of the sedge; otherwise the two species are at first glance similar.

The eggs are laid on overhanging plants and the newly-hatched larvae fall into the water to live in the mud for some months before pupation. The larvae are about 25 mm (1 inch) long and are dark brown. They are carnivorous and move about the lake- or river-bed in search of smaller fauna, even caddis larvae, to eat. Brian Clarke aptly called the alder larva the Ghengis Khan of the aquarium world, so be warned if you intend to keep a few at home for observation. The larvae crawl ashore and burrow in the damp margins to pupate, and the adults emerge after a few days.

The imitation is best fished as a sub-surface pattern on lakes, but on rivers both the sunken and floating imitations are effective. That expert entomologist fly-fisher, David Jacques, was at pains to point out in his book, *The Development of Modern Stillwater Fishing*, that 'during the alder season *and only then*, it is one of the fly-fisher's best flies.'

ALDER LARVA (C. F. Walker)

Hook: Longshank 10
Tail: Ginger hackle-point
Body: Tapered mixed brown and ginger seal's fur

Rib: Gold tinsel
Gills: Sandy hen hackle
Thorax and head: Hare's ear dubbing
Hackle: Brown partridge

ALDER LARVA (Bob Carnill)   Plate 11

Bob Carnill comments: 'I have been fishing this pattern since the late 1960s or early 1970s. It's a good all-purpose "bottom-crawler" pattern, but it really comes into its own during late April. It is usually fished from the bank on a floating line and a long leader. The retrieve should be either figure-of-eight or short, slow draws. The marginal areas are the most productive'.

Hook: Extra long-shank 10

Tying silk: Waxed brown Gossamer
Tail: Bunch of medium-brown cock hackle fibres or one biot quill dyed light brown
Underbody: Lead wire
Body and thorax: Dark chestnut seal's fur
Gills and legs: A small pale ginger hackle tied in by its tip at the tail-end of the abdomen, laid over the back, and secured by its stem at the head-end of the abdomen before the thorax is formed.
Rib: Oval gold tinsel

ALDER LARVA

Hook: Standard or longshank 10
Tying silk: Brown
Body: Copper-wire underbody with dubbed mixed brown and ginger seal's fur over

Hackle: Palmered cream cock hackle with the fibres trimmed on the top and under-sides to about 3 mm
Head: Hare's fur

ADULT ALDER (Charles Kingsley)

This pattern is based on an older one by Alfred Ronalds. G. E. M. Skues spoke highly of it and caught 60 trout in two days on it, most of them over 1 lb.

Hook: 10–12
Body: Peacock herl dyed magenta
Wing: Brown speckled hen
Hackle: Black cock

HEREFORDSHIRE ALDER   Plate 23

This is a popular Welsh Border fly which has proved itself on waters much further afield.

Hook: 10–14

Tying silk: Yellow
Body: Cock-pheasant centre tail feather-fibres
Hackle: Medium blue-dun cock

OUGHTON ALDER

Richard Walker devised this pattern, naming it after a small Hertfordshire stream. It can be fished wet or dry.

Hook: 10–12
Tying silk: Dark brown
Body: Wild goose secondary feather-fibres dyed claret and wound over a varnished shank of tying silk
Wing: Brown mallard, rolled and tied slanting well back
Hackle: Long-fibred black cock

ALEXANDRA   Plate 1

This is a fry-imitating fly fished on both rivers and stillwaters which, according to Courtney Williams, has been around since about 1860. So successful a pattern was it, that it is reputed to have been banned on some waters. It is best fished in the manner of a small fish, in what has been described as dance-time, i.e. slow, slow, quick, quick, slow. It can also be fished as a tandem lure with a tail on the rear hook only and a hackle and wing on the front hook only.

In the dressing known as the **Jungle Alexandra** swan fibres dyed red are replaced in the wings with jungle-cock feathers or a substitute.

Hook: 10–12
Tail: Red ibis or swan fibres dyed red as a substitute
Body: Flat silver tinsel
Rib: Oval silver tinsel
Hackle: Black hen
Wing: Peacock sword herls, flanked either with swan fibres dyed red

ALL ROUNDER

John Ketley devised this pattern as a general sub-surface fly, and he claims success for it when it is used on a top dropper as a hatching-sedge imitation, or as a small fry-imitator. The dressing can be varied by substituting a hen-pheasant wing when the lighter sedges are about or by using a silver body, which seems to do well on cloudy days. I have used this as a late-evening fly with satisfactory results, fishing it slowly just below the surface.

Hook: 10
Tying silk: Black
Tail: Four honey hackle fibres
Body: Flat gold Mylar with five turns of honey cock hackle
Wing: Rolled heavily-barred teal
Hackle: Honey cock

3

AMBER NYMPH

This is one of the patterns devised by Dr H. A. Bell, a nymph-fisher on the Bristol reservoirs during the 1920s and 30s. Bell is very much the father-figure of stillwater nymph fishing. In an era when winged lures were the norm for lake fishing, he devised a series of flies based upon items he found in trouts' stomachs. He set about copying many of the natural food sources in a lifelike fashion. Most of his patterns were entirely new.

Although this pattern is called a nymph, it is in reality probably a sedge-pupa imitation, and certainly it can be fished as one. It has come to be highly regarded over the past sixty years, and in spite of more accurate and complex sedge imitations being available, it continues to have a popular following.

Hook: 10–12
Body: Amber floss silk
Rib: Black tying silk
Wing: Dark red hackle fibres tied fine and close to the body
Thorax (optional): Dark brown or black wool

A variation of this pattern is given below. Whether this was a variant developed by Bell or whether it evolved much later, I am unable to say.

Tying silk: Yellow
Body: Rear half, amber floss or seal's fur; front half, brown or hot-orange seal's fur
Back: Woodcock wing or speckled-brown turkey feather
Legs: Honey-coloured hackle fibres

The larger sizes are used in the early part of the season. The smaller sizes are tied with the orange thorax and are used mid-season onwards.

The Amber Nymph detailed below is one devised by Derek Bradbury, originally for Grafham Reservoir during the 1971 season. It, too, is a fair sedge-pupa imitation.

Hook: Wide-gape 10
Tying silk: Black
Body: Rear two-thirds, amber seal's fur ribbed with narrow orange Lurex; front one-third, dark brown ostrich herl
Back: Dark brown-speckled turkey feather-fibres
Hackle: Brown partridge, sparsely tied
Legs: One fibre of a golden-pheasant centre tail feather tied on each side of the body. These should be tied rear-facing and twice as long as the body.

AMBER SPINNER

An excellent river pattern that can be fished both as a dry fly and below the surface. It is a fair blue-winged olive copy and an imitation of any of the amber-bodied spinners. I have found it a useful grayling fly. As a wet fly it should be fished upstream, because the spent wings are unsuitable for fishing downstream.

AMBER SPINNER (Thomas Clegg) — Plate 19

Hook: 14
Tying silk: White
Body: Orange DFM floss
Rib: Brown Naples silk
Wing: Six lengths of grey DFM floss, equally divided and tied spent
Hackle: Two cock hackles, dyed light blue-grey

AMBER SPINNER (Roger Fogg) — Plate 28

This variation is, according to its creator, best fished on smooth glides below faster water. It is essentially an early-morning and evening fly for use between late April and July. Roger says it works well during falls of the female spinners of the pale watery, spurwings and olive upright.

Hook: 12–16
Tail: Cree cock hackle fibres
Body: Amber seal's fur
Rib: Amber tying silk or marabou floss

Hackle: Generous turns of a cree cock hackle with the upper and lower fibres trimmed off so that the remaining fibres give the impression of spent wings

ANGORA GRUB

Within the fly-boxes of most lowland stillwater fishermen will be at least one pattern devised by Richard Walker. One of his least well known patterns, yet an effective one and one which is easy to tie, is the Angora Grub. It is a general grub or larva imitation which is effective on rivers and stillwaters at any depth, but it is most successful bumped slowly along the bottom when little surface activity is apparent.

Hook: Longshank 8
Tying silk: Dark brown
Body: Optional underbody of lead strips. Wind or dub angora knitting wool (olive-green, amber or any brown shade) over a varnished shank or underbody; ease out the underside fibres with a dubbing needle.
Rib: Flattened clear nylon monofilament of about 20 lb b/s

The back should be trimmed of surplus hair and varnished with coats of clear varnish.

ANNA (GOLDEN and SILVER) Plate 8

These are two lures devised by Taff Price. They should be fished fast. The dressing of the **Golden Anna** is:

Hook: Longshank 6–8
Tail: Swan fibres dyed yellow
Body: Embossed gold tinsel
Wings: Two lemon hackles tied back-to-back with a badger hackle on either side
Cheeks: Jungle-cock

Beard hackle: Lemon yellow cock

The **Silver Anna** is dressed thus:

Hook: Longshank 6–8
Tail: Swan dyed red
Body: Embossed silver tinsel
Wings: Two lemon hackles tied back-to-back with a cree hackle on either side
Cheeks: Jungle-cock
Beard hackle: Scarlet cock

ANTS (*Hymenoptera*)

Ants are basically terrestrial, but some develop wings at mating time in July and August and appear over water in large numbers. Wingless ants may fall on to the water if a nest is near a river-bank.

The ant body is generally red, black or brown, but on the two occasions on which I have experienced the phenomena of flying ants over a river, I have seen only the black variety. I have not had the need to use an imitation on stillwater, but I have found the black patterns useful in mid-summer on northern rivers.

BLACK or BROWN ANT (John Goddard)

Hook: 14
Tying silk: Black or brown
Body: Two small cylindrical pieces of cork, one at each end of the shank. The cork is split, pushed over the shank, bound on and covered with black or brown tying silk. The intermediate sec-
tion is similarly covered with silk and the whole body varnished.
Wings: Two white cock hackle tips tied spent and angled towards the rear
Hackle: Cock hackle to match the body colour

5

BLACK ANT Plate 26

Hook: 14
Tying silk: Black
Body: Black tying silk is built up to form an abdomen and a thorax with a waist in the middle, and then varnished

Wings: Blue-dun or white cock hackle tips tied spent
Hackle: Black cock wound at either the waist or the shoulder

RED ANT

Hook: 14
Tying silk: Red
Body: Crimson silk with a turn of peacock

herl at the tail
Wing: Medium starling
Hackle: Small dark ginger cock

APHIS

These tiny green terrestrial flies are sometimes blown on to a lake or river surface during June and July. If they become available to the trout in large numbers, they are often eagerly devoured. Even when they are not in evidence, I often find, when river fishing in mid-summer, that a small green dry fly will catch fish. The same pattern can do well in October for grayling, but then it could hardly be taken for an aphis. The pattern I use is a Green Wizard (see page 78) with the red tag replaced by a short tail of blue-dun cock hackle-fibres. Roger Fogg tells me that a green version of his latex pupa (see under SEDGES, page 157) kills well when fish are preoccupied with aphis.

The fly below was devised by Derek Bradbury as an imitation of a floating bunch of aphis. For other suitable imitations see ARROW FLY (page 7), GREEN INSECT (page 76) and GREEN MIDGE (page 117).

Hook: 14–16
Tying silk: Olive
Body: Signal-green DRF floss
Wings: White DRF floss, two strands per wing, two or three pairs tied spent along the body
Hackle: Tiny light-olive hackles tied at each set of wings, with all the fibres trimmed from the underside of the body

APPETISER

Bob Church devised this popular lure in 1972. He says it was the first British lure to use marabou in the dressing. Bob claims that it is, as well as being a general attractor, the best-ever fry lure when fished near the surface. I wouldn't argue with a man of Bob's experience of lure fishing. Any fly that has caught a limit totalling thirty-one pounds has to be worth having in the box. This one is a real fish-catcher.

Hook: Longshank 6
Tying silk: Black

Tail: Mixed dark-green and orange cock hackle fibres and silver mallard breast-feathers
Body: White chenille
Rib: Fine oval silver tinsel
Beard hackle: A mixture of dark-green and orange hackle fibres with silver mallard breast feathers
Wing: A generous spray of white marabou herl overlaid with a bunch of natural grey squirrel hair. Gluing the wing roots increases the life of the fly
Head: Black tying silk

ARROW FLY

This river dry fly sometimes works well when aphis are falling on to the water. It is a good CATERPILLAR (*see page 34*) imitation and a useful grayling fly in its smaller sizes. It was devised by A. Courtney Williams and included in his *Dictionary of Trout Flies*.

Hook: 12–14
Tying silk: Green
Body: Emerald tying silk
Hackle: Palmered white cock

ATOM BOMB

A bucktail lure, the origins of which I have been unable to trace.

Hook: Longshank 6–10
Tying silk: Black
Body: Fine to medium silver Mylar tubing
Wing: Yellow marabou fibres with white bucktail and peacock herl over, extending to the tail
Beard hackle: Natural red-brown cock hackle fibres
Head: Black with a white-and-red-painted eye

AUTUMN DUN or AUGUST DUN (*Ecdyonurus dispar*)
See EPHEMEROPTERA

This species of upwinged dun is found mostly on rivers in South Wales, the West Country and parts of northern England. It prefers rivers with stony beds, but is on occasion found in the margins of big, stony lakes. The nymph is a large, flat, stone-clinging type. The duns are large and appear from June to October, being most prolific in July and August.

The duns and spinners are similar to those of the Late March Brown, the former being so similar that only close examination of the veins of the wings enables certain identification.

The male dun has grey wings with black veins. The abdomen is yellow-olive on the upper side, with dark brown bands on the sides. The legs are long and are dark brown-olive, and the two tails are dark grey. The female dun has light fawn wings with black veins. The abdomen is yellow-olive or pale olive-brown on the upper side. The legs and tail are as in the male.

The female spinner (also known as the great red spinner) has transparent wings with dark brown veins. The abdomen is reddish-brown with a darker underside. The two long tails are dark brown and the legs are olive-brown. The male spinner is of little interest.

In addition to the patterns below, the dun can be imitated with a MARCH BROWN (*see page 104*), and the spinner with a RED SPINNER (*see page 154*) or GREAT RED SPINNER (*see page 75*).

AUGUST DUN NYMPH (Thomas Clegg)

Hook: 12–14
Tying silk: Light green
Tail: Yellow guinea-fowl fibres
Abdomen: Signal-green DRF floss
Rib: Copper wire
Thorax: Blue-dun/yellow-olive grass monkey fur
Wing-case: Squirrel-tail hair
Legs: Thorax fur picked out

AUGUST DUN (Roger Woolley)

Hook: 12–14
Tail: Brown ginger cock hackle-fibres
Body: Brown floss silk or brown quill
Rib: Yellow floss
Wing: Pale mottled hen-pheasant wing
Hackle: Brown ginger cock

AUGUST DUN SPINNER (G. E. M. Skues)

Hook: 16
Tying silk: Hot-orange
Tail: Honey-dun hackle fibres
Body: Orange seal's fur
Hackle: Red cock

AYLOTT'S ORANGE   Plate 14

A useful sedge-pupa imitation devised in the late 1960s by Richard Aylott. It works best when fished in a sink-and-draw style on a floating line. An alternative version has a signal-green fluorescent wool body and is a suitable imitation of the green-bodied sedge pupa.

Hook: 12
Body: Arc-chrome DRF wool
Hackle: Natural red cock
Head: Peacock herl tied in front of the hackle

BABY DEER   Plate 8

A hair version of the Baby Doll. Its buoyancy makes it an excellent lure for fishing close to the surface.

Hook: Longshank 8–12
Tying silk: Black
Body: Dubbed white hare's body fur

tapering at each end. A bunch of white deerhair fibres is tied over the back and tied in at the tail with the fibres extending beyond to form the tail in the shape of a fan
Head: Black tying silk

BABY DOLL   Plate 8

An excellent lure, devised in 1971 by Brian Kench. It has become one of the most successful fly patterns ever created. Bob Church, who did much to publicise the fly, says that the fluorescent white wool is a 'key reason why this lure kills an undue share of trout'. He discards each white pattern after a day's use because it collects dirt and loses some of its fluorescent qualities. No stillwater angler should be without a Baby Doll or one of its variants. It can save the day when fished deep and slow on calm and sunny afternoons.

John Goddard believes that the white Baby Doll may be taken for the pupa of one of the larger species of sedge. On occasions I have caught

trout merely by moving the fly as slowly as a twitch every ten seconds.

Hook: Longshank 6–10
Tying silk: Black
Body, back and tail: White nylon Sirdar baby wool
Head: Black tying silk
The white body has been successfully matched with a back and tail of yellow, orange, red, black, green and brown. Other body colours have been used of fluorescent or ordinary baby wool – lime-green, pink, orange and non-fluorescent black. The black variant is known as the UNDERTAKER (*see page 190*). Other versions have suitable beard hackles added, hot-orange in the case of the white Baby Doll.

Richard Walker described a Baby Doll variant called **Nell Gwynne** after a certain 'doll' who became involved with oranges. The dressing is as for the standard white Baby Doll, but includes a back and tail of orange wool and an orange collar hackle.

LEADED DF DOLL

This is a Richard Walker variant.

Hook: Longshank 6–8
Tying silk: White
Body: Varnished shank covered in fluorescent white wool in a cigar-shape; then three layers of lead-foil are tied on top of the shank and given a final layer of wool, building into a fish-shape.
Beard hackle: Cock dyed crimson or hot-orange and trimmed short
Head: Varnished tying silk
The fly is finished by rubbing the body with fine glasspaper to enhance the fluorescent effect.

SPECIAL BABY DOLL

This is a variant tied by expert lure-fisher, Syd Brock.

Body: Stretched black plastic tape for the rear three-quarters of the shank; front quarter, bright-red wool
Back and tail: Fluorescent green wool

BADGER DEMON   Plate 1

A tandem lure useful for fishing deep on the large reservoirs.

Hooks: Two longshank 6–10
Rear hook
Tail: Red ibis or swan fibres dyed red
Body: Flat silver tinsel
Rib: Silver tinsel

Front hook
Body and rib: As for rear
Wing: Two or four badger cock hackles tied back to back and extending to the tail of the rear hook
Beard hackle: Cock dyed bright red
Head: Varnished black tying silk

BADGER SERIES

These are mostly grayling flies which can be fished wet or dry. They have served me well on the northern streams on which I do most of my grayling fishing. I have found them most successful as floating flies rather than wet. All have the badger hackle in common. See also HI C BADGER (*page 84*).

DOUBLE BADGER (Roger Woolley)   Plate 25

A floating pattern which I have found to be one of the best of the series.

Hook: 14–16
Body: Peacock herl

Hackles: Badger cock at either end of the body. The rear hackle should be slightly smaller than the front hackle

RED BADGER   Plate 25

Hook: 14–16
Body: Red floss silk tipped with silver tinsel
Rib: Silver wire through the hackle

Hackle: Palmered badger cock or hen
The **Green Badger** is as above except that it has a green floss body. The **Blue Badger** has a blue floss body.

BADGER RED TAG (Roger Woolley)

This is a variant of the RED TAG (*see page 154*).

Hook: 14–16
Tag: Red wool or floss
Tip: Silver tinsel
Body: Bronze peacock herl
Hackle: Badger wound at the shoulder, not palmered

SILVER BADGER   Plate 25

Hook: 14–16
Tag: Red wool
Body: Flat silver tinsel
Rib: Oval silver tinsel
Hackle: Palmered badger cock or hen
Head: Red wool tag
The **Gold Badger** has a gold tinsel body and rib

BAILIFF'S STANDBY

A lure devised by D. A. Ody. It is one of a number of lures that can be tied with bead bodies of various colours to give the body varying degrees of translucency.

Hook: Longshank 6–8
Tying silk: Black
Tail: Golden-pheasant tippet fibres
Body: Coloured beads (the holes are cut square and lined with silver)
Wing: Grey squirrel-tail fibres
Throat hackle: Hot-orange
Head: Black varnished with a painted eye

BARNEY GOOGLE

Richard Walker created this phantom midge larva imitation. It is highly spoken of by many lake-fishers.

Hook: 12–14 silvered hook
Body: Stretched clear polythene in narrow strips, tied thin
Hackle: A wisp of speckled grey mallard fibres
Eyes: Two small red beads bound in with figure-of-eight turns of tying silk

BANDED SQUIRREL BUCKTAIL (Taff Price)   Plate 10

Hook: Longshank 8–10
Tying silk: Black
Tail: White squirrel tail with a black band, tie in at the black section
Body: Pale mauve wool or white wool tied fairly bulky
Rib: Flat narrow silver tinsel
Wing: Barred squirrel tail (white tip, black bar, brown root)
Throat hackle: Red and white hackle fibres or white bucktail the length of the body with red bucktail tied as a shorter throat

BARRIE WELHAM NYMPH   Plate 14

Barrie Welham says of this pattern:

'In the early 1960s I was visiting a lot of small, clear, stillwater fisheries where one could visually select the quarry and so avoid undersized fish. A nymph that would fall quickly was sometimes required, but a nymph that would sink slowly, to intercept fish feeding just below the surface, was often more useful.

'Around that time Lieut-Col. (Rags) Locke, of tiger-hunting fame, was one of the most successful rods at the famous Two Lakes water, and although he was not 'selecting' fish in the way I tried to do, he still wanted a slow-sinking nymph. To get this performance, Rags used a plain, brown-wool-bodied nymph that he called the BW, Brown Woolly.

'As the tying was developed, the white wing tuft, which soon got dirty, was changed to a white feather hackle and a tail of DFM floss was added. At first the tail was quite long, but this resulted in a lot of false takes and a high proportion of fish hooked outside the mouth. When the DFM material was reduced and shielded, this no longer occurred.

'In 1965 this simple tying caught me a number of big fish, and in the following year my last 50 brown trout of the season – mid-June to September – averaged 3¼ lb, of which 12 were over 4 lb and two over 5 lb. All but three took the BW which, because of the publicity, was now known as the Barrie Welham.'

It is important in tying this pattern to give the body sufficient bulk to provide buoyancy, and the tinsel must be fine enough not to counteract this. Initially, each nymph was tested in a tall measuring glass to check its sinking performance.

As well as proving a successful fly on stillwater, the BW Nymph has also brought good results on rivers for both trout and grayling. It has also taken at least one salmon.

Hook: 10–12
Tying silk: Black
Tail: Short red and yellow DFM floss
Body: Brown wool
Rib: Fine oval gold tinsel
Breathers: A short tuft of white hackle fibres tied back over the body

BARTON BUG   Plate 24

This is a good pattern to represent hatching medium olives. It is fished with the rear half submerged and the front half of the fly floating, in the way that some of W. H. Lawrie's emerging patterns are fished. It was devised by Roy Darlington for some very selective trout taking emerging duns on the Itchen.

Hook: 12–14
Tying silk: Primrose
Tail: Long fur-fibres from a rabbit's neck
Body: Hare's ear fur dressed thinly with a slight thorax
Rib: Fine gold wire round the abdomen only
Hackle: High-quality short-fibred blue-dun cock

BARRET'S BANE   Plate 27

This is a Welsh Border fly of some repute for trout and grayling, and one which I have used to good effect on its home waters. The dressing came from Cosmo Barret, a tackle-dealer in Presteigne, who tied it with a reverse hackle.

Hook: 12–16
Body: Cock-pheasant centre tail fibres
Hackle: Blue-dun cock

BEACON BEIGE   Plate 23

Peter Deane amended and renamed a pattern originally called the Beige, a West Country olive dun imitation. According to Conrad Voss Bark, the original pattern was tied by a member of the Wills family during a period of leave from the Somme in the First World War. Peter Deane regards it as the best-ever olive dun imitation.

Hook: 14–16
Tail: Plymouth Rock cock hackle-fibres
Body: Well-marked stripped peacock eye quill
Hackle: Plymouth Rock cock with a red Indian game-cock wound through

BEASTIE

Plate 2

Geoffrey Bucknall created this lure. It is fished in steady pulls with pauses, usually on a sinking line. The weighted head and marabou wing ensure an attractive sink-and-draw action.

Hook: Longshank 8–12
Tying silk: Black
Body: Black floss
Rib: Flat silver tinsel
Head: Two layers of lead wire (6 mm, ¼-inch long) wound over the thread and varnished black
Throat hackle: Hot-orange marabou
Wing: Long hot-orange marabou with black marabou over, about twice the hook length

Cheeks: Silver-pheasant hackles either side, the central stalk being parallel to the shank. Jungle-cock over

A white version is in the above style, but with the following materials.

Body: White floss silk
Rib: Silver wire
Head: As above, varnished white
Throat hackle: Fluorescent-magenta marabou
Wing: Fluorescent-magenta marabou with two white marabou plumes over
Cheeks: Grey mallard flank feather to face outwards on either side with long jungle-cock over

BEDHOPPER

Plate 2

Freddie Rice, the creator of this series, comments: 'At Datchet and Grafham the bigger brown trout seemed to be near the reservoir bed, hence a fly that would "hop" the bed, leaving small muddy disturbances, seemed advantageous. The Bedhopper was developed in 1970 for this purpose, the leaded head making the fly nose-dive into the mud, while the intermittent upward lift provided the muddy spurts which proved attractive. This action, combined with a "fishy" shape, and the colour options provided in the dressing, proved immediately successful.

'I've had a number of comments that the Bedhopper is the forerunner of the **Dog Nobbler** (*see page 127*) which employs the same lead head,

chenille body, marabou and action. However, I make no such claim.

'A leader of appropriate strength is always needed for heavy leaded flies, and non-splinter Polaroid glasses, or similar, are a wise precaution.'

Hook: Longshank 6–10
Tying silk: Black
Tail: A spray of marabou fibres
Body: Coloured chenille
Wings: Two wings each of coloured marabou fibres. One wing is tied at the head and the other half-way along the back
Head: Fine lead wire overlaid with coloured chenille

The following suggested colour combinations are from Freddie Rice's book, *Fly-tying Illustrated for Nymphs and Lures*:

Tail	Body	Rear wing	Front wing	Head
White	White	White	Olive	Black
White	Grey	Black	Orange	White
Black	Scarlet	White	White	Black

BEES

Plate 22

Although bee-imitations seemed popular with bygone fly-fishers, it is rarely so today. In high summer there may be an occasional opportunity to

use a floating pattern. The imitation is more popular on the Continent, and it is highly rated for chub. See also WASPS (*page 193*).

Hook: 12	**Wing:** Hen-pheasant or partridge flat
Tying silk: Black	across the back
Body: Banded yellow, brown or black	**Hackle:** Furnace cock
seal's fur, mohair or silk	

BEETLES (*Coleoptera*)

In addition to the range of water beetles (see WATER CRICKET and WATER TIGER, *pages 194 and 195*) there are scores of species of terrestrial beetles, some of which sometimes fall on the surface of rivers and lakes. The permutations of size, colour and shape of these are almost endless, but some of the commoner species can be represented by the patterns below. For centuries the imitation has been fished as a dropper on a wet fly cast; the **Marlow Buzz** and **Coch-y-bondhu** are two of the better-known patterns.

Now, in addition to being fished on a team of flies, a suitable imitation is often fished in the nymph style upstream to individual fish or into likely lies. I know of no better pattern for this style of fishing than Eric's Beetle. On numerous occasions a black beetle pattern has turned a potentially blank period of the day into a fruitful one. On many rivers the mid-afternoon period of a bright sunny summer's day is hardly worth fishing. But under just these conditions a small caterpillar or beetle cast under high banks or overhanging bushes has often caught fish for me when they have moved to nothing else.

See also under COCKCHAFER (*page 41*), COCH-Y-BONDHU (*page 40*), CHOMPER (*page 36*), PALMERS (*page 136*), GREEN BEAST (*page 76*) and POACHER (*page 149*).

BLACK BEETLE (John Veniard)

Hook: 12–14	magpie tail feather-fibres
Body: Bronze peacock herl	**Legs:** Black cock hackle
Wing-case: Black cock tail feather or	

BLACK BEETLE (Roger Fogg)

Hook: 14	**Tip:** Silver tinsel
Tying silk: Black or brown	**Wing-case:** Dampened black Raffene over
Body: An underbody of dark floss with	all the back
black ostrich herl over	**Hackle:** Black cock or hen tied sparsely

ERIC'S BEETLE

A pattern devised by Eric Horsfall Turner, a gentleman who could wield both rod and pen with great skill. This fly is a fantastic killer of trout, particularly on hot summer afternoons when nothing is moving. It is fished on a greased leader and allowed to sink just a few inches below the surface. This is one fly I would not wish to be without.

Hook: 8–12
Tying silk: Black
Body: An underbody of yellow wool with bronze peacock herl tied fat wound over. The yellow wool is exposed as a butt at the rear
Hackle: Two turns of black cock or hen

RED-EYED DERBYSHIRE BEETLE

Courtney Williams suggested that this should be fished as a floating pattern, but I understand that it is usually fished wet. In the summer of 1980 I fished as a guest on a club water on the Nidd in North Yorkshire. During a frustrating period when I caught nothing, another rod fished his way upstream casting this fly under trees and in the river margins. He caught four trout when all other flies were being refused. I was using Eric's Beetle, which I usually rate as second-to-none for just these circumstances. It seemed the red beads made all the difference.

Hook: 12
Body: Bronze peacock herl
Hackle: Long-fibred black cock or hen
Head: Two tiny red beads

SAILOR BEETLE

This natural beetle appears from June to August and has a reddish body and dull-blue wings. This is Taff Price's pattern:

Hook: 12

Tying silk: Black
Body: Brown floss
Wing-case: Dark blue Raffene
Hackle: Black

SOLDIER BEETLE   Plate 23

This is similar to the Sailor Beetle, but has a dull yellow body, orange-red wings with bluish tips, and is about 24 mm long. This is G. E. M. Skues' pattern.

Hook: 14
Tying silk: Hot-orange
Body: Bright red-orange seal's fur
Back: Cock-pheasant breast fibres
Hackle: Red cock sparsely tied

BENCH MARK

A bucktail lure useful in dirty water conditions.

Hook: Longshank 6
Tying silk: White
Tail: Hot-orange calf-tail hair

Body: Fluorescent arc-chrome floss
Rib: Fine embossed silver tinsel
Wing: White calf-tail
Collar hackle: Hot-orange cock, rear-slanting

BIBIO   Plate 18

An excellent early-season lake fly. It is most effective as a top dropper dibbled through the surface when fished from a boat. The hackles should be bushy enough to create a little wake on the water and should not be so soft as to collapse against the body when the fly is being retrieved.

Hook: 10–14
Tying silk: Black
Body: Black seal's fur with a middle section of red seal's fur
Rib: Silver wire through the hackle
Hackle: Palmered black with two turns at the shoulder

BI-VISIBLES

A series of highly-visible floating flies devised for fast water or for use in failing light. They originated in the U.S.A. from the vice of E. R. Hewitt in

1898. Hewitt was later to become a notable angling author with three good books to his credit: *Secrets of the Salmon*, *Telling on the Trout*, and *A Trout and Salmon fisherman for Seventy Five years*. In theory, any floating pattern can be made into a Bi-visible by the addition of a white cock hackle in front of the usual hackle. Some of the patterns tied on considerably larger hooks are used for dapping.

BLACK BI-VISIBLE   Plate 26

Hook: 10–12
Tail: Two small black hackle tips
Body: Palmered black cock
Hackle: White cock at the shoulder

The tail and body can be tied with blue, brown, badger or grizzle hackles to produce appropriately-named alternatives

PINK LADY BI-VISIBLE

Hook: 10–12
Tail: Ginger hackle tips
Body: Flat gold tinsel with a palmered

badger cock hackle
Hackle: Yellow or white cock hackle tied at the shoulder

BLACK-AND-ORANGE MARABOU   Plate 6

This stillwater lure, devised by Taff Price, is highly recommended, particularly for the first three months of the season. It is best fished in a steady retrieve close to the bottom.

Hook: Longshank 8–10

Tail: Orange hackle fibres
Body: Flat gold tinsel
Rib: Oval gold tinsel
Wing: Black marabou
Throat hackle: Orange
Cheeks: Jungle-cock

BLACK-AND-PEACOCK SPIDER

One of the greatest influences on stillwater fly-fishing in the 1950s and 1960s was Tom Ivens, author of *Still Water Fly Fishing* of 1952. This is evident in part from the thousands of reservoir and lake fishers who regularly use Ivens' B&P, which has become one of the best stillwater flies of modern times. It is an excellent general fly, catching fish no matter at what depth it is fished.

Ivens wrote that it was deadly fished slowly just a few inches below the surface when trout are head-and-tailing during the evening rise. It is probably taken for a beetle, or a snail when fished near the surface when

snails are about. It is, despite its simplicity, or perhaps because of it, a truly great fly and worthy of a place on any stillwater leader. Few patterns have caught trout so consistently. Perhaps the best catch I have heard of with the Black and Peacock Spider was one by Bob Church and Peter Dobbs who when fishing at Packington in 1976 managed 27 fish between them weighing 44 lb and all for a morning's work with this one fly.

Hook: 8–12
Body: Bronze peacock herl tied fat and tapering to the rear
Hackle: Long-fibred black hen sparsely tied

BLACK-AND-SILVER BUCKTAIL

A bucktail lure of Taff Price's devising.

Hook: Longshank 4–8
Tail: Swan fibres dyed scarlet

15

Body: Flat silver tinsel
Rib: Oval silver tinsel
Wing: Black bucktail
Head: Black with a painted white eye and black pupil

The **Black-and-white Bucktail** is as for the above dressing except that it uses a wing of black bucktail over white bucktail.

BLACK BEAR'S HAIR LURE   Plate 6

John Goddard has described this pattern, devised by Cliff Hardy, as 'an exceptional lure'. The soft bear-hair makes a very mobile wing and enables the fly to be fished slowly with pauses to give life to the wing. In the early season it should be fished deep; in the summer it does well fished fairly fast just below the surface.

Hook: Longshank 8–12
Tying silk: Black
Body: Black seal's fur
Overbody: A 3 mm (⅛-inch) strip of black bear-hair with the skin extending slightly beyond the shank. This is ribbed with oval silver tinsel through the hair so that the hair fibres appear in matuka style

BLAE AND BLACK   Plate 21

This old Scottish wet imitation for the iron blue is still used on Scottish rivers and streams.

Hook: 14

Body: Water-rat or mole fur
Wing: Hen blackbird or dyed starling
Hackle: Body fur picked out

BLACK CHENILLE

Many stillwater lures have black chenille bodies. This one was created by Bob Church in 1970.

Hook: Longshank 6–8
Tying silk: Black
Tail: Black hackle fibres or hackle tip

Body: Black chenille
Rib: Medium silver tinsel
Beard hackle: Black hackle-fibres
Wings: Four black hackles of equal length extending beyond the hook

BLACK GNAT (*Bibio johannis*)   See DIPTERA

The term black gnat is given to a number of species belonging to the flat-winged *Diptera* Order, but *Bibio johannis* is probably the commonest. The differences between the species are so minimal that they need not bother the angler seeking to imitate them with an artificial fly. The naturals are found on the water only as a result of being blown there or after falling after mating. The mating pattern is useful if swarms of paired gnats are in evidence. The larger sizes of the **Knotted Midge** are then useful. The female has a dark brownish-olive body and brownish legs, and the male has a slimmer body and is nearly black. They appear throughout the trout season, from April until September.

See also USD BLACK GNAT (*page 192*) and FOG BLACK (*page 66*)

BLACK GNAT (Freddie Rice)   Plate 28

The imitation of the mating pair can be tied by omitting the wing and tying-in an additional slightly smaller hackle at the rear of the

body.
Hook: 16
Tying silk: Black
Body: Black silk

Rib (optional): Fine silver wire
Wing: About 12 light blue-dun hackle fibres tied at about 35 degrees over the body

Hackle: Black cock or starling breast feather

BLACK GNAT (Jack Hughes Parry)

A Welsh pattern and a simple one to tie.

Hook: 14–16

Body: Grey floss silk
Hackle: Black hen or cock

BLACK GNAT (C. F. Walker)

This is based on earlier pattern by J. W. Dunne.

Hook: 16
Body: Dark turkey tail fibres with a bronze sheen

Wing: Hackle-fibres dyed bottle-green and wine-red (in a ratio of 2:1). The fibres should be thoroughly mixed and tied flat with the points clipped in a V-shape
Hackle: Black cock

BLACK GNAT

A buoyant dressing from the U.S.A.
Hook: 12
Tail: Black hackle fibres
Body: Deerhair dyed black and spun on the tying silk in Muddler style, clipped to shape

Wing: Two white cock hackle tips, rear-sloping
Hackle: Black cock

BLACK JACK

An excellent grayling dry fly that is effective when the fish are smutting. It was devised by York fly-fisherman, Bob Spink, but as far as I know he never had a name for it and he did not tie it particularly for grayling. I gave the pattern a name when I referred to it in *The Grayling Angler*. I know of no better fly for difficult grayling feeding off small surface flies and refusing all artificials.

Hook: 14–18
Body: Brown seal's fur
Wings: Two small wings of dyed hackle fibres, one bright red, the other yellow or light green. They should be set slanting rearwards at about 45 degrees and should be smaller than the hackle.
Hackle: Black cock

BLACK JOE   Plate 18

Scottish loch patterns abound. This one is well recommended as a general nondescript fly usually fished on the top dropper. The fluorescent material greatly improves its attraction in a slightly coloured water or on a dull day.

Hook: 14–16
Body: Rear half, bright red or DRF red floss; front half, black floss or black ostrich herl
Hackle: Long-fibred black hen tied sparsely

BLACK LURES

Dozens of black lures must have been devised over the years. Black Marabous are currently popular and a suitable dressing is given in the section headed Marabou (*page 104*). Other black lures can be found under ACE OF SPADES (*page 1*), BLACK BEAR HAIR LURE (*page 16*), BLACK CHENILLE (*page 16*), and BLACK MAGICIAN (*this page*). Most are early-season patterns, when they are most effective fished deep.

BLACK LURE (John Veniard)

A streamer-style lure sometimes known as the **Black Leech** and an appropriate pattern to represent the natural leeches.

Hook: Longshank 4–8 or two or three standard hooks in tandem

Body: Black seal's fur, wool or floss
Rib: Flat or oval silver tinsel
Wings: Two black cock hackles or hen hackles. Hen hackles give a broad wing, the cock hackles a slim one. Jungle-cock cheeks are a useful addition.

BLACK LURE

A tandem hairwing pattern.

Front hook
Body: Black floss
Rib: Silver tinsel
Wing: Black squirrel-hair extending to the tail of the rear hook
Hackle: Black

Rear hook
Tail: Fluorescent blue floss
Body: Black floss
Rib: Silver tinsel

BLACK MAGICIAN   Plate 6

Angling writer Brian Harris rarely uses lures, but this is one pattern which he says is good for late dusk when all else has failed. It is fished slowly, with long pulls, almost as a nymph. The leaded version should be fished deep and slow, but may also be twitched at speed, the lead keeping it just sub-surface and avoiding wake.

Hook: Longshank 10–12
Tying silk: Black

Tail: Doubled fire-orange DRF floss silk clipped to about 3 mm (⅛-inch)
Body: Optional underbody of lead wire (0.037 mm gauge) varnished after winding over a varnished shank. The overbody is fine black chenille.
Rib: Fine oval, gold tinsel
Throat hackle: Hot-orange cock extending about half-way along the body
Wing: Black marabou turkey fibres about twice the length of the body
Head: Red Cellire varnish

BLACK NYMPHS

There must be dozens of black nymphs, most varying from each other in detail only. None, so far as I am aware, was tied to represent an imitation of a specific nymph or other food source, but all are generally suggestive of food, and trout find them acceptable. They are of most use as stillwater patterns. Three patterns are listed below and a further pattern can be found under COLLYER NYMPHS (*page 41*).

BLACK NYMPH

Hook: 10–16
Tying silk: Black
Tail: Black hackle-fibres

Body: Black floss tapering to the rear
Rib: Silver wire
Hackle: Short-fibred black cock

BLACK BOOBY NYMPH   Plate 11

This is a highly buoyant pattern for fishing just below the surface. Gordon Fraser devised the Booby series and he also tied olive and brown versions.

Hook: Longshank 10–12
Tying silk: Black
Tail: Black hackle fibres

Body: Black seal's fur with a pronounced thorax
Rib: Silver wire
Eyes: Two foam-bead eyes trapped in a stocking mesh either side of the shank just behind the eye. They are tied in with figure-of-eight turns of tying silk with a light dubbing of black seal's fur between the eyes

BLACK FUZZY NYMPH

Hook: 10–14
Tying silk: Black
Tail: Grey squirrel body fibres
Body: Black angora wool well picked out

Rib: Fine silver wire
Hackle: Sparsely-tied grey squirrel body fibres

BLACK SPIDERS

Black spider patterns have always been fished in the rough, faster streams of the hilly areas. Every region has its slight variation on the main theme, so I have selected two of the better-known and well-proven dressings which will take trout nationwide. They are so nondescript that they represent many different terrestrial and aquatic creatures. One essential feature is the sparsely-dressed soft hackle which gives a lifelike impression when worked in the current.

BLACK SPIDER (W. C. Stewart)   Plate 21

This was the favourite pattern of the great Scottish angler, W. C. Stewart, who was never without one on his cast. The tip is a later addition.

Hook: 12–16
Tip (optional): Orange or red floss or silk
Body: Brown tying silk, well waxed
Hackle: Cock starling neck feather palmered half-way down the body

PERRY'S BLACK SPIDER   Plate 21

This is a Welsh pattern

Hook: 12–16
Tip: Flat silver tinsel

Body: Black stripped quill
Hackle: Dark starling

BLACK SQUIRREL

Hook: Longshank 6–12
Tying silk: Black
Tail: A short piece of hot-orange fuzzy nylon wool

Body: Black seal's fur
Rib: Fine oval silver tinsel
Wing: Black squirrel-tail fibres
Throat hackle: Black squirrel-tail

BLAE AND BLACK Plate 17

Small-winged wet flies are popular for fishing in traditional loch-style. This is one of the older patterns still in use. No-one has been able to pin-point the date of its creation, but it seems to be a fly which has evolved from obscure Scottish origins. It is best fished in the early season on the top dropper, and it is likely that in such a position it is taken for a hatching midge-pupa. The **Blae and Gold** and the **Blae and Silver** are in the same series. They differ only in their flat gold or silver tinsel bodies.

Hook: 12–16
Tail: Golden-pheasant tippet fibres
Body: Black tying silk or black seal's fur
Rib: Oval silver tinsel
Wing: Grey duck or small starling feather
Hackle: Black hen

BLAGDON BUZZER

Dr H. A. Bell created this midge-pupa pattern for Blagdon, where he was one of the first stillwater anglers to practise nymph-fishing. This was probably the first stillwater midge-pupa imitation. Hundreds of others have followed.

Hook: 10–12
Body: Black wool tapering slightly
Rib: Flat gold
Breathing filaments: A bunch of white floss silk on top of the hook behind the eye

BLOAS

All these patterns are sparsely-hackled wet spider-type flies of North Country origin for the rough, faster streams of the area. Many have their origins more than 200 years ago when, in a simple fashion, the northern angler sought to imitate the nymphs, emerging duns and drowning spinners in his rivers. Simple these patterns may be, but they are no less effective than the complex constructions we sometimes use today.

These flies are as deadly for trout and grayling as when they were first devised, and they are extensively used throughout the North. The conventional spider hackle at the shoulder is best for downstream fishing, but the semi-palmered style is best for emerging imitations fished upstream or on stillwaters. Bloa is an old name meaning bluish or slate-grey colour.

DARK BLOA

Hook: 14–16
Body: Red-brown silk
Tail (optional): Two black cock hackle fibres

Hackle: Dark feather from a moorhen wing

DARK BLOA Plate 21

Roger Fogg's book, *The Art of Fishing the Wet Fly*, is a modern classic. The author has followed in the steps of Jackson, Pritt and Edmonds and Lee, and has knowledgeably updated many of the old patterns by using more readily obtainable materials. He believes that the Dark Bloa and **Broughton's Point** are one and the same fly, both being part of local

North Country oral fly-tying tradition until the mid-nineteenth century, when the dressings were first recorded. It seems likely that the latter was originally a lake pattern to imitate the claret dun, but now both patterns are used as early-season river flies for March and April.

The dressing below is Roger Fogg's hackled version.

Hook: 14–16
Tying silk: Claret or brown
Body: Dark claret seal's fur
Hackle: Dark grey feather from a jackdaw's throat, or black hen

DARK OLIVE BLOA

This is a pattern from John Jackson's *The Practical Fly-Fisher* of 1854. It has not been improved upon in 130 years.

Hook: 14–16
Body: Lead-coloured silk
Wing: Inside of a waterhen's wing
Hackle: Dark olive or black hen

OLIVE BLOA

This is one of T. E. Pritt's list of *Yorkshire Trout Flies*. He wrote that it was good for cold, windy March, April and May days, and was probably intended to represent the large dark olive. It is still a very good fly.

Hook: 14–16
Body: Yellow silk
Hackle: Lapwing's back feather or substitute (see pattern below)
Head: Orange tying silk.

OLIVE BLOA (Roger Fogg)   Plate 19

A modern counterpart of Pritt's dressing. Colouring French partridge hackles with Pantone pens enables a wide range of hackles to be produced for a variety of hackled spider patterns.

Hook: 14–16
Body: Superfine olive Cobweb thread, pre-waxed
Hackle: A small dull grey hackle from the marginal coverts of a French partridge wing, coloured a dull green-olive with a Pantone pen, shade 104F

POULT BLOA

An excellent trout and grayling fly most frequently used to imitate the pale watery, spurwing and blue-winged olive. Some writers have described it as excelling on cold, dull days. It has done well for me whatever the weather. Like all bloas, it is an old fly, and its dressing can be traced back to 1807. Poult means a young bird or pullet.

Hook: 14–16
Body: Yellow or primrose tying silk with an optional sparse dubbing of natural red fur
Rib: Some tyers recommend a fine gold-wire rib on the dressings that do not have a dubbed fur body
Hackle: Slate-blue feather from a young grouse underwing
Roger Woolley's dressing uses dubbed ginger hare's fur on the body.

SNIPE BLOA
Plate 19

A useful early- and late-season pattern.

Hook: 14–16
Body: Straw-coloured silk or yellow silk sparsely dubbed with mole's fur
Hackle: Feather from the outside of a snipe's wing

STARLING BLOA
Plate 19

Probably a pale watery imitation. The dressing given is Pritt's, and it is recommended by him as being suitable for 'cold, dark days from June to the end of the season.'

Hook: 16–18
Body: Straw-coloured or white silk
Hackle: Lightest feather from a young starling's wing

WATERHEN BLOA
Plate 21

An all-time great North Country fly which, like most of the others in the series, is as effective now as it was a hundred years ago. No northern angler would wish to be without a copy in his fly-box. It is best used as an early-season fly and again at the end of the season, in September and beyond, for grayling. It is a suitable iron blue or dark olive imitation.

Hook: 14–16
Body: Yellow tying silk sparsely dubbed with grey water-rat's fur or mole's fur
Hackle: The inside of a moorhen's wing (originally known as a waterhen)

YELLOW-LEGGED BLOA

A useful May and June pattern. Roger Fogg believes this is a North Country version of the Greenwell Spider.

Hook: 14–16
Body: Well-waxed primrose silk
Hackle: Ginger hen

BLONDIE

A highly visible lure of New Zealand origin.

Hook: Longshank 6–10
Tying silk: White
Tail: A bunch of white mohair yarn, cut and flared
Body: Flat silver tinsel
Wing: White mohair yarn, flared
Hackle: Hot-orange as a rear-sloping collar

BLOOD FLY
Plate 18

This lake wet-fly was devised by Roger Fogg and named after its bright red hackle. Its creator says: 'It had been in my fly-box simply because it looked "interesting", until one warm and breezy summer evening when I knotted it on to the cast in desperation. Fish had been rising on the reservoir quite consistently, yet nothing had managed to tempt them until the Blood Fly came into action. It drew "first blood". Under similar conditions it has always produced fish (particularly rainbow trout), and it is always a useful fly to try when little else "works". Although it does well on the point, it is excellent as a top dropper on a team of three. It makes no pretence at imitation and attracts merely because of its brightness.'

A month after receiving this information from Roger, I found myself fishless under just the circumstances described. I put on a Blood Fly, fished hard for about an hour-and-a-half and caught four trout all within six inches of the surface. Elsewhere on the lake only one other trout was caught for three rods fishing. I have tied up and tried many of the flies sent to me for this book, but none of the newer patterns has worked so dramatically as this one.

Hook: 12–14
Tip: Small flat oval gold tinsel
Body: Rear half, light olive; front half, dark olive seal's fur
Rib: Narrow gold tinsel
Hackle: Blood-red hen

BLUE BOTTLE

This terrestrial fly rarely finds its way on to the water, but one or two fly-creators have found the need to have an imitation. See also HOUSEFLY (*page 85*).

BLUE BOTTLE (Taff Price)

Hook: 12–14
Tying silk: Black
Body: Blue Lurex wrapped with black ostrich herl

Wing: Two blue-dun hackle points tied flat
Hackle: Black cock

BLUE UPRIGHT   Plate 24

A dressing by R. S. Austin which has West Country origins. It can be fished wet or dry (usually the latter) as an imitation of the dark olive or iron blue. G. E. M. Skues suggested replacing the hackle and tail-fibres with a pale honey-dun hackle to make a useful imitation of the lighter olives.

Hook: 10–14
Tail: Medium blue-dun hackle fibres
Body: Well-marked peacock eye quill
Hackle: Medium blue-dun cock or hen

BLUE-WINGED OLIVE (*Ephemerella ignita*)
See EPHEMEROPTERA

Probably the commonest of the upwinged flies. It is found on all types of running water and on some larger lakes. The adults usually appear in mid-June, although in some parts of the country they may be as early as May. Hatches continue into October and November. Hatches usually occur in the evening, but on some rivers afternoon hatches are also seen, and then the imitation is well worth using. The duns frequently emerge immediately below stretches of broken water. C. F. Walker records that the adults sometimes experience difficulty breaking free of the nymphal skin, so becoming easy prey for trout.

The blue-winged olive is a medium-to-large-sized fly with a body of about 9 mm and large wings that slope back slightly over the body. The male's body is orangey or olive-brown. The female's body darkens from olive-green to rusty-brown at the end of its season. The bl.-w.o. is the only olive with three tails. J. R. Harris observes that in neutral or acidic waters the colour of the duns is subdued and they are often smaller. The nymph is a moss-creeping type and is fairly inactive, living on moss-covered stones and obstructions on the river-bed.

Others have commented on how easy it is to recognise the natural, but how difficult it is to imitate it. Many fly-tyers have offered variations on the theme, but I have detailed only those patterns that have been recommended to me. G. E. M. Skues was the first to realise the value of the Orange Quill as an excellent late-evening imitation of the blue-winged olive, and this has long been used on rivers all over the country.

The male dun has dark blue-grey wings and an orange-brown or olive-brown abdomen of which the last segment is yellow. The legs are brown-olive and the three tails are dark grey with brownish rings. The female dun also has dark blue-grey wings and a greenish-olive body changing to rusty-brown later. The legs are dark olive and the three tails are light grey-brown with dark brown rings.

The male spinner is one of the few that are of interest to trout and grayling. The wings are transparent with light brown veins and the abdomen is dark or rich brown. The legs are pale brown and the three tails are fawn with black rings. The female spinner is distinctive with its little green ball-like egg-sac carried at the rear of the abdomen. The wings are transparent with pale brown veins and the abdomen varies from olive-brown to sherry-red. The legs are pale brown and the tails are olive-grey with light brown rings. The female spinner is commonly referred to as the sherry spinner.

In addition to the patterns below, suitable imitations may be found under ORANGE QUILL (*page 133*), PHEASANT TAIL (*page 147*), POULT BLOA (*page 21*), ORANGE SPINNER (*page 133*), RED QUILL (*page 153*), USD PARADUNS (*page 190*), HARE'S LUG AND PLOVER (*page 82*), GREENWELL'S GLORY (*page 77*), NO-HACKLE FLY (*page 128*).

B-W.O. NYMPH (John Veniard)

Hook: 12–14
Tail: Grizzle hen hackle fibres dyed yellow
Abdomen: Heron herl dyed olive
Rib: Gold wire

Thorax: Dark olive seal's fur
Wing-case: Goose breast feather-fibres dyed pale-olive
Legs: One turn of grizzle hen-hackle dyed yellow

B-W.O. NYMPH (Preben Torp Jacobsen)   Plate 15

Hook: 14
Tying silk: Hot-orange
Tail: Three or four brown speckled partridge hackle fibres

Abdomen: A small amount of otter's fur spun on the tying silk
Thorax: Soft red cow's hair
Hackle: Small dark-blue hen hackle

B-W.O. FLYMPH

See under FLYMPHS (*page 65*) for a full description of the method of dressing.

Hook: Longshank Mayfly 14
Tying silk: Primrose or green

Tail: Blue-dun hackle fibres
Body: Dubbed green wool or seal's fur
Hackle: Medium blue-dun

Hook: 14–16
Tying silk: Yellow

Tail: Blue-dun hackle-fibres
Body: Tying silk moderately dubbed with pinkish-beige opossum fur

Hackle: Blue-dun followed by a red game-cock hackle

B-W.O. DUN (David Jacques)

Hook: 14
Tying silk: Orange
Tail: Dark-olive cock fibres
Body: Dirty-olive ostrich herl overlaid with olive PVC

Wings: Coot, set upright
Hackle: Dark-olive cock

B-W.O. DUN (Jim Nice)

A pattern of which its creator wrote: 'A simple pattern, but effective, especially in the early mornings'.

Hook: 12–14
Tail: Blue-dun or olive cock hackle-fibres

Body: Front half, blue DFM floss; then the whole body, including the front half, covered with lime-green DFM floss
Hackle: Blue dun or olive cock

B-W.O. DUN   Plate 28

This pattern was devised by Reg Righyni, who was dissatisfied with available dressings. He says it works better than all the others he has tried.

Hook: 14–16
Tying silk: Yellow

Tail: Blue-dun hackle fibres
Body: Tying silk moderately dubbed with pinkish-beige opossum fur
Hackle: Blue-dun followed by a red game-cock hackle

SHERRY SPINNER (William Lunn)

Dave Collyer says that he finds this as useful on stillwater as on the southern chalk-streams for which it was originally tied.

Hook: 14–16
Tying silk: Pale orange
Tail: Light-ginger cock fibres

Body: Deep-orange floss or hackle-stalk dyed orange
Rib: Gold wire on the floss-bodied version only
Wing: Pale blue-dun hackle-points tied spent
Hackle: Rhode Island Red cock

SHERRY SPINNER (Freddie Rice)   Plate 28

Hook: 14
Tying silk: Light yellow
Tail: Natural buff-barred cree fibres or the same dyed light-olive
Tip: Light-yellow rayon floss
Body: One dark and one light moose-mane hair, the lighter dyed olive-brown

or shades of sherry through to pinkish-red, wound together to give the impression of a segmented body.
Wing: Pale ginger cock hackle fibres wound on and bunched in the spent position
Hackle: Natural light red game-cock

BOOBIES   Plates 5 & 11

These are variations in the dressing of traditional stillwater nymphs, wet flies and lures. The variation is the addition of two large foam beads trapped in a stocking mesh and tied

in behind the eye of the hook with figure-of-eight turns of the tying thread. Almost any stillwater fly can be so adapted. The foam makes the flies buoyant and unweighted patterns can be fished just below the surface film.

Booby-adapted nymphs and lures can be fished in an attractive way on a sinking line. When the line is retrieved, the flies sink, and when there is a pause, they rise in the water to dive again when further retrieved. Some lures may be improved by the painting of eyes on the large beads. The Boobies were named and made popular by Gordon Fraser, a professional fly-tyer from Leicester.

For examples, see under NOBBLER (*page 127*) and BLACK NYMPHS (*page 18*). See also under SUSPENDER MAYFLY NYMPH (*page 109*).

BORDERER

This is a Welsh Border dry fly devised by W. M. Gallichan, a prolific writer. Among other titles, he wrote nine books on angling between 1903 and 1926. This is probably the best known of his patterns. Courtney Williams described it as 'deadly'.

Hook: 14
Tail: Rusty-dun cock fibres
Body: Blue rabbit's fur with a tip of red tying silk
Hackle: Rusty-dun cock

BOWLER HAT   Plate 10

This stillwater lure has also caught salmon and sea-trout. It was devised by Peter Mackenzie-Philps. There seems little doubt that the fluorescent thorax attracts trout and that they aim for this when taking the lure. It seems to be a pattern that has a distant parentage in Richard Walker's Sweeny Todd.

Hook: Longshank 8–10
Body: Black floss with a small thorax of fluorescent-green dubbing
Wing: Black bucktail with a few fibres as an underwing
Head: Large; black tying silk

BOW-TIE BUZZER   Plate 15

Frank Sawyer was a river-keeper on the Wiltshire Avon where he spent much of his life keenly observing trout and grayling and the fly-life of his river. He was an expert nymph-fisher, an informative writer and an original creator of artificial flies. All his patterns show that he was aware that trout could be duped by general imitations, even caricatures of the real nymphs, but he was doubly aware of how those patterns ought to behave beneath the surface to emulate their natural counterparts.

This pattern is a buzzer (midge-pupa) and gnat-larva imitation. The fly is not tied to the leader, but the tip of the leader is passed through the down-eye of the hook and a tuft of white nylon wool is tied on and pulled up to the eye. The knot and the wool ensure that it is not pulled through the eye. On being retrieved, the fly spins in the water, imitating the larger species of midge-pupae as they struggle in the surface film.

Hook: 12
Tying silk: None
Tail: Pheasant tail fibres
Body: An underbody of gold-coloured copper wire is wound on to give also a slight thorax and is then overlaid with flat silver tinsel. Copper-wire is used to tie in the materials. The overbody of four or five cock pheasant-tail fibres is wound on so that the silver tinsel is visible through it.
Bow-tie: A small tuft of white nylon wool

BRADSHAW'S FANCY

Plate 20

An excellent grayling fly devised for northern rivers about a century ago. It is now used throughout the country. Reg Righyni includes it on the point of his favourite three-fly cast.

Hook: 14–16
Tying silk: Purple

Tag: Crimson wool or floss
Body: Copper peacock herl
Hackle: Norwegian or hooded crow (pale blue-dun)
Head: Two turns of crimson wool or floss, or a small tag similar to that at the rear but slanting forward at 45 degrees

BREATHALISER

Plate 7

A stickleback imitation and general stillwater lure devised by Alec Iles and based on an earlier Canadian lure.

Hook: Longshank 8
Tail: Black hen hackle fibres
Body: Flat silver tinsel

Wing: Two hot-orange hackles with two Green Highlander hackles on the outside tied in streamer style
Eyes (optional): Jungle-cock tied in close to the head
Collar hackle: Badger
Head: Black varnish

BROUGHTON'S POINT

Tradition has it that Broughton was a Penrith cobbler who fished Coniston Water and Ullswater in the mid-nineteenth century. Although Broughton's name is associated with this dressing, it seems likely that the pattern had been around for some time as an almost identical fly (except for the addition of a tail) is given in John Jackson's *Practical Fly-Fisher* of 1854. Jackson called it the Dark Bloa. It is likely that Broughton's Point was a lake fly to imitate the Claret Dun

nymph, which is fairly common in the relatively acid waters of the Lake District. The dressing remains an excellent lake fly for this purpose. It is also a useful trout and grayling fly.

Hook: 12–14
Body: Dark-claret or ruddy-purple silk
Wing: Medium-blae starling wing feather
Hackle: Black hen

Courtney Williams includes a smaller secondary red hackle, but this is not as the original dressing or as quoted by Jackson, T. E. Pritt or Edmonds and Lee.

BROWN BOMBER

Dave Collyer created this first cousin to his ACE OF SPADES (*see page 1*). Both are excellent matuka-style lures.

Hook: Longshank 4–10
Tying silk: Brown
Body: Brown chenille

Rib: Heavy copper-wire
Wing: Brown hen-hackle tied in matuka-style with a bronze mallard overwing the length of the hook.
Hackle: Two bunches of cock-pheasant centre tail fibres tied one on either side

BROWN NYMPHS

There are a number of general brown nymph imitations, some of which go under other names. See COLLYER NYMPHS (*page 41*), IVENS BROWN NYMPH (*page 90*), and PHEASANT-

TAIL NYMPH (*page 147*). The pattern below is an olive nymph imitation useful on river and stillwater. It was devised by Jim Nice.

Hook: 14
Tail: Three brown-olive cock hackle-fibres
Body: Opaque PVC dyed brown, each turn just overlapping
Thorax: Brown seal's fur or brown herls
Wing-case: Brown feather-fibres
Hackle: Brown-olive hen.

BROWN FUZZY NYMPH   Plate 14

A pattern by Roger Fogg which he describes as 'An alternative sedge-pupa imitation which works best on rivers or stillwaters in the summer evenings when sedges are about'. It is fished just below the surface and allowed to drift. It is based upon the SOMETHING AND NOTHING (*see page 176*) and should have a rough and unkempt appearance.

Hook: 10–14
Tying silk: Brown
Body: Brown seal's fur taken near the bend
Rib: Stripped peacock quill or herl dyed pale watery olive
Hackle: Two turns of brown hen clipped short
Wing: Any grey feather tied as normal and clipped to a short stub.

BROWN-AND-YELLOW NYMPH

Bob Church recommends this pattern in his book, *Reservoir Trout Fishing*. It was devised by John Wilshaw, editor of *Trout and Salmon*. It is recommended when sedges are hatching or are expected.

Hook: Longshank 8
Tail: Pheasant tail fibres
Body: Rear two-thirds, brown seal's fur; front one-third, yellow seal's fur
Rib: Narrow gold tinsel
Hackle: Short-fibred yellow cock.

BROWN OWL   Plate 21

This old North Country pattern is still a useful spider-type of wet fly. It is effective when the willow flies are about, but can be profitably employed throughout the season as suggestive of stoneflies and sedges.

Hook: 14
Body: Orange tying silk
Hackle: A reddish feather from the outside of a brown owl's wing, sparsely wound

BROWN TROUT STREAMER   Plate 8

This imitation, created by Taff Price, may well prove useful on stillwaters where small brown trout are stocked or breed naturally.

Hook: Longshank 4–8
Tail: A tuft of olive-green hackle fibres
Body: Thin, tapering green floss

Rib: Flat gold tinsel or Lurex
Wings: Six cock hackles – two fiery-brown tied back-to-back, two dark-olive either side, and two badger on the outside
Beard hackle: Dark green-olive with a few long strands of white hackle fibres tied under the olive to body length

BUCKTAILS

The collective name for lures or fry-imitating lures with wings of animal hair. Bucktail (deer) was originally the commonest material, but now squirrel, stoat, bear, monkey, calf and almost any other animal hair is used. These lures were developed in the U.S.A. and became popular on our reservoirs. Marabou wings have largely superseded bucktail.

The conventional wing has a bunch of hair flat over the back, extending beyond the hook-bend. A single colour may be used or a combination of two or three, one over the other or mixed. Double-winged versions have a shorter front wing, with a second wing half-way down the body, the front wing overlapping the second. The life of the fly is greatly increased if the wing roots are soaked in varnish or quick-drying glue and allowed to become tacky before being bound to the shank. All patterns have a varnished head which is sometimes improved with a painted eye.

For examples see, BANDED SQUIRREL BUCKTAIL (*page 10*), YELLOW BUCKTAIL (*page 204*), BLACK-AND-SILVER BUCKTAIL (*page 15*), ORANGE BUCKTAIL (*page 132*), and SWEENY TODD (*page 184*).

BUFF BUG

On lakes and reservoirs aquatic beetles of various sorts often figure in the trout's diet. They mainly inhabit the shallower areas, and imitations should be fished near the bottom or near weed-beds. This pattern is an imitation of the striped-back aquatic beetle.

Hook: 12
Tying silk: Brown
Body: Light-brown wool or ostrich herl
Back: Oak turkey
Paddles: Two strands of oak turkey swept back and tied in at the shoulder or half-way along the body

BUFF BUZZER   Plate 13

This pattern was devised by Steve Parton, who comments: 'This is a good mid-summer middle dropper nymphing pattern. Do not use it before the start of June. It is best fished in a figure-of-eight style until the light has really faded. Then it can be most effective thrown in front of rising fish and retrieved in twitches. The reason for its effectiveness is probably that it is an excellent imitation of the pupal form of a green-bodied sedge that appears around that time of year.'

Hook: 10–24 sproat bend
Body: Swan herl dyed palest beige
Rib: Gold wire
Thorax: Seal's fur dyed normal beige (ginger/pink)
Wing-case: Body herl butts

BULLHEAD   Plate 3

The small fish known as the bullhead is found in many lakes and rivers. The excellent imitation given below is by Taff Price. Also see **Sculpin Muddler** under MUDDLERS (*page 122*).

Hook: Up-eyed salmon hook 8
Underbody: Copper-wire
Body: Mixed hare's fur and green seal's fur

Rib: Wide oval gold tinsel
Wing: Brown squirrel flanked by dyed olive-brown hackles
Cheeks: Dark game-bird feathers, one tied flat on top of the fly, and one on each side of the wing
Head: Spun deerhair, large and clipped to shape

BUMBLES

An old series of flies, probably of Derbyshire origin. The palmer-style hackles suggest an ancestry earlier than the fifteenth century. Bumbles were no doubt originally fished wet, but they are now also fished as floaters. F. M. Halford, recalling the pattern's use on the Test, describes it as 'the priceless Bumble'. As well as being a trout fly, it is an excellent grayling pattern.

CLARET BUMBLE

Hook: 12–14
Body: Claret silk
Rib: A strand of peacock sword herl
Hackle: Palmered furnace cock or hen
The **Furnace Bumble** is as above except that it has an orange floss body.

The **Red Bumble** is as above except that it uses a red floss body.
The **Ruby Bumble** is as for the Claret Bumble except that it uses a palmered pale blue-dun hackle.

HONEY-DUN BUMBLE   Plate 21

Body: Salmon-pink floss
Rib: A strand of peacock sword herl

Hackle: Palmered honey-dun cock or hen

PURPLE BUMBLE   Plate 21

A grayling fly recommended by Reg Righyni for use when iron blues are on the water.

Body: Purple silk
Hackle: Palmered blue-dun

STEELY-BLUE BUMBLE

An excellent grayling fly.

Body: Alternate bands of orange, light-orange and cherry-coloured floss silk

Rib: A strand of peacock sword herl
Hackle: Steely-blue hen or cock

YELLOW BUMBLE   Plate 21

Body: Primrose floss silk
Rib: A strand of peacock herl

Hackle: Palmered blue-dun hen or cock

BURLEIGH   Plate 16

Loch Leven used to be one of the best three or four stillwater fisheries on the U.K. mainland. Sadly it is no longer as prolific a trout water as it once was, but a number of flies developed there have survived and are still killing Scottish loch trout. This is one of them. Tom Stewart, a knowledgeable Scottish fly-fisher, suggested that it fished well either on the point or as a dropper and that it was at its best from early June onwards.

Hook: 10–14
Tail: Ginger hackle fibres
Body: Well-waxed yellow silk
Rib: Silver wire
Wing: Starling wing feather tied low over the body
Hackle: Ginger hen

BUTCHERS   Plate 17

A series of attractor flies for both stillwater and river. They have been catching trout for more than 150 years. The Butcher was originally known as **Moon's Fly**, but the name was changed about 1838 to the name of the trade of one of its co-inventors, Moon and Jewhurst. It is generally accepted as being a small fry imitation, although John Goddard believes that fished slowly under the surface film it could be taken for an orange-and-silver midge-pupa. Courtney Williams suggested in his *Dictionary of Trout Flies* that it is a good grayling dry fly, but I don't know of its use as such today. It is without doubt an effective general attractor pattern on river, loch or reservoir. A number of variants have been developed.

Hook: 10–14
Tail: Red ibis or swan dyed red
Body: Flat silver tinsel
Rib: Oval silver tinsel
Wing: Blue mallard, crow wing or magpie tail feather
Hackle: Black
The **Teal-Winged Butcher** has a wing from a barred teal feather.
The **Bloody Butcher** has the black hackle replaced with a scarlet one.
The **Gold Butcher** is as the standard dressing except that it has a gold tinsel body and gold rib

KINGFISHER BUTCHER Plate 17

Hook: 10–12
Body: Flat gold tinsel
Rib: Oval gold tinsel
Tail: Kingfisher wing feather-fibres or substitute
Wing: Black hen or as for the standard dressing

Hackle: Orange cock
This pattern tied with a whitish-grey squirrel-tail hairwing is known as **Morning Glory**.

POLY BUTCHER

This is a Bob Church variation of the original. The polythene body makes the fly very durable and Bob writes of having a fly unmarked after it had taken thirteen trout.

Hook: Longshank 6–10
Tail: Red cock hackle fibres

Body: Red tinsel or red silk covered with clear polythene strips
Wing: Black squirrel-hair with black marabou
Eyes: Jungle-cock or substitute
Hackle: Cock, dyed red

CADDIS   See SEDGES

CAENIS or BROADWING   See EPHEMEROPTERA

The six species within this family are known as the angler's curse because of the difficulty in tempting fish feeding upon them into taking an artificial. Three species are confined to rivers. Of the remaining species, one is extremely small, fairly uncommon and appears only at dawn, while the other two are similar and found on stillwater.

The family is common throughout Britain on slow-moving rivers and lakes, but it is principally on stillwater that the prolific hatches appear. The nymphs inhabit the bottom mud or silt. The adults are the smallest of the *Ephemeroptera*. They are easily recognised by their cream bodies, broad whitish wings and three tails. They usually hatch in the early mornings or evenings between May

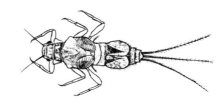

and September. Trout seem to prefer the spinners, which are considerably whiter than the duns. The males have much longer tails than the female.

The difficulty of catching trout on the artificial cannot be understated. Not only does the fly have to be very small, but frequently so many spinners are on the water that it must be by sheer chance that a trout selects the artificial. A further difficulty is that duns and spinners appear over the water at the same time, as the adult life lasts only about ninety minutes. Fishing a hatch or fall of spinners can be frustrating. Sometimes artificials 'work', and at other times they fail completely.

Some fly-tyers tie imitations on hooks as small as size 24 or 26 and claim success with them. I can claim moderate success when dropping down to these sizes. The difficulty then becomes not rising the fish, but hooking and playing them.

For further imitations see GODDARD'S LAST HOPE (*page 71*), ENIGMA (*page 57*), GREY DUSTER (*page 79*), LUCKY ALPHONSE (*page 102*), and POLYSTICKLE (*page 140*).

CAENIS NYMPH (Roy Masters)

Hook: 16
Body: White seal's fur

Rib: Fine oval silver tinsel wound close and tight

CAENIS NYMPH (Bob Carnill)   Plate 15

Bob Carnill comments on his dressing: 'This nymph stems from the middle to late 1960s. It was first used with success on Eye Brook Reservoir. I usually fish with a team of three when I anticipate a caenis hatch. However, the pattern often continues to catch even after the trout have turned their attention to the hatching duns. I usually tie the nymph slightly larger than the natural, and for a better hook-hold and surface penetration, short-dress it on a size 14 hook. The caenis nymph is fished just sub-surface on a floating line and a light leader. The retrieve should be a slow figure-of-eight.'

Hook: 14–16
Tying silk: Brown
Tail: Three brown partridge hackle fibres or tail fibres
Body: Drab-brown swan, goose or heron herl
Rib: Stripped peacock quill
Thorax: Hare's ear fur
Wing-case and thorax cover: Biot quills from the narrow side of a heron primary feather, tied with the broad ends facing rear over the body and tied in at the head and rear of the thorax. Trimmed and shaped (rounded) so that they extend half-way down the body.
Legs: Partridge fibres

CAENIS DUN (Frank Sawyer)

Hook: 18–20
Tying silk: Special midge thread
Tail: Short cream cock fibres
Body: Mole's fur

Thorax: Stripped black ostrich herl, shiny side uppermost
Hackle: Three turns of a very small dark-blue hackle

CAENIS DUN (J. R. Harris)

Hook: 16
Tying silk: Brown

Tail: Cream cock fibres
Body: Cream-coloured herl or floss silk

Hackle: Pale-cream cock or henny cock tied in by the butt with some of the downy fibres still on the shank, and wound slightly toward the tail, taking up about one-third of the shank

CAENIS SPINNER (Stuart Canham)

Hook: 18
Tying silk: Fine special midge thread
Tail: Three white cock hackle fibres
Body: White polythene
Thorax: A single turn of brown condor or turkey herl
Wings: White hen hackles cut out with a wing-cutter and tied spent
Hackle: White cock trimmed along the bottom edge

CAENIS SPINNER (C. F. Walker)

Hook: 16
Tail: White cock saddle hackle fibres
Body: White seal's fur
Rib: Silver tinsel
Wing: Pale blue-dun hen hackles
Hackle: Short-fibred white cock

CAENIS SPINNER

Also known as the **Deerhair Spinner**.

Hook: 14–16
Tail: Three strands of white deerhair
Body: White wool or silk
Rib: Black tying silk
Thorax: A dab of black varnish
Wing: White deerhair tied spent

CAHILLS

The Cahill, Light Cahill and Dark Cahill are North American dry flies developed in the 1880s by Daniel Cahill, a New York railroad worker. They are extensively used throughout their home country and they have successfully carved a niche for themselves on some of our rivers.

Hook: 10–14
Tail: Brown cock hackle-fibres
Body: Peacock eye quill
Wing: Speckled mandarin flank fibres tied in a single upright bunch-wing, or in a split V-shape
Hackle: Brown cock

DARK CAHILL

A fair imitation of the large summer dun.

Hook: 10–12
Tail: Mandarin duck breast fibres
Body: Muskrat fur or any fine brown fur
Tip: Gold tinsel
Wing: Mandarin-duck fibres tied upright or in a split V-shape
Hackle: Brown cock

LIGHT CAHILL Plate 25

Hook: 10–12
Tail: Mandarin-duck breast-fibres or fibres of the hackle used
Body: Creamy fox fur or pale cream-grey wool
Wing: Mandarin-duck breast or flank fibres tied upright or in a split V-shape
Hackle: Brownish-grey or buff cock

CAHILL BUCKTAIL LURE

This resulted from the North American trend of developing a good dry fly into a stillwater lure. It should be fished slowly and steadily just below the surface in coloured water.

Hook: Longshank 10

Tying silk: Black
Tail: Brown hackle fibres
Body: Grey fur
Wing: Brown-barred squirrel-tail
Hackle: Brown cock

CAMPBELL'S FANCY Plate 16

One of a few North American fancy lake flies which have been introduced into Great Britain. It is recommended for fishing in a wave on a bright sunny day and as a summer evening pattern.

Hook: 8–14
Tail: Golden-pheasant crest feather
Body: Flat gold tinsel
Rib: Gold wire on the larger sizes only
Wing: Barred teal feather
Hackle: Coch-y-bondhu

CARDINAL Plate 18

This stillwater fly is really a fancy fly, although it may be taken for a bloodworm.

Hook: 8–12
Tying silk: Scarlet or black

Tail: Red ibis substitute
Body: Scarlet floss silk or seal's fur
Rib: Fine gold or silver wire
Wing: Swan or duck dyed scarlet
Hackle: Cock, dyed scarlet

CARDINELLE

A highly-visible fluorescent stillwater lure.

Hook: Longshank 6–12
Tying silk: Red
Body: Arc-chrome fuzzy nylon

Wings: Fluorescent-orange marabou with magenta marabou over
Hackle: Long yellow cock tied as a rear-sloping collar

CARROT NYMPH

This was introduced by G. E. M. Skues as being devised by the Novice, one of the fictional characters from his angling stories. Although it is a tongue-in-cheek pattern, it does catch fish. The way has been opened up for the **Parsnip Nymph**, which should be a good imitation of a maggot!

Hook: 14–16
Tail: Green parrot feather-fibres or substitute
Body: Rear one-third, pale yellow wool; middle third, hot-orange wool; final third or thorax, greenish seal's fur
Hackle: Short-fibred olive-green dyed hen

CATERPILLARS Plate 14

It is a common sight in summer to see small caterpillars descending from trees on slender gossamer threads. The slightest breeze breaks the thread and they may be blown on to any nearby water. Larger caterpillars are more likely to fall in the water from plants and grass on the bankside, and the artificial is best fished near overhanging trees and bushes. Floating and sinking patterns have been devised, but I prefer to use a slow-sinker as most naturals falling to the water rarely float on the surface. Often in mid-summer, there is a mid-afternoon period of inactivity.

Two patterns work better than most to change a trout's apathy into avarice. One is Eric's Beetle, the other is a small caterpillar. Both sometimes seem too tempting for a fish to pass them by.

See also CHENILLE GRUB (*this page*) and PALMERS (*page 136*).

CATERPILLAR (John Roberts)

Hook: Longshank 12–14 with a slight downward bend imparted to give the impression of the caterpillar wriggling
Body: A layer of floss silk covered with matching heron herl or ostrich herl (white, green or brown)
Head: Peacock herl

CATERPILLAR (John Roberts)

Hook: Longshank 8–10 with a bend imparted
Tying silk: Brown
Body: Brown chenille with golden- pheasant tippets bound on to the underside in three evenly-spaced bunches.
Head: Bronze peacock herl

FLOATING CATERPILLAR (Richard Walker)

Hook: Longshank 10
Underbody: Varnished polythene foam
Overbody: Dyed ostrich herl over the wet varnish. Suitable colours are brown, black, white and green.
Rib: Crimson or buff silk soaked in diluted Durofix adhesive and allowed to dry

CHENILLE GRUB   Plate 14

This is Roger Fogg's caterpillar or general grub imitation. A weighted version lands with a 'plop' that often draws attention to itself as a natural caterpillar might falling on to the water. In *The Art of Fishing the Wet Fly*, Roger Fogg writes of a small wooded bay on a reservoir he fishes, where trout regularly feed on caterpillars blown on to the water. The difficulty was casting to trout that were well-protected by overhanging branches. Roger finally managed to get his brown Chenille Grub into the water beneath the branches and a 3¼ lb trout was the result. He also took three brown trout the next evening from a river on the same pattern.

Terrestrial insects and grubs often figure in the diet of trout. Their imitation should not be overlooked, particularly if fish are feeding but the usual nymphs or dry flies are being refused.

Hook: 12–14
Tying silk: Black
Body: White, green, yellow or brown chenille, attached to the shank behind the eye only with the remainder left free to move in the water.
Head: Black tying silk

CHEW AND BLAGDON LURE

A three-hook tandem lure devised by Tom Saville.

Rear hook
Tail: Swan fibres dyed red
Body: Flat silver tinsel
Middle hook
Body: Flat silver tinsel

Front hook
Body: Flat silver tinsel
Wings: Badger hackles tied back-to-back the length of the three hooks
Hackle: Brown

CHEW NYMPH

Thomas Clegg, author of an interesting little book, *The Truth about Fluorescents*, 1967, devised this general stillwater nymph pattern incorporating some fluorescent materials.

Hook: 8–10
Tying silk: Red

Tail: Three short neon-magenta DRF floss fibres
Body: Mole's fur tied fairly fat
Rib: Neon-magenta DRF floss
Back: Mottled turkey feather-fibres
Legs: Brown hen hackle.

CHIEF

Roy Masters tied this lure for Chew and Blagdon reservoirs and based it upon the Chief Needabeh.

Hook: Longshank 8
Tag: Silver tinsel
Body: Scarlet Firebrand floss silk
Rib: Oval silver tinsel

Wing: Two yellow hackles tied back-to-back with two scarlet slim-pointed cock hackles outside and with jungle-cock cheeks on each side
Hackle: Mixed scarlet and yellow as a beard
Head: Black varnish

CHIEF NEEDABEH   Plate 7

A streamer lure of North American origin.

Hook: Longshank 6–10
Tag: Silver tinsel
Body: Scarlet floss
Rib: Oval silver tinsel
Wing: Two yellow cock hackles tied

back-to-back with two orange hackles outside with jungle-cock at the shoulder (optional)
Collar hackle: Mixed yellow and scarlet cock
Head: Black varnish

CHOMPERS   Plate 12

An excellent range of impressionist patterns devised by Richard Walker to represent a number of food sources. The variations and their natural counterparts are listed below. Each should be fished in a manner to imitate the intended natural. The white version has been my most useful pattern, usually fished on a greased leader fairly close to the surface. The series is the antithesis of all that exact imitation represents.

There could hardly be a simpler pattern, nor a more broadly imitative one.

Hook: 10–14
Body: Body herls as below, or wool of the appropriate colour. Optional underbody of lead-foil strips
Back: Coloured Raffene tied in at the head and tail
The following patterns can be used to represent various natural fauna.

36

Back	Body material	Tying silk	Imitation
Clear	Golden yellow ostrich	Black	General imitation
Brown	Olive ostrich	Olive	General imitation
Brown or white	White ostrich	White	General imitation
Pale buff	Buff ostrich	Brown	Shrimp
Pea green	White ostrich	Olive	Small corixa
Black	Peacock herl	Black	Beetle
Speckled turkey	Golden yellow ostrich	Black	General imitation

CHRISTMAS TREE   Plate 1

A popular lure on the big Midlands reservoirs, where the tandem versions are much-used by boat fishers. The original single-hook was devised by Les Lewis for Rutland.

Hook: Longshank 6–10
Tying silk: Black
Tail: Fluorescent-green wool or floss
Body: Black chenille
Rib: Oval silver tinsel
Wing: Black marabou
Cheeks: Red fluorescent wool or floss

The white tandem variant was evolved by Steve Parton on Rutland Water where, after a fairly unspectacular start, it took three large brown trout in about nine casts in blazing sunshine and near flat-calm conditions. For the next three seasons it was rarely absent from Steve's leader when he was boat fishing, and it has accounted for more than 800 trout to his rod alone. It should work on big waters throughout the country.

The dressing for both hooks of the tandem is the same.

Hook: Longshank 6–10
Tying silk: Black
Tail: Arc-chrome fluorescent floss
Body: White chenille
Rib: Oval silver tinsel
Wing: White marabou
Cheeks: Green fluorescent wool tied above the wing.

In the black tandem version the tails are replaced by neon-magenta wool. It has a black body and wing.

CHURCH FRY   Plate 10

This fry-imitating pattern was devised by and named after its inventor, Bob Church. It was first fished in 1963 at Ravensthorpe when trout were feeding on perch fry. It is an excellent pattern for use throughout the season, even when no perch fry are in evidence.

Hook: Longshank 4–10
Tying silk: Black
Tail: White hackle fibres
Body: Orange floss or chenille
Rib: Flat gold tinsel
Wing: Natural white-tipped grey squirrel-tail hair extending just beyond the bend of the hook
Beard hackle: Orange or crimson hackle

CINNAMON AND GOLD   Plate 17

This winged wet fly is used mainly on stillwaters as an imitation of the cinnamon sedge pupa (*see under* SEDGES, *page 157*) as well as being a useful general pattern for a three-fly leader. An alternative dressing has a yellow wool body ribbed with oval gold tinsel.

Hook: 10–12
Tying silk: Black
Tail: Golden-pheasant tippets
Body: Flat gold tinsel
Rib: Oval gold tinsel
Wing: Cinnamon-dyed or natural hen-wing quills
Hackle: Cinnamon hen

CINNAMON QUILL

This old-established dry fly is fished as a general spinner imitation, suggestive of the female spinners of the MARCH BROWN (*page 104*), IRON BLUE (*page 87*), BLUE-WINGED OLIVE (*page 23*), PALE WATERY (*page 135*) and OLIVES (*page 129*).

Hook: 14–16
Tying silk: Sherry spinner
Tail: Ginger cock hackle fibres
Body: Pale cinnamon quill
Hackle: Ginger cock

CLARET BUMBLE   Plate 16

This is a different fly from those in the BUMBLE series (*see page 29*). T. C. Kingsmill Moore, the author of that beautiful book, *A Man May Fish*, held this lake pattern in high esteem. I suspect that it is not so commonly used now.

Hook: 10–12
Tail: Golden-pheasant tippets
Body: Claret seal's fur with a palmered black cock and claret cock wound together
Rib: Oval gold tinsel
Head hackle: Blue jay, slightly longer-fibred than the body hackle

CLARET DUN (*Leptophlebia vespertina*)
See also EPHEMEROPTERA

The claret dun is fairly common on some stillwaters. It prefers acidic water and is rarely found on rivers. The reddish-brown nymph is slow-moving and lives among stones and moss on the bottom, usually in shallow water. The adults appear in May and June, often around midday. The female spinners are usually encountered in the early evening. The species is similar to the slightly larger sepia dun, which has the same habitat but appears later in the season. The size of the adults seems to vary across the country. J. R. Harris describes them as being as large as the large dark olive, John Goddard records them as medium to large, and C. F. Walker as being medium to small.

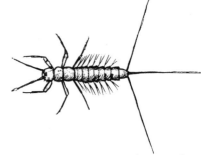

The male dun has dark-grey wings with pale hindwings. The abdomen is dark black-brown with a grey-black underneath, the last three segments having a claret tinge. The legs are dark black-brown and the three tails are dark grey-brown. The female dun has dark-grey wings with pale-buff hindwings. The abdomen is dark brown with a claret tinge. The three tails are dark brown, as are the legs.

The female spinner has transparent wings with pale-brown veins. The abdomen is brown tinged with claret. The legs are pale to medium brown and the three tails are pale brown with light black rings. The male spinner is of no interest as it dies over land without returning to water.

The nymph can be imitated with a PHEASANT-TAIL NYMPH (*page 147*) or BROUGHTON'S POINT (*page 27*) and the dun with an IRON BLUE DUN (*page 87*), or with those patterns below. Small versions of the GROUSE AND CLARET (*page 80*) or MALLARD AND CLARET (*page 102*) also take fish when the duns are hatching.

CLARET NYMPH (C. F. Walker)

Hook: 14
Tail: Black hen fibres as long as the body and well splayed out
Body: Dark brown seal's fur mixed with a little ginger fur and well picked out for the gills

Rib: Silver tinsel
Thorax and wing-case: Black seal's fur
Legs: Dark brown hen

CLARET NYMPH (John Henderson)   Plate 15

Hook: 14
Tying silk: Dark claret
Tail and body: Cock-pheasant tail fibres dyed dark claret

Rib: Gold wire
Thorax: Dark claret seal's fur
Hackle: Two turns of dark dun hen

CLARET DUN (J. R. Harris)

Hook: 24
Tying silk: Claret
Tail: Dark blue-dun cock hackle fibres
Body: Dark heron herl dyed claret, or claret mohair mixed equally with mole's fur

Rib: Fine gold wire
Hackle: Dark blue-dun cock clipped with a V-cut out underneath

CLARET DUN (John Henderson)

Hook: 14
Tying silk: Claret
Tail: Very dark rusty-dun cock hackle fibres

Body: Very dark claret seal's fur
Rib: Fine gold wire
Hackle: Very dark rusty-dun cock

CLARET SPINNER   Plate 24

Hook: 14
Tying silk: Black
Tail: A bunch of honey-dun or badger hackle fibres
Body: Dark claret floss or seal's fur
Rib: Fine gold wire

Wings: Light honey-dun or badger cock hackle wound full and bound in bunched spent wings, or wound full with the upper and lower hackles cut away
Hackle: None

CLYDE SANDFLY   Plate 20

This is a Scottish imitation of the Gravel Bed. In some areas sandfly is the name given to a species of sedge, but this is not a sedge imitation.

Hook: 12–14
Body: Black silk
Wing: Hen-pheasant centre tail, without the black bars, laid flat across the back
Hackle: Long-fibred black cock

COACHMAN

The Coachman and its many variants make it probably the most widely used trout fly. It is known in one of its various guises to fly-fishers through-out the world. The original was devised in the first half of the nineteenth century, and was probably named after the occupation of its inventor.

Thomas Salter's *The Angler's Guide* of 1814 says: 'There is a fly very much used at Watford, in Herts, called Harding's Fly, or the Coachman's; the merits of such flies experience will teach how to appreciate'.

Its merits are still evident today. It is an excellent general fly for both river and lake, and, in its larger sizes, for sea-trout. It can be fished wet or dry. Wet it is a passable hatching sedge copy; dry it can be fished as a moth imitation. Some of the more extreme variations have taken place across the Atlantic, where Coachman variants are held in high esteem. The Royal Coachman Bucktail (below) is one example.

COACHMAN   Plate 23

Hook: 8–16 (the larger sizes for sea-trout)
Tying silk: Black or brown
Body: Bronze peacock herl
Wing: White duck or swan fibres
Hackle: Natural light-red cock or hen
A wingless version has a white cock hackle with a shorter natural red cock in front or wound together.

The **Leadwing Coachman** is as above, but with a wing of grey duck or starling wing. The **Grayling Coachman**, which is always fished dry, has an additional red wool tag and often the wing is of white hackle fibres slanting over the body or set upright.

HACKLE-POINT COACHMAN (Dave Collyer)   Plate 23

A floating pattern which Dave Collyer says has probably accounted for more fish for him than any other.

Hook: 10–14
Tying silk: Red spinner
Body: Bronze or green peacock herl

wound over wet varnish for durability
Wing: White cock hackle points tied semi-spent
Hackle: Ginger or natural red cock with the underside trimmed flat in line with the hook-point

ROYAL COACHMAN   Plate 17

The 1878 variation by the American John Haily changes the pattern into a fancy one.

Hook: 8–14
Tying silk: Black

Tail: Golden pheasant tippets
Body: In three parts – peacock herl, red floss, peacock herl as for pattern below
Wing: White duck or swan
Hackle: Light red game

ROYAL COACHMAN BUCKTAIL

Hook: Longshank 8–10
Tail: Golden-pheasant tippets
Body: Peacock herl at either end of the body for a short length only; red floss in

the middle
Wing: White bucktail
Cheek: Jungle-cock
Throat hackle: Brown

COCH-Y-BONDHU   Plate 19

This terrestrial beetle has been imitated by fly-fishers for centuries. Its Welsh origin is betrayed by its name, meaning 'red with black trunk'. The natural is sometimes blown on to the water in June, but the fly can be fished successfully throughout the season.

Courtney Williams devoted five pages of his book to the fly. It is an effective beetle imitation and general river wet fly. The dressing is so generally nondescript that it passes as a variety of beetle species.

Hook: 12–14
Tying silk: Black
Tag: Gold tinsel
Body: Bronze peacock herl
Rib (optional): Red floss silk
Hackle: Coch-y-bondhu (red-game hackle with a black centre and black tips).

A West Country pattern is detailed below. It is reputed to be a good grayling fly.
Hook: 14
Body: Bronze peacock herl
Wing-case: Long strands of golden-pheasant tippets tied so that the black rib of the tippets is on top of the body
Hackle: Coch-y-bondhu

COCKCHAFER

This is a terrestrial beetle sometimes found on the water. It is similar to the Coch-y-bondhu, but is larger, being about 25 mm long, and has a barred black and grey underbody. It appears in May and June. The pattern below is from John Henderson.

Hook: 8
Tying silk: Brown
Tail: Two light-dun cock hackle-points

about 16 mm (¾ inch) long
Body: Oval-shaped cork with a flat underside. A groove is cut in the cork, the shank is glued and the cork pushed over the shank. This is painted dark grey.
Wing-cases: Two cock-pheasant breast feathers (brownish-red) which are heart-shaped with black edges, tied on top of each other over the back of the body
Hackle: Large natural red cock

COLLYER NYMPHS   Plate 15

A series of general stillwater nymphs devised by Dave Collyer. They are extremely effective as general imitations and I have successfully used the brown and green versions on both rain-fed rivers and chalk-streams. On stillwaters they are best fished slowly near weedbeds on which one expects to find natural nymphs.

Hook: 10–12

Tail: The tip of the body feather-fibres
Thorax: Ostrich herl dyed as for the body
Wing-case: Body fibres taken over the thorax and tied in at the head
Body: Swan herl dyed olive and ribbed oval gold tinsel for the **Green Nymph.** Cock-pheasant centre tail fibres ribbed oval gold tinsel for the **Brown Nymph.** Natural heron herl ribbed oval silver tinsel for the **Grey Nymph.** Turkey herl dyed black and ribbed fine silver Lurex for the **Black Nymph.**

COLONEL DOWNMAN'S FANCY   Plate 17

As its name suggests, this is wholly a fancy lake fly. It is used mainly on Scottish lochs.

Hook: 12–14
Tying silk: Black
Tail: Teal fibres

Body: Black floss
Rib: Silver tinsel
Wing: Blue jay wing with a small jungle-cock eye on each side
Hackle: Black cock

CONNEMARA BLACK   Plate 17

Like Guinness, the Connemara Black is a black Irish export that has been well received on this side of the Irish Sea. It is a lake and river fly that is also used, in its larger sizes, for sea-trout and salmon and as a dapping fly. It is an excellent general stillwater pattern which is probably best fished in its smaller sizes just below the surface on the top dropper.

Hook: 6–12
Tying silk: Black
Tail: Golden-pheasant topping
Body: Black wool, seal's fur or ostrich herl

Rib: Oval silver tinsel
Wing: Bronze mallard shoulder feather
Hackles: Black cock or hen with a throat hackle of barred blue jay feather

COPPER HOPPER

Muddler variations abound on both sides of the Atlantic. This British fly was devised by Terry Griffiths and is based upon the American Hopper patterns. It is heavily leaded to overcome the buoyancy of the deerhair head. It is fished deep on a sinking line and retrieved slowly. It is not unusual for takes to come in the form of a couple of shy knocks followed by a more confident 'thud' on the fly-line. It could well be taken for a small fish grubbing about on the lake-bed.

Hook: Extra longshank 8
Tying silk: Brown
Tail: A loop of the body material
Body: Copper glitter yarn ribbed with a red game-cock hackle
Wing: Brown-barred squirrel overlaid with mottled peacock wing tied flat
Head: Dome-shaped natural deerhair in Muddler style on the front one-third of the shank with a few underside fibres trailing to the rear

CORIXAE

The best-known member of this family is the lesser water boatman. Corixae are found predominantly on stillwaters and are widely distributed throughout the country. They vary in size, but some reach 12 mm (½-inch) in length and all have shiny backs and two long hind-legs which resemble oars. The coloration of the backs varies depending upon the species, but brown is the dominant colour, with shades of yellow, grey and dark brown blended in. The underbody is invariably white.

Corixae have a preference for shallow water as they have to return to the surface to take in air, held in a bubble under the wings. Artificials incorporating a flash of silver in the dressing to represent the bubble are often more successful than those without this refinement. Corixae prefer to be near weed-beds, where they can find food and protection, but they are found in open water. Although some 30 species are known, their value was largely overlooked until the last 20 years. Imitations are useful throughout the season, but their greatest effectiveness is during the August and September period.

Some of the patterns listed are buoyant and the best way to fish them is on a sinking line or sink-tip. The artificial can be made to dive towards the bottom as it is retrieved. During pauses between retrieves the buoyant fly heads towards the surface – all very lifelike.

CORIXA (Arthur Cove)

Hook: Low-water salmon 8–10
Body: White silk or floss tied on the front half or two-thirds of the shank

Back: Cock-pheasant tail fibres
Hackle: Sparsely-tied white hackle as a throat only

CORIXA (Roger Fogg)   Plate 12

Hook: 10–14
Tying silk: Brown
Tag: Silver tinsel or Mylar

Body: An underbody of lead-foil covered with a dubbing of dirty-white or pale-lemon angora wool

Rib: Fine silver wire
Back: Pale-orange raffia stretched over the back and stroked with a brown Pantone pen to give a mottled finish
Hackle: Two bunches of brown hen fibres at either side of the body

CORIXA (D. Ashmore)

The silver body gives a good impression of the natural's air-bubble.

Hook: 12–16
Tying silk: Black
Body: An underbody of lead-foil. Over this is wound a plump body of silver Mylar to a point half-way along the shank.

Here a strand of black ostrich herl is tied in across the top of the shank and trimmed at each side to suggest the paddles. The Mylar is continued to the head
Back: Black Raffene

CORIXA EGG MASS (John Henderson)

This is a pattern for when trout are feeding on corixa eggs among weeds.

Hook: 10
Tying silk: Green
Body: Green polymer dubbing (to represent a strand of weed)
Rib: Gold tinsel
Hackle: Palmered fluffy white feather dyed yellow, wound almost to hide the body

LARGE BROWN CORIXA (Richard Walker)

Hook: 10
Body: White floss silk tied fat
Rib: Flat silver tinsel
Tip: Silver tinsel
Back and paddles: Brown speckled turkey feather-fibres

The small green corixa can be copied with a size 14 hook to include a back and paddles of pale olive-green swan herl. The yellow corixa is tied with a primrose floss silk body and olive-green feather-fibres for the back and paddles.

PLASTAZOTE CORIXA (Dave Collyer) Plate 12

A buoyant pattern.

Hook: 12–14
Body: A rectangular piece of plastazote slotted on to the shank, glued and shaped with a sharp knife
Back and oars: Pheasant tail fibres, with the oars extending well beyond the bend

COVE NYMPH Plate 14

This nymph pattern was devised by Midlands stillwater nymph expert, Arthur Cove. In *Stillwater Flies, Vol III*, Taff Price describes Arthur Cove as 'a human heron, so still he stands, very slowly retrieving his flies in a figure-of-eight retrieve and allowing the natural drift of the water to work his flies. He is the most patient of anglers'. There are lessons to be learned from such an attitude and technique.

The Cove Nymph is an impressionist nymph, probably being taken for a midge-pupa, sedge-pupa, small fry and possibly other sub-surface food sources. In addition to the pattern below, it can be tied with dyed seal's fur of the following colours as alternatives for the thorax: black, grey, olive, claret, orange, red, yellow, amber or brown. The original pattern is best and most popular for general use, but for water green with algae the orange or green thorax version works better. The pattern was originally intended to be fished on the end of a long leader and inched slowly across the bottom, but it takes fish higher in the water, too.

Hook: Standard shank 6–12

Body: Ruddy pheasant tail fibres extending round the bend
Rib: Fine copper wire wound in the normal manner or criss-crossed along the body
Thorax: A round ball of rabbit's under-body fur
Wing-case: Pheasant tail fibres

COW-DUNG FLY (*Scatophaga stercoraria*)

A flat-winged terrestrial species, a member of the *Diptera*. The flies are yellow and hairy and their principal habitat and breeding ground, cow dung, hardly makes them appealing. Nevertheless, there are occasions when trout seem to find them attractive. The imitation given was devised by Taff Price. It should be fished wet just below the surface.

Hook: 12
Tying silk: Yellow
Body: Mixed yellow and olive seal's fur
Wing: Cinnamon hen wing
Hackle: Light ginger, tied on the underside only

CRANE-FLY (*Tipulidae*)

Nearly 300 species of crane-fly or daddy-long-legs are known. Many of them are found in the vicinity of water, as some species are semi-aquatic. They are poor fliers and from June to September crane-flies are often found struggling on the water surface. The artificial is of particular value as a stillwater pattern when fished in a wave. During hot, flat days of mid-summer, this large mouthful often seems a stimulus to lethargic, cruising fish.

One July morning on Leighton Reservoir I watched a canny septuagenarian angler catch three good trout on a suitable imitation. All the fish rose to the floating imitation, knocked it under the water and then turned to devour it. The old chap knew a thing or two, and each time a trout splashed at the fly he watched for a second sub-surface swirl before tightening. If trout are rising to the artificial, but are not being hooked, it is worthwhile not to react to the first splashing rise, but to wait until the second sub-surface swirl as the trout turns to take the drowned fly. This is fine if your nerves can stand it. An alternative is to fish a wet pattern such as the Stan Headley version given below, which I can thoroughly recommend.

Some of the patterns below have specific leg appendages. The natural insect has six legs, but it is better to tie in more than this on the artificial as invariably they break off when a fish is being played. I doubt if trout can count up to six, and additional legs make the fly last longer.

CRANE-FLY (Richard Walker)

Hook: Longshank 8–10
Body: Pale cinnamon turkey fibres
Wings: Two badger cock hackle points tied slanting over the body and well divided
Legs: Eight cock-pheasant tail fibres knotted in two places and trailing to the rear
Hackle: Pale ginger grizzle

CRANE-FLY LARVA   Plate 11

Taff Price devised this pattern to imitate the larvae of the semi-aquatic species which live in the stagnant lake margins.

Hook: Longshank 8
Tying silk: Brown
Body: Wool or silk underbody with yel-

low latex dental dam wound over
Rib: Oval gold tinsel
Hackle: A small clipped white hackle

DADDY-LONG-LEGS (Geoffrey Bucknall) Plate 22

Hook: Longshank 10
Body: Brown floss
Legs: Strong knotted black or grey nylon

monofilament
Hackle: Ginger cock
Wing: Ginger cock hackle-tips tied spent

WET DADDY (Stan Headley) Plate 16

Stan Headley comments: 'For anyone who has spent a frustrating day trying desperately to keep an artificial "Daddy" floating on the surface, this pattern is a gift from Heaven. It is fished in standard wet-fly style and will kill fish whether it is retrieved fast or slow. It is an absolute must from August through to September or whenever trout expect the occasional Daddy to appear. I've had fish to it in June, during a very patchy trickle of naturals. It works very well indeed, and usually a lot better than any

floating artificial. I've experimented with added refinements such as knotted pheasant-tail fibres as legs, tied in at the tail, and hackle-tips for wings, but none made any appreciable improvement to an already excellent fly.'

Hook: Longshank 10–12
Tying silk: Black
Body: Natural raffia
Rib: Fine gold wire
Hackle: Large brown partridge hackle and golden-pheasant tippet feather, mixed

CREE DUSTER Plate 28

This dry fly was devised by Roger Fogg, who uses it on stillwaters, where it has caught a number of large rainbow trout. It floats well and is highly visible. Roger tells me that it fishes well in May and June. I have used it on only two rivers, but on both occasions two brown trout and an out-of-season grayling were duped by it. I have yet to try it on stillwater, but Roger Fogg speaks highly of it.

Hook: 14
Tying silk: Brown
Tail: Cree hackle fibres
Body: Pale blue rabbit's underfur and hare's ear equally mixed. The body should be fairly short
Hackle: Two cree cock hackles tied back-to-back so that the duller sides face each other. Three turns of each produces a generous hackle

DAILY DUN

Eric Horsfall-Turner devised this copy of a Pale Watery Dun. The name of the pattern could have given rise to some head-scratching in the future had not Donald Overfield recorded for us in *50 Favourite Dry Flies* that the angora rabbit's fur came from a pet belonging to Horsfall-Turner's cleaning daily.

Hook: 18
Tying silk: Light olive
Tail: Dark ginger cock hackle fibres
Body: Angora rabbit's fur dyed light yellow
Wing: Bunched mallard breast fibres slanting forward
Hackle: Dark ginger cock

The Wormfly is an old reservoir pattern, and Richard Walker tied this version of it. He suggested that it should be fished from a boat on to the waves coming off a dam wall. The stiff hackles help to prevent the hook catching on the dam wall, and they cause the fly to bounce in a lively way off the stones. Richard Walker claimed that fishing it the length of the dam in a good wave usually brings several good fish.

Hook: Longshank 8–12
Tag: Yellow or arc-chrome fluorescent wool
Bodies: Peacock herl
Hackles: Two, one at the shoulder and the other in the middle of the shank between the divided body, both natural red cock

DAMSEL-FLY (*Odonata zygoptera*)

The adults of this large stillwater species appear during May to August, at the same period as the dragonfly. They are distinguished from the latter by the way the wings are closed when at rest. They are poor fliers and rarely venture far from water. The adults are occasionally of interest to trout, but the nymphs are more eagerly taken.

The nymphs are slim, browny-green and live among weeds, where they are well camouflaged from predators. It is likely that their colour darkens as the season progresses. They swim with a distinctive wiggle towards the shore before crawling up vegetation and splitting their skins to emerge as adults, usually blue or green.

It is when the naturals are making this bankward journey that the sunken artificial is best employed. During the early season the nymphs are quite small, 12–14 mm long. Before emerging they may be as long as 40 mm, and it is these that the nymph-fisher usually imitates. Green-bodied lures or green traditional patterns such as the Woodcock and Green seem likely to be taken for the larger nymphs. See also WIGGLE NYMPH (*page 199*).

DAMSEL NYMPH (Peter Lapsley) Plate 14

This is the early-season version. It is sufficiently generally imitative to be taken not only for a damsel nymph.

Hook: 8
Tying silk: White
Tail: Three pale-olive cock hackle tips
Body: Pale-green seal's fur tied sparsely with a slight taper to the rear
Rib: Fine silver wire
Legs: One turn of an olive hen hackle

The pattern below is a mid- to late-season imitation which Peter Lapsley says is one of his two most frequently used flies for small lakes. The other is the Gold-ribbed Hare's Ear. He fishes it on a slow-sinking line or leaded on a long leader and a floating line. Peter advocates a careful watch on the line as most takes come on the drop.

Hook: Longshank 8–10
Tying silk: Green
Tail: Three medium-olive cock hackle points about 6 mm (¼-inch) long
Abdomen: Olive, green or brown seal's fur
Rib: Fine oval gold tinsel
Thorax: As for the abdomen, but tied fatter
Wing-case: Cock-pheasant centre tail fibres with the rear fibres clipped short (3–6 mm long) and sticking out to the rear and slightly to each side
Legs: The points of eight hen-pheasant tail fibres divided four each side
Head: Varnished tying silk

DAMSEL NYMPH (Peter Gathercole)

Hook: Longshank 8–10
Tail: A small tuft of marabou dyed olive
Body: Finely-dubbed olive marabou (keeping the body slim)
Rib: Fine gold or copper wire
Thorax: As for the body, tied thicker

Wing-case: Olive feather-fibres
Legs: Non-fluffy olive marabou fibres
Eyes (optional): The melted ends of brown nylon monofilament of about 30 lb b/s

BLUE DAMSEL ADULT   Plate 22

This is a pattern tied by Captain Jack Sheppard and amended by Pat Russell.

Hook: Longshank 12
Tying silk: Blue
Body: This is extended in the manner of a tail with blue feather-fibres held together near the bend by varnish. The body on the hook is completed with an underbody of blue fluorescent silk with dubbed blue seal's fur wound over.

Wing: Two cape badger cock hackles tied in the spent position
Hackle: Cock hackle dyed blue and wound on either side of the wings

DAMSEL NYMPH (C. Kendall)   Plate 14

Hook: Longshank 8
Tying silk: Green
Tail: Three olive cock hackle points, set in a triangular shape
Abdomen: Seal's fur or any fine dubbing, 10 parts olive, 1 dark olive, 1 golden olive, 1 white
Rib: Fine gold wire
Thorax: As for the abdomen without the rib, dubbed in front of the rear pair of legs and both sides of the front legs and round the eyes

Back: Olive dyed duck or similar fibres over the thorax
Legs: Olive dyed partridge flank or neck feather fibres, in four bunches, two each side at the rear and half way along the thorax
Eyes: Brown monofilament nylon with melted ends in a dumb-bell shape, tied in at the front of the thorax.

ADULT DAMSEL-FLY

Professional fly-tyer Dave Tait devised the following pattern which incorporates an unusual detached body. He comments: 'It was during the 1979–80 season that the Flyline Damsel was evolved after two fellow Gloucestershire fly-fishers had prompted me to develop a damsel-fly imitation which would take the damsel-feeding trout in Wiltshire's Lower Moor Fishery, particularly during those hot sunny days when trout could be seen trying to catch the blue male damsels in the air.

'The Flyline Damsel is best cast to margin-feeding trout which are patrolling a particular beat. Watch out for any floating plant or weed where damsels are seen to alight. Study of such plants may show that the trout visit them solely to try to pick off the damsels, which may well be only a matter of inches above the surface.

'A few fishermen each season take numbers of fish on this damsel pattern during trying days when trout are not really on the feed due to hot sunshine. It is usually during these hot days that sedges, buzzers and other fly-life are not in evidence because of the heat. During such days, the natural damsels are abundant, and this is when this pattern scores. Time after time, I have caught trout during heatwave conditions by leaving this damsel pattern afloat near or on top of a small weed patch which has been visited regularly by patrolling fish.'

BLUE MALE FLYLINE DAMSEL Plate 22

Hook: 10
Tying silk: Black
Body: A detached body made from an old No 7 or No 8 floating line, dyed blue and ribbed with black tying silk with a small butt of silk at the end

Wings: Four black cock hackle points in two groups of two in a V-shape
Hackle: Black or grizzle cock
Eyes: Ethafoam balls covered in stocking mesh and tied in with figure-of-eight turns to secure and separate them

DAPHNIA

So small are these tiny creatures that individually they are impossible to imitate, but they are important and do form a large source of food on some of the bigger stillwaters. In *Reservoir Trout Fishing*, Bob Church goes so far as to suggest that at Grafham daphnia are the most important food available to trout.

The problem of being unable to imitate them has been overcome largely by the considerate attitude of trout, which seem to find orange lures and nymphs attractive when gorging themselves on daphnia. During the summer billions of light-sensitive daphnia move up and down at various depths depending upon the brightness of the sun. On a typical sunny day the daphnia will be nearest the surface during the late evening, throughout the night and in early morning. When the sun rises they will sink deeper. If the weather is dull but warm then it could well be that the upper layers will hold vast quantities of daphnia throughout the day. Find the daphnia and you'll probably find trout.

For suitable patterns to fish when daphnia are in evidence, see under ORANGE LURES (*page 131*) and ORANGE NYMPHS (*page 132*), GREEN THROAT and ORANGE MUDDLERS under MUDDLERS (*page 122*).

DARK OLIVE (*Baetis atrebatinus*)   See *Ephemeroptera*

This is a species of upwinged dun with a preference for alkaline streams. It is found on the rivers of southern England and on some northern rivers, but it is rare in the rest of the country. The nymph is an agile darting type and the medium-sized adults appear during the first two months of the season and again in September and November. They are similar to, but smaller than, the large dark olive. On the tributaries of the Rye in North Yorkshire it is the earliest upwinged fly of the season, with significant hatches in the late morning and early afternoon in the first weeks of April.

The male dun has grey wings and a dark olive-brown abdomen, with the last segment of the underside yellowish. The legs are pale olive and the two tails are dark grey-olive.

The female is similar to the male except that the tails are greyer. The female spinner has transparent wings. The upper abdomen is dark reddish-brown with paler rings and the lower abdomen is light olive. The legs are brown-olive and the two tails grey-olive with faint red rings. The male spinner is of little interest.

KITE'S IMPERIAL (*page 94*) is a suitable imitation, as are some of the general olive imitations under OLIVES (*page 129*) and the medium-sized patterns of the LARGE DARK OLIVE (*page 96*).

DARK OLIVE DUN (Thomas Clegg)

Hook: 14
Tying silk: Olive
Tail: Cock hackle fibres dyed dark olive
Body: Dubbed dark-olive wool

Rib: Electron-white DRF floss
Hackle: Slate-blue and dark brown-olive cock hackles wound together

DAWN-AND-DUSK LURE   Plate 10

Freddie Rice created this lure. He comments: 'Black has long been successful in fly-dressing materials so in the early 1970s I coupled this with a hair tyed in a fish-shape to produce a pattern particularly successful in early morning and late evening, hence the name. It does best moved at a steady medium pace in the top six inches of water, for which purpose I fish it sedge-style with the rod-tip held up. An occasional stop allows the fly to sink a little, and then I revert to the steady pace. In the smaller sizes, with a shortened body, it has proved itself as a Tadpole, best fished fairly slowly in the shallows around weed-beds, but with the rod-tip "waggled" to provide the appropriate movement.'

Hook: 6–12
Tying silk: Black
Body (optional): Lead-wire under the body, covered by black floss. If the weight is omitted, build up the body
Overbody and tail: Black squirrel-tail hair tied in at the head, swept back surrounding the body and tied in at the rear, allowing the ends to become the tail-fibres. The body is varnished

DAZZLER

One of H. A. Rolt's grayling dry flies. Rolt, to his eternal credit, is one of the few authors to devote an entire volume to the grayling (*Grayling fishing in South Country Streams*, 1901). This southern chalk-stream fly must have caused a few raised hackles with its scarlet and gold colours, so often a stimulus to grayling. It hardly falls into the category of an imitation, but such is the fickleness of grayling that, although they may refuse copies of natural flies, they can be duped by fancy patterns bearing little resemblance to the real thing.

Hook: 14–16
Tag: Scarlet ibis or substitute
Body: Rear half, flat gold tinsel; front half, peacock herl
Hackle: Badger cock dyed ruby-red

DIPTERA

These flat-winged flies are the largest Order of flies of interest to the fly-fisherman, but only a relative handful concern both fish and fisherman. Some of the Order never venture near water, but those that do, or are aquatic are the CRANE-FLY (*page 44*), REED SMUT (*page 175*), BLACK GNAT (*page 16*), MIDGE (*page 113*), COW-DUNG FLY (*page 44*), DIXA (*page 50*), HOUSEFLY (*page 85*), HAWTHORN FLY (*page 83*), HEATHER FLY (*page 84*), and PHANTOM MIDGE (*page 145*).

All members of the Order have two transparent wings that lie flat across their backs. Each is considered separately under its own heading.

DITCH DUN (*Habrophlebia fusca*)　See *Ephemeroptera*

The distribution of this upwinged species is fairly local and limited to ditches and slow-moving rivers. The nymphs are dark reddish-brown with three tails at least as long as the body and are laboured swimmers. The duns are similar to the iron blue dun, but have three tails and appear during June and July. Their value to the fly-fisher is minimal. However, Oliver Kite deemed them to be of sufficient interest and offered this dressing for the nymph.

Hook: 14–16
Tying silk: Purple
Tail: White cock hackle fibres
Abdomen: Dark heron primary herls
Rib: Fine gold wire
Thorax: Underbody of copper wire covered with dark heron primary herls

Legs: Blue-dun fibres
A pattern for the dun omits the copper-wire underbody and has a full blue-dun cock hackle. A spinner dressing is as for the dun except that the body and thorax are of pheasant tail fibres dressed thinly.

DIXA (*Dixa aestivalis*)　See DIPTERA

The following patterns are imitations of *Dixa aestivalis*, a mid-summer species thinly distributed on some stillwaters in the southern counties. They are of the Diptera Order of flat-winged flies and are within the Chaoborus family of Phantom Flies. The adult *D. aestivalis* is fairly easy to identify with its black body, yellow legs and a head that has three black stripes. Within the area of their localised distribution they are known to prove popular with trout. All three patterns were devised by Alec Pearlman, who brought them to notice in an article in *Trout and Salmon* magazine in February 1978.

Nymph
Hook: 10–12
Tying silk: Black or olive
Body: Black ostrich herl clipped short
Rib: Fine silver wire
Thorax: A mixture of lemon-yellow and light olive seal's fur, with a gap between the body and thorax
Legs: Thorax material well picked out, or olive-yellow cock hackle fibres
Head: Generous turns of yellow-green silk

Wet fly
Hook: 10–12
Tying silk: Black or olive
Body: As for the nymph but slightly longer
Thorax: Two turns of yellow-green silk
Leg hackle: Yellow-green cock
Wing: Moorhen wing, blae side out
Head: Two turns of yellow-green floss silk

Dry Fly
As for the wet pattern, except that it has a full hackle and wings of yellow-green cock hackle-points tied at 45 degrees and slightly split.

DODDLERS　Plate 6

That prolific fly-tyer, Freddie Rice, produced this series of lures to be fished deep on a sinking line with a slow, constant retrieve. Freddie Rice comments: 'I wanted a largish fly to get well down, without resorting to lead or copper weighting, for the better rainbows in the lakes I fish at Effingham in Surrey. A salmon iron got the fly well down, while the marabou wing gave it a sleek, fish-like appearance. Casting into deep water, I took a number of good fish, several taking on the drop as the iron settled. A good 6 lb leader is needed to resist the strain on the eye knot'.

Hook: Low water salmon 2–4
Tying silk: Black

Colour combinations:

Tail (Squirrel)	Body (Chenille)	Rib (Tinsel)	Beard (Squirrel)	Wing (Marabou)	Overwing (Marabou)
Scarlet	White	Silver	Olive	White	Black
Orange	Black	Gold	Black	White	Olive
Green	Grey	Silver	Orange	White	Black
Natural	White	Silver	Scarlet	White	Olive

DOGSBODY   Plate 23

In 1924, Harry Powell, a famous Welsh fly-dresser of the Usk valley, created this general river dry fly. Courtney Williams suggests that it is best used from April to mid-June and again in September, but Donald Overfield finds it an excellent general-purpose fly to be fished 'with every confidence of success'. The fly was named after the body material was obtained from a family pet from one of the customers in Powell's barber's shop. Create your own variant by combing your own dog, cat, gerbil or chimpanzee!

Hook: 12–14
Tail: Pheasant tail fibres
Body: Camel-coloured dog's hair spun on brown tying silk
Rib (optional): Oval gold tinsel
Hackle: Plymouth Rock followed by a second natural red cock, or wound together

DOG NOBBLER   See NOBBLERS

DOOBRY   Plate 18

A useful pattern for those reservoir fishermen who like to take their fish in traditional style. The mixed head hackle produces that extra sparkle which can prove the undoing of wary fish. Stan Headley, who devised the fly, suggests that it is best used on the bob, often with a standard Zulu on the tail. It is effective for brown trout and sea-trout in stillwaters and excels in coloured water on bright days, and in gin-clear water on dull days.

Hook: 8–12
Tag: Fluorescent red wool
Body: Flat gold Mylar or tinsel
Body hackle: Black cock contra-ribbed with gold wire
Head hackle: Two, hot-orange first, then wound over with black hen

DOTTEREL SERIES   Plate 20

A series of old North Country wet flies. The silk body colour is varied to imitate the nymphs of various up-winged duns and stoneflies. Golden plover is a suitable substitute for the dotterel, which is a migratory bird rarely seen today. The soft hackle feather can be tied at the shoulder only or semi-palmered a third of the way along the shank. Tied in the latter manner, the flies are profitably fished upstream just below the surface where they give a good impression of an emerging dun or drowned adult.

Hook: 12–16
Body: Silk of one of the following colours: orange, red, yellow, purple, claret, brown, slate, green, olive
Hackle: Golden plover; small wing feather, pale brown or dark ash with yellow tips

It has been suggested that the orange body is possibly a stonefly imitation, the yellow a pale watery, and the green a sedge.

This is one of only two named patterns of my own. It was originally tied to catch deep-lying grayling, but it has also caught a good many trout. It was named after the small North Yorkshire stream on which it was first tried. I have caught scores of chalk-stream grayling on it, a few over 2 lb, and trout to 4 lb. I caught my biggest grayling, 2 lb 6 oz, on it from the Driffield Beck. It came during a short period in which I made five casts and had three memorable grayling for a total of 6 lb 1 oz.

My original dressing had a small red tag as I thought this would prove more attractive to grayling. However, I seem to catch far more rainbow trout on the tagged version. Grayling seem to prefer the tagless version.

Hook: 10–12
Tying silk: Brown
Body: An underbody of copper or lead wire. Rear half, a mixture of orange and pink seal's fur; front half, orange and brown seal's fur.
Rib: Fine gold tinsel or copper wire
Tag (optional): A small stub of red wool

DRAGONFLY (Odonata anisoptera)

The nymphs are large, growing to almost 50 mm long, and live among mud and stones on the lake- or river-bed. They are carnivorous, feeding even on small fish. They normally move slowly, but they have the ability to dart forward rapidly to attack prey. Their coloration is dull and blends with the lake-bed.

The adults appear from May to the end of August. They are attractive, but are rarely taken by trout. The nymphs are more usefully imitated. The adult is distinguished from the damsel-fly by its wings, which are held open at rest. The damsel-fly closes its wings. They are stronger fliers than the damsel-flies and are often found some miles from the nearest water. See also GREEN PALMER (*page 137*) and WONDERBUG (*page 201*).

DRAGONFLY NYMPH

A simple pattern to dress is this version of Richard Walker's Chomper.

Hook: 10
Tying silk: Green

Body: Green ostrich herl
Tail: Green marabou fibres
Back: Green Raffene on the front half of the body only

DRAGONFLY NYMPH (Taff Price)

This pattern may be weighted if desired and small amounts of fluorescent material included in the body dubbing.

Hook: Longshank 8–10
Tying silk: Black

Tail: Two spiky goose quill fibres dyed olive
Body: Dubbed brown and olive wool mixed equally
Rib: Yellow silk
Hackle: Brown partridge
Head: Peacock herl

DRAGONFLY NYMPH (B. Curtis)

Hook: Longshank 6
Tying silk: Olive

Tail: Three cock-pheasant tail fibres trimmed

Body: Underbody of green wool; overbody of mixed mustard-coloured and grass-green seal's fur
Rib: Olive pre-stretched PVC
Back: The back of the body is marked with an indelible brown felt-pen
Wing buds: V-shaped green/brown PVC rear-facing from the rear of the thorax

Thorax case: Green goose or heron fibres
Legs: Two millinery pin heads enclosed in a nylon stocking mesh

A more buoyant pattern can be tied to keep the fly off the bottom or weed by tying in the booby style. See BOOBIES (*page 25*).

DRIFFIELD DUN Plate 24

The Driffield Beck is a delightful chalk-stream tucked away in east Yorkshire. This fairly old dry fly is named after it. No one knows for sure what it is intended to represent. Some sources have suggested it is a spider-type of fly or a Whirling Blue Dun, but Driffield-born angling historian, Donald Overfield, discounts these. He has been unable to trace its origins, but tells me that on the Driffield Beck the fly is of most use when the pale wateries are about.

Hook: 14–16
Tail: Ginger hackle fibres
Body: Mole's fur
Rib: Yellow silk
Wing: Pale starling wing
Hackle: Ginger cock

DRONE-FLY (See also DIPTERA)

This member of the Diptera Order is sometimes of sufficient interest to trout to warrant fishing an imitation. The larval and pupal stages of some species are at least part aquatic. The adults are bee- or wasp-like in appearance. The larvae of the commoner stillwater species are known as rat-tailed maggots and they inhabit the muddy bottom of the shallows. Their grey bodies are about 12–20 mm long and have a long breathing tube which extends to the water surface. The female adult returns to the surface to deposit her eggs.

I have yet to see a trout caught on an imitation, but if Richard Walker and Cyril Inwood saw fit to devise imitations, they must have some value.

RAT-TAIL MAGGOT Plate 14

The larva imitation devised by Peter Thomas. It should be fished slowly along the lake-bed.

Hook: 12
Tail: Long white swan fibres

Body: White fluorescent wool tied slim
Rib: Stripped buff cock hackle stalk
Thorax: Two turns of medium-brown ostrich herl

DRONE-FLY (Richard Walker)

To be fished just below the surface.

Hook: 12
Abdomen: Yellow wool or fluorescent wool tied fat
Rib: Broad black wool
Thorax: Black wool tied smaller than the abdomen

Wing: Blue-dun cock hackle points tied slanting over the back
Hackle: Dyed yellow cock sparsely tied
Head: Crimson silk with a single bright red ostrich herl round it

DRONE-FLY (Cyril Inwood)

A floating pattern.

Hook: 12–14
Tying silk: Red
Body: Yellow chenille tied fairly fat
Rib: Bronze peacock herl

Wing: Two white cock hackle tips tied split and rear-sloping
Hackle: Medium-brown cock
Head: Red silk tied small

DUNKELD Plate 16

Originally a salmon fly. Its smaller sizes are used for sea-trout and lake trout. Its origins are obscure, but a similar fly was mentioned by Francis Francis in *A Book on Angling* in 1867. It has survived so long because it is a good attractor pattern on both Lowland reservoirs and Highland lochs.

It is generally fished on the tail of a leader as an imitation of a small fish, or on the middle dropper, in which case the retrieve should be fairly slow. A variant is tied as a longshanked lure. The tandem version is detailed below.

Standard pattern

Hook: 10–12
Tail: Small golden-pheasant crest
Body: Flat gold tinsel
Rib: Oval gold tinsel
Hackle: Palmered orange cock
Wing: Brown mallard shoulder feather with jungle-cock on either side

Tandem

Rear hook
Tail: Golden-pheasant crest
Body: Gold tinsel
Rib: Oval gold tinsel

Front hook
Body and rib: As for the rear
Wing: Brown mallard flank feather with jungle-cock cheeks
Hackle: Hot-orange

DUN SPIDER Plate 21

A renowned Scottish wet pattern of W. C. Stewart, one of his successful trio of spider patterns that killed thousands of brown trout. I don't think the dressing is commercially available now, but there is no reason why it should not still catch trout. What it was taken for did not interest Stewart; he was content to know that it was sufficiently generally imitative to suggest a variety of nymphs and emerging duns.

Hook: 12–16
Body: Well-waxed yellow tying silk
Hackle: Soft dun, or ash-coloured feather palmered part way down the body. Originally a dotterel wing feather was used, but the inside of a starling wing is a suitable substitute

DUSKY YELLOWSTREAK (*Heptagenia lateralis*)
See EPHEMEROPTERA

This upwinged fly has a localised distribution on upland lakes and smaller rivers in Devon, Wales, the north of England and Scotland. The nymphs are stone-clingers and are usually found fairly close in to the water's edge. The medium-sized dun has dark grey wings, a dark grey-brown body and two tails. A distinguishing feature is the yellow streak on each side of the front of the thorax. The spinner has an olive-brown body with the same yellow streak. The flies appear from May to September.

No artificials are tied specifically to represent the species. However, in his book, *Trout Flies of Stillwater*, John Goddard suggests a DARK WATCHETT (*page 194*) to represent the emerging dun, an IRON BLUE QUILL (*page 87*) for the dun, and a PHEASANT-TAIL SPINNER (*page 146*) for the female spinner, all on size 14 hooks.

EARLY BROWN (*Protonemoura meyeri, Nemoura variegata*)
See STONEFLIES

These stoneflies have a preference for faster water and they are most prolific and of the greatest importance in the north of England. The nymphs are about 9 mm long and live on moss-covered stones. The adults, which appear from February to May, have small reddish-brown bodies with brown-grey wings. The head has a distinctive pale bar across the top. The wet fly given below is Roger Fogg's dressing. He also has a dressing for the floating imitation in which the hackle below is replaced with a dun-coloured cock hackle.

Hook: 14
Tying silk: Red spinner
Body: Reddish-brown seal's fur tied slim

Hackle: Slate-coloured coot, palmered half-way down the body

EARLY OLIVES

The early olive is a popular name for the large dark olive. See LARGE DARK OLIVE (*page 96*). Most imitations are known by the latter name, but the following two dressings are known thus.

EARLY-OLIVE NYMPH (Geoffrey Bucknall)   Plate 19

Hook: 12–14
Tying silk: Dark grey
Tail: Dark-olive cock fibres
Abdomen: Water-rat or mole fur
Rib: Fine gold wire

Thorax: Dark-olive seal's fur
Wing-case: Waterhen feather-fibres
Legs: The ends of the wing-cases divided either side of the thorax

EARLY-OLIVE DUN (Roger Woolley)

Hook: 14
Tail: Fibres of the hackle used
Body: Blue rabbit, water-rat or mole fur

Rib: Gold wire
Hackle: Medium or dark blue-dun cock

EASY-TIED TROUT SNACKS   Plate 9

Freddie Rice developed this series of lures for his fly-tying students in 1971. Their simplicity belies their catching powers.

Hook: Longshank 6–10

Tying silk: Black
Tail and body: Rayon or floss silk
Rib: Gold or silver, or Goldfingering
Beard hackle: Cock or hen hackle fibres
Wing: Squirrel tail

Colour combinations:

Tail and body	Beard hackle	Squirrel wing
Black	Red	Hot orange
Scarlet	Black	Black or natural
Hot orange	Red	Black or natural
Yellow	Hot orange	Brown
Green	Black	Black or hot-orange

EDSON DARK TIGER

This is a bucktail lure from North America which, along with the Edson Light Tiger, is making an appearance on our reservoirs. Dave Collyer wrote that these two are 'good, and I mean *really* good fish-takers'. They do well on the bigger stillwaters.

Hook: Longshank 6–10
Tying silk: Black
Tail: Barred guinea-fowl or mandarin-duck fibres
Body: Yellow chenille
Wing: Brown bucktail with jungle-cock cheeks
Throat hackle: Scarlet cock

EDSON LIGHT TIGER

Hook: Longshank 6–10
Tying silk: Yellow
Tip: Narrow gold tinsel
Tail: Barred mandarin-duck fibres
Body: Bronze peacock herl

Wing: Yellow or honey bucktail with jungle-cock cheeks
Gills: Two scarlet cock hackle points tied as underwings on each side of the under-body

EMIDAS

A few American dry flies have made the successful transition to British waters. This is a highly visible series devised for fishing on fast water. The Badger Emida is detailed below. The Brown Emida and Claret Emida differ only in their palmered brown and claret hackles.

Hook: 12–14
Tip: Embossed silver and gold tinsel
Body: Deerhair spun on the tying silk and clipped fairly short
Wing: Short grey duck feather set upright
Hackle: Palmered badger cock.

ENDRICK SPIDER   Plate 14

Simple patterns so often turn out to be the best, and the Endrick Spider gives weight to that premise. It is a general pattern attributed to John Harwood. Peter Mackenzie-Philps lists it in his catalogue and writes of it: 'Of all the flies we have ever tested on them (*his own rainbow trout*), this is outstandingly the best . . . We could hardly believe the confidence with which fish grabbed this fly, on the drop, swung gently in the current, or twitched – it made no difference.' I I can vouch for its trout-taking qual-

ities after giving it a thorough trial. It is one of those patterns that represent nothing at all, yet it is a fair impression of something aquatic and edible.

Hook: 8–10
Body: Lead or copper-wire underbody covered with cock pheasant-tail fibres tapering to the rear
Rib: Copper wire
Tail and hackle: Brown partridge hackle
An alternative dressing has a silver wire rib and a grey partridge hackle and tail.

This is an excellent pale watery dun imitation devised by Pat Russell. It is a good riser of trout and grayling. In Pat Russell's own words: 'It is a very good "bringer-upper" for fish which can be seen lying doggo. Sometimes an apparently non-feeding fish can be brought on to the feed after it has been covered five or six times ... The fly came about after I served an apprenticeship with Dick Walker and Peter Thomas in my old home town of Hitchin. We would wander up the River Oughton and wait for a particular fish to rise. As soon as it showed, Dick would cover it with his Ghost Swift Moth and it would be at the net and released for a repeat performance in a day or two. That fly had so much feather on it, and was so big, that some of us called it the Chicken Fly, as we reckoned he was casting the whole bird! That was in the early fifties. When I went to live in Topsham in Devon, I required a dry fly which would ride the ripples on the River Creedy, which could be seen and which caught fish. The Enigma did just that. The Mark II version is somewhat like a small version of the Ghost Swift Moth without wings. It is tied palmer-fashion and floats rather well.'

The Enigma is a useful Caenis copy, and a slight variation on a pattern being used to represent the Caenis is to include a few turns of tying silk on each side of the hackle to represent the thorax.

Hook: 14–18
Tying silk: Brown
Tail: Pale-cream cock fibres
Body: Cream cock hackle stalk
Hackle: Top-quality glassy pale-cream cock.

EPHEMEROPTERA
See pages 60–63

Unlike most other Orders of flies of interest to fishermen, this group has no common collective name. The term Mayfly is sometimes applied to all the members of the Order, but this leads to confusion with the two species *E. danica* and *E. vulgata*, which are more particularly known as Mayfly. They are sometimes called upwinged duns because of the way the adults carry their wings perpendicularly when at rest. They are of the greatest importance to the fly-fisher. Stillwater trout feed to a lesser extent on the nymphs, duns and spinners of the Order, but river trout and grayling consume these species in considerable quantities. Their value to the fly-fisherman has never been under-estimated, and most of the natural flies the dry-fly-fisher attempts to imitate belong to the Order.

All members of the Order, from the Caenis, the smallest, to the Mayfly, the largest, have physical characteristics and aspects of their life-cycle in common. The eggs are laid on the surface of the water and immediately sink to the river- or lake-bed, where they stick to stones or weed. The female spinners of the Baetis species, which include the iron blue, medium and dark olives, lay their eggs directly on underwater objects by crawling down reeds and stakes, etc. Depending upon the species, and the water temperature, the eggs hatch after an incubation period of between a few days and many weeks.

The length of time spent at the nymph stage varies greatly between species. Some remain nymphs for only two to three months, while the Mayfly nymph, *E. danica*, takes up to two years to mature according to some authorities. The time taken is greatly affected by water temperature. Nymphs of the same species hatching from eggs in October may take nine months to mature over a cold winter, but nymphs hatched in the early summer may take only two to five months.

The nymphs generally live on or close to the river-bed. Some, like the Mayfly nymph, burrow in mud, while others, such as the blue-winged olive, crawl along the bottom among weeds and stones. Yet others cling to vegetation. Most nymphs are extremely agile. Some swim in a jerky stop-start motion, others in a steadier, slower movement. Their growth is by a series of moults or a shedding of the outer skin. One species passes through twenty-seven different nymphal stages, but most go through far fewer. Finally the mature nymph is ready to leave its watery habitat to take to the wings which have been forming beneath its skin.

The mature nymph rises to the surface where, temporarily trapped in the surface film, it emerges into its winged state, the dun. It pauses on the surface while its wings dry. Generally speaking, the warmer the air temperature, the quicker the dun dries and leaves the surface. On cooler, damp days the dun lingers on the surface for some minutes, and in early spring and in autumn the duns often remain on the water for quite a while. Most duns spend between twenty-four and thirty-six hours as sub-imagos, but the Caenis has a total adult lifetime of about ninety minutes.

Characteristic features of the adults of the Order are that they carry their wings upright when at rest, and that they have six legs, two or three tails, and a segmented body. They are thus distinguished from any other fly on the water. The dun is, as its name suggests, a rather sombre colour. Spring or autumn hatches are frequently darker-coloured than the mid-summer hatches of the same species. Additionally, the air temperature on the day of the hatch may affect the colour of the duns; the cooler the air, the darker the colour of fly.

The dun moults and the metamorphosis from sub-imago to imago, from dun to spinner is complete. The legs and tails become longer, the body brighter, and the wings shiny and transparent. The colour of the spinners of a species may vary. The reasons are unclear, but most spinners darken with age, and the females darken after mating, which they do in flight.

The males of most species die over land and are of little interest to the fly-fisher, but the females return to the water, on which they lay their eggs. They then die on the surface, and the spent spinners, their wings trapped horizontally in the water, drift downstream to be devoured eagerly by the trout. Spent spinners of the Baetis species are likely to be found below the surface, because the females lay their eggs under water. Such is the sad end to a life-cycle that has been a battle for survival through four different stages.

The species of greater or lesser interest to trout and grayling are listed on pages 60–63. They are examined in more detail elsewhere under their common names. The differences between some species is minimal and evident only on close examination. No trout could determine some of these differences or tell apart the sexes of some species, but I have detailed them to aid identification.

EPSOM SALT   Plate 9

This is a minnow-imitating lure evolved by Freddie Rice's fly-tying class in 1973. Its success is due partly to the colouring and partly to the fact that it is a softish mouthful and not subject to immediate rejection as are some harder-bodied lures. Best results are achieved by fishing it along the bottom in a series of short, sharp jerks interspersed with longer, smooth draws.

Hook: Longshank 6–10
Tying silk: Hot-orange
Body: Rear two-thirds, medium-green or natural seal's fur; front one-third, a mix-ture of red and orange seal's fur
Rib: Silver wire
Tail and back: Five to eight strands of peacock herl tied in at the rear and trimmed to form a tail
Collar hackle: Hot-orange

FEATHER DUSTER

A once popular dry fly by this name has fallen from favour. The pattern that has inherited the name is one of the many recently developed marabou-winged lures. This particular one is for use on the larger reservoirs. It uses more marabou than other lure, which gives it an unusual action in the water. The bulk of the wing enables the lure to hang in the water, hardly sinking at all. The slowest of retrieves is sufficient to enliven the marabou. The lure can be fished deep and slow, either as an early-season pattern, or on those terrible hot, still summer days when fish are hard to come by.

Hook: Longshank 6–8
Tying silk: To match the wing colour, or red for the white version
Tail and wing: Black, white, orange or yellow marabou. Ten or twelve plumes each with their butt ends spun between wetted finger and thumb into a shuttle-cock. The first is tied in just slightly round the bend as the tail. The remainder are tied-in over a layer of silk along the back and finished with a varnished head of tying silk

FEBRUARY RED (*Taeniopteryx nebulosa, Brachyptera risi*)
See STONEFLIES

For some obscure reason these members of the stonefly Order are also known as Old Joan. The first species is common in parts of the north of England, Scotland, Wales and in the west of England. It is the only stonefly that does not live up to its name, as it prefers to inhabit the vegetation of slower-moving waters. The nymph varies in size between 8 mm and 12 mm.

The adults are between 7 mm and 11 mm and appear from February to April. The female is larger than the male with longer red-brown wings with two dark bands. The last three segments are also red-brown. The second species is similar and common and does inhabit stony-bedded rivers. The adults begin to appear in March and continue into July.

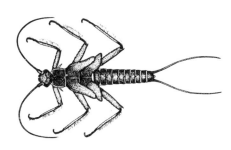

FEBRUARY RED (John Veniard)

A wet pattern.

Hook: 14
Body: Reddish-claret mohair at the tail; remainder lightish-brown mohair.
Wing: Speckled hen wing
Hackle: Dark grizzle-dun cock

Common name	Scientific name	Distribution	Habitat	Type of nymph	Appearance
Autumn dun	*Ecdyonurus dispar*	North and west of England; South Wales	Stony rivers; occasionally in lake margins	Stone-clinging	June–October
Blue-winged olive	*Ephemerella ignita*	Widespread	All types of rivers; some large lakes	Moss-creeping	May–November
Caenis	*Caenis horaria, C. marura, C. moesta, C. rivulorum, C. robusta*	Widespread	Lakes and rivers	Mud-inhabiting	May–September
Claret dun	*Leptophlebia vespertina*	Widespread, but localised	Slow-moving rivers; lakes; preference for slightly acidic water	Slow-moving on moss and stones	May–July
Dark olive	*Baetis atrebatinus*	South, south-west and north of England	Alkaline rivers	Agile-darting	April–May; September–October
Ditch dun	*Habrophlebia fusca*	Widespread, but localised	Slow-moving streams	Laboured swimmer	May–September
Dusky yellowstreak	*Heptagenia lateralis*	Scotland; west, south-west and north of England	Smaller rivers and upland lakes	Stone-clinging	May–September
Iron blue	*Baetis niger, B. muticus/ pumilis**	All areas except parts of south-east	Rivers	Agile-darting	April–November
Lake olive	*Cloën simile*	Widespread	Stillwaters	Agile-darting	May–October
Large brook dun	*Ecdyonurus torrentis*	Widespread, but localised	Smaller stony streams	Stone-clinging	March–September
Large dark olive	*Baetis rhodani*	Widespread	Rivers	Agile-darting	February–May and September–November
Large green dun	*Ecdyonurus insignis*	North and west of England; South Wales	Rivers	Stone-clinging	May–October
Large spurwing	*Centroptilum pennulatum*	Localised in South Wales, south and north of England	Alkaline rivers	Agile-darting	May–October
Large summer dun	*Siphlonurus lacustris, S. alternatus/ linnaeanus*, S. armatus*	Scotland, north of England, Wales	Stillwaters	Agile-darting	May–August
Late March brown	*Ecdyonurus venosus*	Widespread, except South and East	Rivers	Stone-clinging	April–October
March brown	*Rithrogena germanica/ haarupi**	Localised in Wales, Scotland, north of England	Rivers	Stone-clinging	February–April
Mayfly	*Ephemera danica, E. vulgata, E. lineata*	Widespread	Rivers and stillwaters	Mud-inhabiting	April–November
Medium olive	*Baetis buceratus, B. tenax, B. vernus*	Widespread in alkaline water	Rivers	Agile-darting	April–October

Approximate time of emergence	Place of emergence	Appearance (dun)	Anglers' names
Daylight	On water surface; on stones, etc, partly out of water	Large; two tails; grey or light fawn wings	August dun, great red spinner
Daylight and dusk	On water surface	Medium-large; three tails; bluish wings	Sherry spinner
Dawn and dusk	On water surface	Very small; three tails; creamy-white overall	Broadwings, angler's curse
Daylight	On water surface	Very dark grey wings; three tails; dark brown body	—
Daylight	On water surface	Medium; two tails; grey wings; olive/brown body	—
Daylight	On stones, etc, partly, out of water	Small; three tails; blue/black wings	—
Evening	On water surface	Medium; two tails; very dark grey wings	Dark dun
Daylight	On water surface	Small; two tails; blue/black wings	Jenny spinner, little claret spinner
Daylight	On water surface	Medium; two tails; grey wings	—
Daylight	On water surface; on stones partly out of water	Large; two tails; mottled wings	Great red spinner
Daylight	On water surface	Large; two tails; pale grey wings	Early olive, large spring olive, blue dun, large red spinner
Evening and dusk	On water surface; on stones partly out of water	Large; two tails; light fawn mottled wings	—
Daylight	On water surface	Medium-large; two tails; blue-grey wings	Large amber spinner, blue-winged pale watery
Daylight	On stones partly out of water	Large; two tails; grey wings	—
Daylight	On water surface; on stones partly out of water	Large; two tails; fawn wings	Great red spinner
Daylight	On water surface	Large; two tails; fawn wings	Great red spinner
Daylight	On water surface	Large; three tails; grey wings	Green drake, grey drake, spent gnat
Daylight and dusk	On water surface	Medium; two tails; grey wings	Blue dun, olive dun, red spinner

Common name	Scientific name	Distribution	Habitat	Type of nymph	Appearance
Olive upright	*Rithrogena semicolorata*	Western half of the country	Rivers	Stone-clinging	April–September
Pale evening dun	*Procloëon bifidum/ pseudorufulum**	Widespread in alkaline water	Rivers	Agile-darting	April–November
Pale watery	*Baetis fuscatus/ bioculatus**	South of England, parts of Wales and north of England	Alkaline rivers	Agile-darting	May–October
Pond olive	*Cloëon dipterum*	Widespread	Stillwater and slow-moving streams	Agile-darting	May–October
Purple dun	*Paraleptophlebia cincta*	North and west of England	Rivers	Agile-darting	May–August
Sepia dun	*Leptophlebia marginata*	South and north England, Scotland	Slow-moving rivers and lakes	Laboured-swimmer	April–May
Small dark olive	*Baetis scambus*	Widespread, preferring alkaline water	Rivers	Agile-darting	February–November
Small spurwing	*Centroptilum luteolum*	Widespread, but not Wales	Alkaline rivers and some stillwaters	Agile-darting	May–October
Yellow evening dun	*Ephemerella notata*	North, west and south-west of England	Moderately-paced rivers	Moss-creeping	May–June
Yellow May dun	*Heptagenia sulphurea*	Widespread	Rivers	Mainly stone-clinging	May–October

*The scientific name has been changed comparatively recently and may differ from that used in other fly-fishing text-books. Both new and old names are therefore listed in this table, the alternatives being separated by an oblique stroke. The first name is that now accepted, the second is the earlier scientific name. Reference: *A Key to the Adults of the British Ephemeroptera*, by J. M. Elliott and U. H. Humpesch, 1983, published by the Freshwater Biological Association.

FEBRUARY RED (Roger Fogg) — Plate 21

This pattern has its roots in one of Alfred Ronalds' dressings which Roger Fogg has updated. He tells me that it succeeds as an imitation of any of the small brown stoneflies, and that as an early-season pattern it has caught for him larger fish than the more popular patterns, such as the Partridge and Orange. It is recommended as top dropper of a three-fly cast fished upstream.

Hook: 12–14
Tying silk: Dark orange
Body: Claret and brown seal's fur, dressed slim
Rib: Brown tying silk
Hackle: Woodcock hackle over a third of the body on the wet fly. Reddish-brown cock hackle on the dry fly

FEBRUARY RED

A floating pattern.
Hook: 14

Body: Peacock quill dyed claret
Hackle: Rusty blue-dun cock

62

Approximate time of emergence	Place of emergence	Appearance (dun)	Anglers' names
Daylight and evenings	On water surface	Large; two tails; dark blue/ grey wings	Yellow upright
Evenings	On water surface	Small; two tails; pale grey wings	Little pale blue dun
Daylight	On water surface	Small; two tails; pale grey wings	Golden spinner
Daylight	On water surface	Medium; two tails; dark grey wings	Apricot spinner
Daylight	On water surface	Medium; two tails; blackish-grey wings	—
Daylight	On water surface; on stones partly out of water	Medium; three tails; brownish-grey wings	—
Daylight	On water surface	Small; two tails; medium dark grey wings	July dun, small red spinner, olive dun
Daylight	On water surface	Small; two tails; grey wings	Little amber spinner, little sky-blue dun
Late evening	On water surface	Medium-large; three tails; pale yellow body	—
Late evening/dusk	On water surface	Medium-large; two tails; yellow body	Yellow hawk

For a winged version, two dark-brown grizzle cock hackle-tips can be tied flat over the back of the pattern above.

FIERY BROWN
Plate 16

With more than 500 years of angling literature on which to look back, it is not surprising that we can trace some of the flies in present use back to their origins centuries ago. Although the Fiery Brown is generally accepted as an Irish lake-fly, it is likely that its real origins are English. Courtney Williams suggested that Charles Cotton's seventeenth-century pattern, **Bright Brown**, might be its ancestor.

In recent years the dressing has been so widely adapted that there is no 'correct' formula. Courtney Williams' pattern has a body of reddish-brown seal's fur. Other sources also give the one body colour, but include a tag of orange floss. The dressing below is a modern one. See also Fiery Brown under SEDGES (*page 157*).

Hook: 8–12
Tying silk: Brown
Tail: Golden-pheasant tippets
Body: Rear one-third, hot-orange seal's fur; front two-thirds, fiery-brown seal's fur
Rib: Gold wire
Wing: Bronze mallard
Hackle: Fiery-brown

FINGERLING

A fry-imitating reservoir lure that should be fished to imitate the manner of a small fish.

Hook: Longshank 6–8
Tying silk: Black

Tail: Hackle fibres dyed red
Body: Embossed gold tinsel
Wing: Five golden-pheasant tippets tied to show the three black bars
Throat hackle: Light-red cock

FIRE BALLS   Plate 9

A series of lures from Peter Mackenzie-Philps, of Wetherby. Their design is based on the Muddler series, the only difference being the head material. Recommended head colours are orange, pink, yellow, white, red (all fluorescent) and buff. The lure is intended for rainbow trout, but it has also caught brown trout and sea-trout, and steelhead in the U.S.A.

Hook: Longshank 4–8
Body: Gold tinsel or Lurex
Wing: Black squirrel-tail
Head: Fireball fluff in a very large head. This material is available only from Mackenzie-Philps

FISH FRY

In the latter half of the season on many stillwaters trout search the margins for shoals of fry, minnows and other small fish. It is not uncommon to see a commotion in the water, with small fish jumping out and the wake of trout chasing them. Another tell-tale sign that a shoal of fry is about might be seagulls swooping over the area of the shoal and feeding on the fry. The larger brown trout of many fisheries often fall to a suitable imitation at the end of the season. Trout feed on small fish throughout the year and an imitation has always a chance of success. Suggested artificials include MUDDLERS (*page 122*), CHURCH FRY (*page 37*), PERCH FRY (*page 144*), APPETISER (*page 6*), MINNOW STREAMER (*page 119*), FINGERLING (*this page*), and POLY-STICKLE (*page 149*).

FLASHABOU PRETTY DOG   Plate 2

A relatively new lure devised by professional fly-tyer Dave Tait, of Gloucestershire. It has attained widespread popularity among reservoir fishers. The Flashabou material is now being incorporated into other lures.

Dave Tait says of his lure: 'The Flashabou Pretty Dog is an improved version of a lure called the Pretty Dog which I developed during 1981. The original pattern had a marabou tail with a chenille body and bead-chain eyes. During 1983, I obtained a new material called Flashabou from America. It is in fact a fine, limp tinsel

and it was incorporated in the Pretty Dog. Flashabou comes in many colours, and it was obvious that it had a great deal to offer.

'Pretty Dog lures were the first U.K. lures to incorporate Flashabou, and during the first trials some very good catches were made from South Cerney's Rainbow Lake. However, it was when big trout started to be caught that the full potential of Flashabou was realised.

'During the long, hot summer of 1983 Flashabou took a number of trout at times when other lures were catching nothing. Fish of 9 lb 13 oz,

8 lb 12 oz and 6½ lb were taken during a four-day spell at South Cerney.

'During 1984, a fuller appreciation of the lure's potential was gained. For instance, a seven-fish bag was taken at Chew Valley lake, the best of which was 7 lb-plus. Trout and salmon fell to the Flashabou Pretty Dog. A 9 lb-plus brown trout was taken at Rutland on it only a matter of weeks after the fly was introduced nationally. I also took three 8 lb rainbows during one busy day at a small fishery called Brook Farm in Gloucestershire.

'Yellow Pretty Dogs were the original flies of that name, and this is my favourite lure colour.

'I always fish the Pretty Dog on a sinking line, because I can then fish all the water layers. Floating lines do produce fish, but I think that correct depth and possibly better presentation is gained by using a sinking line. The lure should be fished slowly, because stripping tends to destroy its action. Slow-retrieving gives that undulating flashing of the Flashabou tail that trout find so irresistible.

'Some anglers tend to call the Pretty Dog a Dog Nobbler. This is incorrect, because the lure does not have a painted lead-shot head. Dog Nobblers do not have Flashabou tails, either.

'I would suggest that a mix of colours is advisable in the tail. Two or three colours of Flashabou combined with the marabou tail give a nice flashing colour spectrum.'

Hook: 6–8
Tying silk: To match the body colour
Tail: Marabou plus strands of Flashabou, the colour of your choice
Body: Coloured chenille
Rib: Oval silver tinsel
Eyes: Bead-chain from a sink-plug chain

Tinsel strips can be used effectively as an alternative to Flashabou. These are not as soft and as mobile as Flashabou, but they do provide a workable and cheaper alternative.

FLUE BRUSH   Plate 22

This is an interesting fly devised by Lynn Francis. It is easy to see how the name originated, but what the trout take it to be, I'm at a loss to say. It fishes well in August and September as an ungreased point fly in a wave.

Hook: 8–12
Tying silk: Brown
Body: Palmered white, green and red hackles
Rib: Fine copper wire

FLYMPHS

Between the sub-surface mature nymph and the adult dun on the surface is an intermediate stage when, in the surface film, the wingless nymph changes in a matter of seconds into the winged dun. At this critical and vulnerable moment, the nymphs/duns become attractive targets for feeding fish. Various patterns have been devised to represent this important stage. This series of aptly-named flies was devised by an American, V. S. Hidy, to imitate the struggling insect emerging through the surface film. All his patterns are wingless and use soft-to-medium hen hackles, unless they are intended for use on turbulent water, when a stiffer hackle is needed. All the hackles are tied rear-slanting. The fly bodies are tapered from body fur spun between two strands of tying silk. For the detailed patterns see under IRON BLUE (*page 87*), TUP'S INDISPENSABLE (*page 188*), BLUE-WINGED OLIVE (*page 23*), PALE EVENING DUN (*page 134*) and STONEFLY (*page 180*).

FOG BLACK Plate 20

This was one of T. E. Pritt's patterns which, without the wing, was known as the **Little Black**. In addition to being a fair trout fly and Black Gnat copy, it is also an excellent grayling fly. Indeed, Pritt considered this to be his favourite top dropper for the species. Some fly-fishers may scorn the use of so old a pattern, but a number of grayling fishers of my acquaintance, some with more than forty years' experience on northern streams, rate this fly highly. Norman Roose, president of the Grayling Society, holds the fly in high esteem.

In an article in the society's newsletter he explained how the Fog Black received its name. Fog is the name given in Upper Wharfedale to the short lush grass which grows after haymaking, and the small black member of the Diptera Order which inhabits the grass often finds its way on to the water.

Hook: 12–14
Body: Dark purple silk
Rib: Magpie or ostrich herl
Wing: Starling wing quill as a substitute for the bullfinch originally specified
Hackle: Starling neck feather

FOOTBALLER Plate 15

This midge-pupa imitation devised by Geoffrey Bucknall was probably the first of the more modern style of buzzer dressing. It was originally tied for Blagdon reservoir in the 1960s. The original pattern used black horsehair, but red, green, orange, brown, olive and claret have followed and the materials have been revised. No breathing filaments were tied on the original, but they have been added since. The name developed from the original black-and-white stripped pattern, which looked like a football strip. Perhaps the ideal fly to fish in a team! Geoffrey Bucknall's revised dressing is as follows:

Hook: 8–16 standard or caddis hook
Tail: White fluorescent floss
Body: Stripped black-and-white hackle-stalks wound side-by-side from about half-way round the bend. They should be wound from the tips, so that the body thickens towards the thorax
Thorax: Grey seal's fur
Head: Two turns of bronze peacock herl
Breathing tubes: A tuft of white fluorescent floss forward over the eye

FORE-AND-AFT

This is not a pattern of fly so much as a style of dressing a dry fly developed on the Kennet by Horace Brown earlier this century. In addition to the head hackle, a slightly smaller hackle, often of a different colour, is wound in at the rear of the body. This causes the fly to float with its body well clear of the surface, resting only on the hackle-tips and imitating the natural upwinged fly, of which only the legs would be on the water.

FREEMAN'S FANCY Plate 16

Courtney Williams records the inventor of this lake fly as Captain W. Freeman, who first tied it about 1900. Williams rated it highly: 'No other fly can approach it' when a brightly-coloured pattern is required. Still-water fishing has developed dramatically since Williams wrote that, but winged wet flies in the traditional style are still popular and catch thousands of trout each season.

Hook: 8–12
Tail: Orange toucan or substitute
Body: Flat gold tinsel

Wing: Brown mallard with jungle-cock cheeks
Hackle: Magenta cock or hen

FROGHOPPER

This is a mid-summer terrestrial fly, the larvae of which live in cuckoo-spit found on plants and grass stems. For the rare occasions on which the adults are found on the water, Taff Price has devised a suitable imitation based upon the Jassid imitation tied by the American, Vincent Marinaro.

Hook: 14–16
Body: Brown palmered hackle clipped short at the top
Back: Two stiff mottled feather tips forming a roof over the back

FROG NOBBLERS See NOBBLERS

FROGS

This unlikely food source has been imitated by this pattern from Taff Price. It should be fished close to the surface. Although I have read reports of big trout taking frogs, I have never seen one do so, despite fishing frequently at two lakes that, during spring, seem to have more frogs than trout. Perhaps the Frog would succeed as a pike fly!

Hook: Longshank 4–6
Body: Clipped deerhair tied fairly bulky and coloured with indelible felt-pens, green on top and yellow underneath
Legs: Two sets of legs widely divided at the front and rear of the body. Green bucktail for the front, and yellow for the rear; or a mixture of both for both sets of legs

FUNNEL-DUNS Plate 26

Neil Patterson lives on the banks of the Kennet and is a keen observer of both fish and fly-life. His Funnel-duns were evolved from the thinking behind John Goddard's and Brian Clarke's USD Paraduns, in that he realised the basic idea of the bend of a dry-fly hook facing downwards was second best to having a fly that would float with the hook upside down, point in the air and beyond a trout's view. Neil modestly says that the dexterity needed for the USD Paraduns was beyond him and he set about devising an easier alternative. He wrote in *Trout Fisherman* magazine:

'In the beginning, the Funnel-dun set out to put to rights three basic design faults I believed afflicted the

traditional dry-fly tying method. First, that dry flies require the sort of quality cock hackle that I couldn't find. And when I did, couldn't afford. Second, that the traditional mounting of the hackle at right-angles to the shank ingeniously helped the fly to sink. In this 90-degree position, the full weight of the hook and fly bears down on the needle-sharp hackle-point piercing the surface skin. Third, that in the trout's window, the natural's thorax in outline – clearly visible from an underwater tank vantage – is absent on the traditional dry-fly pattern.

'It was while experimenting with how to mount the hackle so that the fly is supported on a broader base that the idea of "funnelling" the hackles over the eye – therefore offering up the flattened edge of the hackle flues to the surface – first came about.

'Tying-in a standard small dry-fly hackle at the eye and pulling it forward made the fly too long in profile. And winding the silk over the roots of the flues to hold them in position shortened the hackle, leaving me with prickly stubs.

'To overcome this problem, I experimented by winding in the hackle a third of the way down the hook-shank, not at the head, using larger hackles than those you'd use to dress a dry fly Halford fashion. By using these longer hackles, I found I was no longer dependent on capes that sported a luxurious spread of tiny hackles. Instead, I was plucking feathers from an area on a cape rarely used by dry-fly dressers – the zone you'd reach if (God forbid) you were to tie your olives on size 8s or 10s. Even a ten bob Indian cock cape has a super-abundance of these. And I had a stack of these in a bottom drawer.

'The drawback about these hackles is that, although the points and stems of each individual flue are as sharp and as bright as a top-grade Metz, at the foot of the flue, where it meets the stalk, they seem to wear woolly socks. They have fuzzy, flimsy bases. This, I discovered, softens when the fly gets wet or a fish crunches it, causing the hackle to lose its spring and shape and collapse pathetically along the body.

'However by "funnelling" them forward, and winding turns of silk over the roots to hold them sloping over the eye, you cover the woolly bases up, leaving the crisp, sharp stems to support the fly, flues that won't fold up under stress. To keep these "funnelled" hackles at 45 degrees over the eye, like an umbrella part blown out by the wind, I dubbed on a lump of fur in front of the hackle, in the vacant third between the

hackle and the eye.

'One thing led to another, logically and naturally. I was now tying grade A dry flies from streamer capes. I had broadened the base of the fly where hackle meets surface, taking the weight off the pin-prick hackle-points. I had added a thorax which, as well as giving the fly a more realistic outline, also served an important function. And I had added it in exactly the place it is on the natural, in front of the wings at the head . . . Since the Funneldun is a system, a method of tying a dry fly – and not a pattern – you can tie any fly you like, even patterns of your own making . . .

'Because the hackles protrude slightly in front of the Funneldun, making it a little longer than if it were tied by the conventional method, if I want a size 14 fly, I tie it on a 16. For a 16, I tie on an 18, and so on. This is a bonus. It means the hook is smaller and lighter in proportion to the fly-size. With less iron to carry, the Funnenduns float like balsa wood. And I don't add ribbing as extra ballast aboard.

'Don't be terrified of whip-finishing at the tail. It's easier than at the head. There's no wing or hackle to get in the way . . . When you tie in the the tail, tie it a little way round the bend, but not too much, otherwise the fly will rest on the body, rather than on the tail tips. After your first effort, you'll get to judge this distance according to the hooks you use.

'While the fly is still in the vice, cut out a small "V", by clipping off a few small hackle flues at the base, from the top-side of the hackle. This will be the underside of the fly when you chuck it on the table and it flips monotonously upside down.'

If you insist on adding wings, Neil suggests that feather-fibre wings are the best and recommends the breast-feathers of teal, widgeon or mallard.

'Take the breast feather and peel off the flues, leaving the tip. Secure this lightly on the underside of the hook after you've tied in the dubbed thorax. Pulling the stem through the loose turns of silk, judge the height of the wings. Then figure-of-eight round the base to hold the wing upright. I like to let it slope slightly forward towards the eye. Clip the butt and continue the Funneldun as prescribed.

'The Funneldun allows me to fish upside-down flies without turning me inside out at the vice. It allows me to fish upside-down flies all the time to every fish.'

Dave Collyer comments on this style of dressing: 'I may be wrong, but I think that this Funneldun method of tying dry flies could well be the biggest advance in dry-fly design and improvement since the advent of the eyed hook.' And they were invented in the mid-nineteenth century!

FURNACE   Plate 24

This is an old southern chalk-stream dry fly which F. M. Halford described as 'a very favourite hot-weather pattern'. Despite this, I doubt whether I would have included it here had I not read that Dave Collyer finds it to be an 'excellent winter grayling fly'.

Hook: 14–16
Tying silk: Light brown
Tail (optional): Furnace cock fibres
Body: Orange floss
Rib: Peacock sword feather herl
Hackle: Furnace cock

FUZZY-WUZZY   Plate 10

An early-season stillwater pattern to be fished deep and slow. It is modelled on the WORMFLY (*page 203*).

Hook: Longshank 6–10
Tying silk: Black

Tail: Black squirrel-tail
Body: Chenille of any colour tied in two, three or four sections. Suggested colours are black, scarlet, orange and dark green.
Hackle: Black cock at the shoulder and between the body sections

THE GERROFF   Plate 14

John Goddard created this pattern for small, clear stillwaters and clear, slow-moving rivers. Its first outing accounted for two limit bags of twelve trout totalling 49 lb for two rods. The fly was so named because unwanted smaller fish took the slow-sinking fly time and again before larger fish took it. The fly was christened by the angler shouting 'Gerroff'. John Goddard suggests that its success is due to the small body on a large hook which allows the fly to sink slowly, which trout seem to find irresistible.

Hook: 10–14 slightly longer shank than standard
Body: Mixed olive-brown and pink seal's fur (three : one) tied on the front half of the shank
Back: A strip of clear PVC or latex over the top of the body

GHOSTS

A series of streamer lures from the U.S.A. The third pattern is probably the most popular.

BADGER GHOST

Hook: Longshank 6–8
Tail: Yellow or orange hackle fibres
Body: Black floss
Rib: Embossed silver tinsel

Throat hackle: Yellow or orange hackle fibres
Wing: Four dark badger hackles

BLACK GHOST   Plate 10

Tail: Golden-pheasant crest fibres
Body: Black wool
Rib: Silver tinsel
Throat hackle: Golden-pheasant crest

fibres or yellow hackle
Wing: Four white hackles with jungle-cock cheeks

BLACK GHOST

This is Syd Brock's version. It should be fished fairly fast.

Hook: Longshank 6–8
Tying silk: Black
Tail: Yellow cock hackle fibres
Body: Black wool or stretched black PVC

Rib: White stiff plastic tape about 1.5 mm wide
Wings: Four matched white cock hackles extending just beyond the tail
Throat hackle: Yellow cock hackle fibres

GINGER QUILL   Plate 24

For more than a hundred years a fly of this name has been representing the pale watery and lighter olive duns. Some of the earlier patterns had upright wings, but more recent dressings omit these in favour of an optional blue-dun hackle at the head, in front of the ginger.

Hook: 14
Tying silk: Brown
Tail: Ginger cock hackle fibres
Body: Natural or lightly-dyed, well-marked peacock quill
Hackle: Ginger cock

GINGER SPINNER   Plate 24

The Ginger Spinner is a general spinner imitation suitable for representing a variety of natural upwinged spinners on rivers. This particular dressing was devised by G. E. M. Skues.

Hook: 14–16
Tail: Pale sandy-dun cock fibres
Body: Pale-orange seal's fur on hot-orange tying silk
Rib: Gold wire
Hackle: Pale sandy-dun cock

G. J. FINGERLING   Plate 9

Freddie Rice developed this lure and chose to try it at Grafham. With water lapping over his wader-tops, he took pike after pike up to 18 inches when fishing out into the reservoir. The lure excels when fry are driven into the margins by gorging trout. It should be fished in a short, jerky retrieve, followed by a slow-sinking of the fly, as if a small fish were injured.

Hook: Longshank fine-wire 6–8
Tying silk: Hot-orange
Tail and back: Bronze peacock herl tied in at the rear and trimmed for a tail
Body: White floss covered by medium-sized gold or silver Mylar tubing
Beard hackle: Hot-orange hackle fibres
Head: Scarlet floss

GLOWDOLLS

Plate 8

The Baby Doll has many variations. These fluorescent variants were devised by Peter Mackenzie-Philps. He claims that 'using a Fireball head on a Baby Doll gives a lure which our rainbows rush 10 yards to grab'. The Dollybody and Fireball fluff are available only from Peter at Wetherby.

Hook: Longshank 4–10 or Stronghold 8
Back and tail: White Dollybody
Body: White Dollybody
Head: A large head of Fireball fluff. Suggested fluorescent colours are orange, pink, yellow, white and red and non-fluorescent buff

GLOWSTICKLE

This is a Richard Walker variant of his own Polystickle. The luminescence is activated by shining a torch over the fly. The fly is particularly good when fished at dusk.

Hook: Longshank 6–8

Body: Luminous plastic strip, wound to produce a carrot-shaped body
Tail: White cock hackle fibres
Hackle: Sparsely-tied white cock
Head: Black tying silk

GODDARD'S LAST HOPE

Plate 23

This is John Goddard's imitation of the pale watery dun. It is also effective when other small flies are on the surface, including the Caenis.

Hook: Fine-wire 16–18
Tail: At least six of the hackle fibres
Body: Pale-yellow tying silk overlaid with buff condor herl or Norwegian goose-breast feather-fibres. Light-coloured herls are used for the early season and dark grey from mid-June onwards
Hackle: Short-fibred dark honey-dun cock

GODDARD'S RED or GREEN LARVA

Plate 12

Few angling writers have influenced fly-fishers over the last twenty years as much as John Goddard, and it is fitting that this book includes a number of his more widely-used patterns. This is his imitation of the large midge larvae found in the muddy lake or reservoir bottom. He suggests that it is best fished by allowing it to rest on the bottom and giving the line an occasional slight twitch.

Hook: Longshank 8–12
Tying silk: Brown
Tail: Red ibis quill or substitute about 12 mm (½-inch) long from the curly section, or the curved tip, of a cock hackle dyed red or green
Body: Crimson or olive condor herl covered with fluorescent floss of the same colour
Rib: Narrow silver Lurex
Thorax: Buff condor herl

GOLDEN-EYED GAUZEWING

Plate 26

This highly visible dry fly is useful for fishing at dusk. It was created by Taff Price and uses a material not usually associated with wings.

Hook: 10–12
Tying silk: Pre-waxed yellow or green nylon

Body: Fluorescent-lime silk slightly tapering to the rear
Wing: Two pieces of lime-green Raffene cut to shape, sprayed with artist's fixative and allowed to dry. Tie-in at 30 degrees over the back of the body
Hackle: Cock dyed light green

GOLDEN OLIVE Plate 17

A number of Irish lough patterns have become established lake flies in the U.K., and the Golden Olive is one of the better known. It is a useful general pattern, particularly when lake olives are about. Michael Rogan, son of the original tyer of the fly, suggests that the body colour is improved by using a mixed dubbing of 3:1 yellow and orange seal's fur.

Hook: 8–12
Tail: Golden-pheasant crest feather
Body: Golden-olive seal's fur
Rib: Oval gold tinsel
Wing: Brown mallard flank feather
Hackle: Golden-olive cock or Rhode Island Red cock

GOLDIE Plate 10

This bucktail lure was created by Bob Church in 1976. It was originally tied for the brown trout of Rutland. Bob comments: 'They love it.' He recommends a tandem version for use on a lead-core line from a boat.

Hook: Longshank 6–10
Tail: Yellow hackle fibres
Body: Gold tinsel
Rib: Gold wire
Wing: Yellow goat or skunk-hair with black goat- or skunk-hair over
Throat hackle: Yellow hackle fibres
Head: Black varnish

GOLD-RIBBED HARE'S EAR

A fly with origins way back beyond the last century. Whether fished as a nymph or a floater, it is an excellent medium olive or dark olive copy, and as a general impressionist nymph and dun it probably has no peer. It is a killer wherever olives hatch, whether on river or stillwater.

It was originally tied without a hackle, with merely the body fibres picked out for legs. F. M. Halford was later responsible for the addition of wings. But no matter how one chooses to fish the fly, and with which dressing, it is one of the few really dependable patterns. It is possibly taken also for a sedge-pupa when fished just below the surface. Although Halford later discarded the fly, probably because it was just too nondescript for his liking, he believed it to be the most killing pattern used on southern chalk-streams in his time. Many writers over the years have described the wingless version as one of the best-ever nymph-suggesting imitations. I subscribe to this view, as I have taken dozens of river and lake trout with it fished just below the surface.

A **Hare's Ear** or **Hare's Lug** is known throughout the country with minor variations in the dressing.

GOLD-RIBBED HARE'S EAR

Hook: 14–16
Tail (optional): Three long body strands
Body: Dark fur from the base of a hare's ear spun on yellow tying silk
Rib: Flat gold tinsel
Legs: Long body fibres picked out
A hackled version can be tied with a rusty blue-dun cock or hen.

AMERICAN GOLD-RIBBED HARE'S EAR

Only the Americans could tie this nymph pattern without actually using any hare's ear fur. Peter Lapsley tells me that he uses this as an imitation of the lake olive nymph and comments that it is 'one of the most deadly patterns I know.'

Hook: 12–14
Tying silk: Black or brown
Tail: Hare's body hair
Body: Hare's body hair
Rib: Oval gold tinsel
Thorax: Hare's body hair with some strands picked out for legs
Wing-case: Dyed black turkey-tail fibres

GORDON

The Gordon and Quill Gordon are both North American flies named after their creator, Theodore Gordon, the father-figure of American fly-fishing. Few dry-fly fishers across the breadth of North America fail to give space in the fly-box for these patterns. Both are excellent general flies taken for a variety of naturals. Over the last seventy years these have become the most famed of all American trout flies. Various dressings have appeared in print, largely because Gordon varied the dressings to match the different species hatching. I believe the dressings given are close to the original.

GORDON

Hook: 12–14
Tail: Speckled mandarin flank fibres (brown mallard as a substitute)
Body: Gold floss silk
Rib: Gold tinsel
Wing: Bunched speckled mandarin flank fibres
Hackle: Badger cock
A wet version is sometimes tied with a hen hackle and a flat gold tinsel tip.

QUILL GORDON

See also NO-HACKLE QUILL GORDON (*page 128*)

Hook: 12–14
Tail: Three summer-duck feather-fibres (brown mandarin)
Body: Dark stripped bi-coloured peacock quill (for spring use); lighter-coloured quill for summer use
Wing: Summer-duck feather-fibres set upright
Hackle: Smoke-grey cock, or dark-blue dun (spring use); or pale honey-dun (summer)
Mallard fibres with a brownish-olive tinge make a good substitute for summer-duck.

GOVERNOR Plate 24

This originally was a beetle pattern invented by T. C. Hofland in the late 1830s which has been amended over the years.

Hook: 12–14
Body: Green peacock herl
Rib (optional): Fine oval gold tinsel
Tag: Gold tinsel
Wing: Starling wing quill. An alternative version has a light hen-pheasant wing
Hackle: Natural red or ginger cock

GRAFHAM GREY LURE Plate 1

Plate 1

A three-hook tandem lure devised by
Tom Saville.

Rear hook
Tail: Golden-pheasant crest
Body: Grey fur or wool
Rib: Silver wire
Middle hook
Body and rib: As for the rear hook

Front hook
Body and rib: As for the rear hook
Wing: Two badger cock hackles tied back
to back
Cheek: Jungle-cock
Hackle: Badger

GRASSHOPPER

The Americans have produced some lifelike imitations of the natural grasshopper. Laying one in my hand, I almost expect it to leap into the air with a click of its heels. I doubt if quite so realistic an imitation is needed, and I think the two patterns given will be sufficient for the rare occasions on which you may feel obliged to fish an imitation. If, like me, you have no experience of using them, I suggest you try the one you find easiest to tie.

GREEN GRASSHOPPER (Taff Price)

Hook: Longshank Mayfly 12
Tying silk: Green
Body: Clipped deerhair coloured green
with an indelible felt-pen
Wing: Swan dyed green

Legs: Two cock pheasant tail fibres
Head: Bronze ostrich herl
A brown version is tied with a brown-coloured deerhair body, oak-turkey wings and a brown ostrich herl head.

GRASSHOPPER (Richard Walker)

Hook: Longshank 8
Body: Fine-grain polythene foam, split and glued to the shank and trimmed to shape
Back: Brown Raffene or pheasant tail fibres

Legs: Two swan primary feather-fibres dyed medium-brown and tied one on each side of the head
Beard hackle: Eight to ten pheasant tail fibres tied short

GRAVEL BED (*Hexatoma fuscipennis*)   See DIPTERA

A member of the Diptera Order, this flat-winged terrestrial lives in its pupal state in gravel or sand-beds at the edges of rivers. Their closeness to the water inevitably means that some of the adults end up on the river, and they can often be seen swarming over the surface. The adult is delicate and looks like a small crane-fly. Its body is brownish-grey with two heavily-veined brownish wings. It appears on warm days from late April until early June. Northern fly-fishers particularly find the imitation of value. See also CLYDE SANDFLY (*page 39*).

GRAVEL BED

A wet pattern.

Hook: 12–14
Tying silk: Purple
Body: Stripped peacock sword feather quill with the tying silk exposed at the shoulder
Wing: Hen pheasant tail fibres, laid almost flat along the back
Hackle: Long-fibred black cock

GRAVEL BED (Roger Fogg) Plate 27

A dry fly with a Parachute hackle.

Hook: 12–14
Tying silk: Lead-coloured or grey silk well-waxed with dark wax
Body: Lead-coloured tying silk with a thorax of mole fur
Hackle: Good-quality black cock tied so that the shiny side faces upwards and the fibres bend downwards

GRAYLING FIDDLER Plate 25

Although Eric Horsfall Turner was not a prolific angling writer, the exceptional quality of his work made up for this. His book, *An Angler's Cavalcade*, is well worth reading. He spent much of his life fishing the streams of North Yorkshire and one of his great loves was the autumn grayling. I once had the pleasure of sitting next to Eric at an angling dinner. During the meal he produced a small box of flies and among the Eric's Beetles were a couple of Grayling Fiddlers. They were beautifully tied and looked just right for difficult grayling. Sadly, despite a few hints from me, they all remained in his fly-box. I have tried the pattern on occasion and always caught fish. A size 18 hook was originally suggested, but I find this difficult to dress. More importantly, I haven't found the grayling to be deterred by the increase to a size 16.

Hook: 16–18
Body: Brown tying silk taken round the bend just short of the barb and dubbed with red wool or DRF floss. The body should be slightly shorter on the size 16
Hackle: Small grizzle cock

GRAYLING STEEL BLUE Plate 23

An excellent grayling fly created by Roger Woolley. It can be fished wet or dry. My preference is dry. This pattern is effective wherever grayling are found, not just on the Derbyshire streams that Woolley fished.

Hook: 14
Body: Peacock herl tied thin
Rib: Gold wire through the hackle
Tip: Three turns of orange tying silk and a tiny tip of silver tinsel
Hackle: Palmered bright-blue grizzle cock

GREAT RED SPINNER Plate 26

The great red spinner is the name given to the female spinners of the Late March Brown, March Brown and Autumn Dun. These are two patterns to represent them.

GREAT RED SPINNER (J. R. Harris)

Hook: 12–14
Tying silk: Claret
Tail: Dark rusty-dun cock fibres
Body: Dark red or claret seal's fur
Rib: Gold wire
Hackle: Dark rusty-dun cock tied half-spent

GREAT RED SPINNER (Roger Woolley)

Hook: 12–14
Tail: Natural red cock fibres
Body: Red seal's fur
Rib: Gold wire
Wings: Two medium-blue cock hackle tips or hackle fibre bunches, tied spent
Hackle: Natural red cock

GREEN-AND-ORANGE NYMPH   Plate 11

I have found this small nymph of use on small weedy lakes in mid-summer. By fishing it close to the weeds, one can take fish seeking refuge in the shade offered from the summer heat.

Hook: 12–14

Tying silk: Orange
Tail: Pheasant tail fibres
Body: Green ostrich herl
Rib: Fine silver wire
Thorax: Orange seal's fur
Wing-case: Pheasant tail fibres

GREEN BEAST

A water-beetle larva imitation devised by Alan Pearson. Most water-beetle larvae live close to the lake-bed and this pattern should be fished at an appropriate depth in a slow, steady retrieve.

Hook: 8–10
Body: Grass-green floss silk tied fat
Rib: Fine silver thread
Tail: Short green feather-fibres
Hackle: Brown partridge

GREEN DF PARTRIDGE   Plate 11

Richard Walker created this fluorescent, bug-like pattern for trout and grayling in rivers and stillwaters. It is probably taken for a variety of larvae and other food sources. On a number of rivers the bigger fish spend most of their time close to the bottom. The weighted version is ideal for fishing to them.

Hook: 10–16
Body: Optional underbody of lead-foil strips; lime-green DF wool tied fat
Rib: Silver thread
Hackle: Sparse brown partridge
Head: Black varnished tying silk

GREEN INSECT

Principally a grayling fly, this is also a useful green APHIS imitation (*page 6*). It is fished wet or dry. The red tag is common to a number of grayling flies. Its inclusion is important and similar flies without the flash of red often fail when those with some red in the dressing are catching fish. Red has been proved to be a stimulus to many members of the animal kingdom. The grayling seems not to be an exception.

Hook: 14–16
Tag: Red wool or silk
Body: Bright green peacock herl

Hackle: Small grey or blue-dun cock or hen

GREEN LUREX NYMPH Plate 14

A nymph version of Tom Iven's Jersey Herd, amended by Roger Fogg. He ties it as a flashy pattern for catching stillwater trout lying deep and sulking during hot sunny spells.
Hook: 8–14

Tying silk: Brown
Body: Lead-foil underbody wrapped with bright-green Lurex (becoming hard to obtain)
Hackle: Brown hen
Head: Peacock herl

GREEN PETER Plate 13

There is a sedge that hatches on Irish loughs during July and August known as the Green Peter (*Phryganea varia*), which I believe is unknown or extremely rare in the U.K. Irish patterns are beyond this book's scope, but in the last decade this artificial fly has come to be used on British stillwaters with great success. In Ireland it is fished both as a floater and as a wet fly on the top dropper, but it is principally as the latter that it is used over here. The pattern given is the standard wet dressing. The dry fly sometimes has a palmered red cock hackle.

Hook: 8–10
Tying silk: Brown
Body: Pale green seal's fur
Rib: Gold wire or black Naples silk
Wing: Hen-pheasant centre tail
Collar hackle: Natural red cock

GREEN RABBIT

A Richard Walker pattern for stillwater and river trout and grayling. It is remarkably similar in use and design to the Green DF Partridge. It is fished as a nymph on rivers. On stillwaters it is best fished with long slow pulls.
Hook: 8–14

Tail: Any buff or brown feather-fibres tied short
Body: Optional lead-foil underbody; a mixture of 2:1 wild black rabbit's fur and lime-green fluorescent wool, with the fibres well picked out
Rib: Fine gold thread
Hackle: Short-fibred brown partridge

GREENWELL'S GLORY Plate 24

Probably the most famous of all British trout flies. It was originally developed for the Tweed by Canon Greenwell and James Wright in 1854. Its continued popularity is due entirely to the fact that it is an excellent general imitation of all the olives. Depending upon the fly-size, and the shade of its dressing, it can represent all the olives and can be used when the iron blue is on the water. It was first tied as a winged wet pattern, but now it is tied as a floating fly, nymph, spider wet-fly and even as a lure. Because there is barely a week during the season when olives of one sort or another are not hatching, the pattern can be reliably used from March to October. If one were restricted, as a river fisherman, to one pattern all season, I doubt if one could do better than choose the Greenwell. Although it was devised as a river fly, it is also an excellent representation of the lake olive and pond olive.

The original pattern is listed first.

Hook: 14
Body: Waxed yellow tying silk
Rib (optional): Gold thread
Wing: Inside of a blackbird's wing (starling is a modern substitute)
Hackle: Coch-y-bondhu hen

The **Woodcock Greenwell** is as above except that it uses a woodcock wing. The **Greenwell Spider** omits the wing and has a longer-fibred coch-y-bondhu or furnace hen hackle.

GREENWELL

A floating variant.

Hook: 14
Tail: Furnace-cock hackle-fibres
Body: Waxed yellow tying silk
Rib: Gold wire

Hackle: Furnace cock with a medium blue-dun in front
An alternative dressing has a Greenwell hackle and tail fibres.

GREENWELL LURE

A tandem lure.

Rear hook
Body: Silver tinsel
Rib: Silver wire

Front hook
Body: Silver tinsel
Rib: Silver wire

Wings: Four Greenwell hackles (or coch-y-bondhu or furnace) tied back to back and extending to the tail of the rear hook
Hackle: Greenwell tied as a throat

GREENWELL NYMPH   Plate 19

Hook: 12–16
Tail: Coch-y-bondhu hackle fibres
Body: Waxed yellow silk or floss
Rib: Gold wire

Thorax: Grey or blue-grey fur
Wing-case: Grouse hackle-fibres with the ends turned down as legs

GREEN WIZARD   Plate 25

A grayling dry fly which does well in its smaller sizes on the rivers and streams I fish in North Yorkshire. Small green-bodied flies are sometimes attractive to grayling. This is one pattern that I've found effective. No doubt its usefulness is not restricted to that most prolific of grayling counties.

Hook: 14–16
Tag: Red wool
Body: Light-green floss
Hackle: Blue-dun cock

GRENADIER

One of the earliest of the modern reservoir flies. It was tied by Dr H. A. Bell for Chew and Blagdon. It can be fished successfully at various depths, although no one has offered an acceptable suggestion as to what it is intended to represent. In *The Super Flies of Still Water*, John Goddard suggests that it is better as a second-half-of-the-season pattern, to be fished on a dropper and retrieved slowly on a slow-sink line. He emphasises its usefulness fished in such a manner on hot, calm days.

Hook: 12–14
Body: Hot-orange floss or seal's fur
Rib: Oval gold tinsel
Hackle: Two turns of ginger or light furnace cock (sometimes palmered)

An excellent dry fly, this is a killing pattern for trout and grayling on both rivers and stillwaters. The smaller sizes are useful midge and caenis imitations, the medium sizes are a general floater and stonefly imitation, and the larger sizes can represent a moth. A Parachute version seems to work even better than does the shoulder-hackled version.

Courtney Williams suggested that it is also taken as an early olive, occasionally as a Mayfly, and sometimes as a needle-fly. He wrote: 'As a general utility dry fly for trout and grayling, the Grey Duster is one of the best – perhaps *the* best – pattern known to me. Certainly it is the only fly which has nearly tempted me to become a "one-pattern" angler. It has not succeeded in doing that, but I find myself using it for days on end, because it will tempt fish with such regularity that it is difficult to find anything better.' Many fly-fishers would go some way to echo those sentiments. It is a useful fly throughout the season.

Hook: 10–14
Tail (optional): Badger cock hackle fibres
Body: Blue-grey rabbit's fur
Hackle: Badger cock

GREY FOX

Preston Jennings was the first American to publish a really valuable guide to the entomology of that country and of the suitable imitations for the fly fisher. *A Book of Trout Flies*, published in 1935, has become a classic. This is one of Jennings' flies used on both sides of the Atlantic. John Goddard and Brian Clarke have suggested this variant for U.K. streams.

Hook: 10–14
Tying silk: Yellow
Tail: Honey-dun hackle fibres
Body: Light ginger quill
Hackles: Three – dark ginger, light ginger, grizzle cock, all long-fibred

GREY GOOSE NYMPH   Plate 15

A Frank Sawyer nymph tied to imitate the nymphs of the spurwings, pale watery and blue-winged olive. As with all Sawyer's nymph patterns, no attempt is made to imitate the legs of the natural. It is in this respect that Sawyer differs from many other fly-creators. He maintained that nymphs in the flow of the current hold their legs close to their bodies and that the tail was the means of propulsion. Sawyer's great emphasis was upon the overall size and shape of the nymphs and the materials used. This resulted in rather impressionistic caricatures designed to be fished fairly deep and with slim, weighted bodies which allowed a rapid entry into the water.

The Grey Goose nymph is principally a river pattern. A few friends and I have used it to good effect in small, clear lakes in mid-summer, but I'm not sure what it is then taken for. The dressing is similar to that of Sawyer's Swedish Nymph, but the goose herls used are not as dark as those on the latter.

Hook: 12–16
Tying silk: None (use the copper wire)
Tail: Grey goose fibres
Body: Grey goose wing fibres and golden-coloured copper wire wound together over a layer of copper wire. Additional weighting can be added by including a copper-wire thorax underbody
Thorax: Body fibres doubled and re-doubled and tied in with the copper wire

GREY SPINNER

Plate 23

This is a general spinner imitation created by Dave Collyer.

Hook: 14
Tail: White cock hackle fibres

Body: A strip of barrel teal wound on
Wing: Grizzle cock hackles tied spent
Hackle: Badger cock

GRIZZLE MINK

Plate 26

This nondescript dry fly from the vice of Neil Patterson fulfils his fly-tying philosophy: 'Why wait for a trout to make your fly more effective by pulling it about with its teeth? Do it yourself at the vice . . . The more bits hanging off my flies, the more fur flying, hackles ruffling; the more base grubbiness a fly has, the more my fins, like the trout's, bristle. Few flies can claim to be as downright scruffy as the Grizzle Mink. And it's this feature, on a blustery early-season day, that makes a prim-and-proper fly take on the appetite appeal of a lump of wood. If it has nothing else going for it, a roughly tied Grizzle Mink lives. It has life!'

Neil relates how on one occasion Stewart Canham caught an amazing total of forty Kennet trout in one session on the same fly. Neatness certainly doesn't count for much in this dressing. In an article in *Trout Fisherman* magazine, Neil commented: 'In the years I've been fishing the Grizzle Mink, it has proved to be a fly of enormous adaptability. As a dry fly on lakes, to imitate adult midge, lake and pond olives, it has trout rising as if on tracks. In Normandy, a small gang of converts fish it even through the Mayfly season on size 10–12 hooks. In New York State, on a size 20, I took (but lost) my only trout of the day on a pounded public water where the trout are claimed to have microscopes for eyes.

'Due to its popularity, there have been many variations of the Grizzle Mink, the correct tying understandably blurring *en route* . . . But before you leap to the vice, throw all the text-books out of the window. I cannot stress enough that untidiness and pure scruff are the keys to successful Grizzle Mink tying.'

The correct dressing is:

Hook: 14–18
Tying silk: Brown
Tail: A bunch of grizzle whisks
Body: Dun-coloured mink fur charged with longish hairs, some of which should stick out through the rib. Do not trim.
Rib: Fine gold wire
Hackles: Red cock wound through grizzle for the early-season; ginger cock wound through grizzle during summer

GROUSE SERIES

A range of lake flies with grouse wings. The combination of colours is extensive and is broadly similar to those in the mallard, teal and woodcock series, all of which differ, in the main, in their wing material. With the exception of the pattern given, the flies in this series can be found in the section headed MALLARD SERIES (*page 102*). The grouse-wing material is from the speckled tail feathers. The **Grouse and Yellow** is a useful sedge-pupa copy, the **Grouse and Claret** is a fair representation of the sepia dun and claret duns and their nymphs.

GROUSE AND PURPLE

Hook: 8–14
Tail: Golden-pheasant tippets
Body: Purple seal's fur

Rib: Oval gold tinsel
Wing: Grouse tail feather
Hackle: Black

HALF STONE

Originally a West Country wet pattern, this is now widely used as a dry fly. The original wet version is probably a good imitation of a hatching dun or a sedge-pupa rising to the surface.

Hook: 12–14
Tying silk: Cream
Tail: Blue-dun hackle fibres

Body: Rear two-thirds, yellow floss; front one-third, mole fur
Hackle: Blue-dun, which may be wound in the normal manner or palmered through the mole fur

A version using a honey-dun hackle and tail fibres is known as the **Honey Half Stone**.

HANNINGFIELD LURE

A Richard Walker tandem lure, which its creator described as also being deadly for perch. Although I have never used this lure, I once shared a boat on Malham Tarn, a beautiful limestone lake in North Yorkshire.

My partner did not seem to be concerned with the excellent trout in the tarn, but he caught perch up to 3 lb by the sackful. This was the pattern he used.

Rear hook
Tail: Hot-orange cock hackle wound on and trimmed
Body: Fluorescent white wool
Rib: Silver thread

Front hook
Body: White fluorescent wool
Rib: Silver thread

Wing: White goathair topped with speckled turkey or mottled peacock wing feather-fibres extending to the tail
Throat hackle: Short bright-blue hackle with a hot-orange hackle tied more fully behind the blue
Head: Black silk

HARDY'S FAVOURITE   Plate 18

Devised by J. J. Hardy of the famous fishing-tackle firm, this is a well-established Scottish loch-fly usually fished on the point or as a bob-fly.

Hook: 10–12
Tail: Golden-pheasant tippets
Body: Claret floss

Rib: Peacock herl
Wing: Woodcock wing
Hackle: Grey partridge breast feather
An alternative dressing has a tail of brown mallard fibres and a wing of brown turkey-wing fibres.

HARE'S LUG AND PLOVER   Plate 21

This old wet fly is described by Roger Fogg, author of *The Art of the Wet Fly*, as 'an excellent early-season pattern. It kills well on rivers such as the Derbyshire Wye when the large dark olive is emerging'. It imitates any of the emerging olives, and is a useful stillwater pattern when the lake olive and pond olive are about. It works well on rivers if it is dressed Stewart-style and fished upstream just below the surface film, suggestive of the emerging dun freeing itself from the nymphal shuck.

The origins of the fly are obscure, but it has been used for at least two centuries on Derbyshire streams. Never let the age of a trout fly deter you from using it. I would rather pin my faith in a pattern that has survived decades, even centuries of anglers' use, than in some of the one-season wonders we are bombarded with in the angling press. Despite its age, the Hare's Lug and Plover has the distinction of catching Roger Fogg's biggest number of trout in one day's river fishing. He says: 'I even approached the kind of number boasted about by Stewart himself in the nineteenth century', and in those days they assessed the catches by the score, not by the brace!

Hook: 12–16
Tying silk: Brown or primrose (varied to alter the olive shade)
Tip (optional): A small tip of flat gold tinsel
Body: Hare's ear fur tapering to the rear
Rib: Gold wire
Hackle: Golden plover (mouse-coloured with yellow tips)

HARRAY HORROR   Plate 18

This is an Orkney pattern devised by Stan Headley. I liked the look of the copy Stan sent me so much that I tied up a couple for fishing some of the Yorkshire lakes and reservoirs. Fishing it in the manner he advised, I caught trout at the two places where I used it, and I don't doubt its potential elsewhere. Stan devised it while trying to come up with an acceptable pattern for the mating shrimp. It has subsequently proved a first-class bob-fly in bright conditions. It sparkles in the water and its wet appearance is totally at odds with the dry. Stan comments: 'Kingsmill-Moore would have loved this fly'.

Hook: 10–12
Body: Dark greenish-brown olive ostrich herl, tapering towards the bend
Rib: Fine gold wire
Body hackle: Hot-orange cock
Head hackle: Mixed hot-orange hen and a hen hackle the colour of the ostrich herl body

HATCHING NYMPHS

The emerging dun struggling to leave its nymphal shuck and penetrate the surface film is a prime target for a feeding fish. The inch below the water surface is probably the most critical and most exciting inch of water for both fish and fly-fisherman. It also offers the greatest challenge to the fly-dresser. On many occasions sodden artificial dry flies have sunk below the surface and have been greedily snapped up by trout and grayling. Has the dry fly become a nymph, or is there something in between?

A few fly-tyers have offered different methods of imitating the hatching nymph or emerging dun. The style suggested by W. H. Lawrie is listed under some natural patterns. See IRON BLUE (*page 87*) for an example. See also SUSPENDER MIDGE (*page 115*) for John Goddard's suggestion, or under BOOBIES (*page 25*). The appropriately named FLYMPHS (*page 65*) are another example of an answer to the problem.

Richard Walker suggested this variation of the standard dressing which could be applied to many nymph patterns. A bunch of cock hackle-fibres is tied in to emerge from the top of the thorax. The fibres are tied vertically, but the wing-case material is laid through them so that they are split and spread out. The colour of the hackles should match the wing-colour of the natural dun.

HAWTHORN FLY (*Bibio marci*)   See DIPTERA

This important terrestrial fly has been copied by fly-fishermen for centuries. It is of value to both river and lake fishermen when the adults are blown on to the water in late April and May. The fly has a large black hairy body about 12 mm (½-inch) long, with a pair of long trailing hindlegs which make it distinctive. Most artificials are fished dry, although on stillwaters an imitation fished just below the surface often does well. There is no doubt that on some fisheries the Hawthorn is of some significance. Fishing a pattern on the leeward bank of a stillwater on a breezy May day is the most likely time for success. If naturals are falling on to the water, it is usually not long before trout realise and take advantage of them.

HAWTHORN FLY (Preben Torp Jacobsen)   Plate 27

The well-known Danish fly-tyer, Preben Torp Jacobsen, was a vet before his retirement. Few occupations could provide a better opportunity of procuring some of the more exotic furs and feathers. The original materials for this fly came from Copenhagen Zoo. Condor herls, like many other once-popular materials, are now scarce or on the prohibited list. Ostrich herl is a suitable replacement.

Hook: 12
Tying silk: Brown
Body: Black condor herls twisted on the tying silk
Hackles: Two black cock hackles
Legs: Two black condor herl tips tied in just to the rear of the hackles so that they trail backwards and downwards

HAWTHORN FLY (Taff Price)

Hook: Wide-gape 10–12
Body: Shiny-black rayon floss
Rib: Fine silver wire
Legs: Two knotted black pheasant tail fibres
Thorax: Black seal's fur
Wing: Grey duck tied flat over the back
Hackle: Black cock

HAWTHORN FLY (John Henderson)

Hook: 12
Tying silk: Black
Body: Black polymer dubbing
Rib: Fine gold wire
Hackle: Palmered black cock trimmed to between 3–6 mm (⅛–¼ inch) and black cock at the shoulder
Wing: Two light-grey hackle points

HAYMAKER

Dave Collyer devised this lure for water thick with algae. Such conditions often demand an orange or yellow lure.

Hook: Longshank 6–10
Tying silk: Yellow
Tail: Bright yellow marabou
Body: Yellow chenille
Overwing: A small bunch of yellow marabou
Underwing: Yellow marabou
Head: Yellow varnish with a painted red eye with a black centre

HEATHER FLY (*Bibio pomonae*)   See DIPTERA

This is similar to the Hawthorn Fly except that the tops of the legs are a reddish colour. It is a more localised species, commonest in Scotland, parts of Wales and the North of England where heather grows. Heather flies are sometimes found on the water surface during their most prolific months, July and August. In some parts of the country it is also known as the *Bloody Doctor*. The scarcity of patterns indicates that it is of not as great value as the Hawthorn Fly.

Hook: 12
Body: Black ostrich herl
Hackle: Coch-y-bondhu

HENDRICKSON

An American dry fly originally tied by Roy Steenrod to represent the upwinged dun *Ephemerella subvaria*, unknown in the U.K. However, the two patterns below are both useful general patterns and are being offered by some British fly-tyers.

DARK HENDRICKSON   Plate 25

Hook: 12–14
Tail: Squirrel-tail fur or dark blue-dun hackle-fibres
Body: Dark blue-grey fur
Wing: Mandarin-duck speckled flank feather-fibres set upright
Hackle: Dark blue-dun cock

LIGHT HENDRICKSON

Hook: 12–14
Tail: Squirrel-tail fur
Body: Cream-coloured fox belly fur
Wing: Mandarin-duck speckled feather-fibres set upright
Hackle: Light blue-dun cock

HI C SERIES

A series of highly-visible dry flies suitable for fishing fast, rough water. The double hackle makes them good floaters. Some of the series are variants of imitations of natural flies; others are general patterns.

HI C BADGER   Plate 24

Hook: 12–14
Tail: Natural red hackle fibres
Body: Black silk
Hackles: Small blue-dun, natural red, badger cocks
The **Hi C Black** has a black hackle in place of the badger

HI C PALE WATERY   Plate 24

Tail: Olive hackle fibres
Body: Yellow silk
Hackles: Natural red with a blue-dun in front

HI C RED SPINNER

Tail: Cream hackle-fibres
Body: Red silk overlaid with a thin layer of clear PVC or polythene
Hackle: Natural red with a blue-dun cock in front

HOT PANTS Plate 12

Freddie Rice devised this fly after reading of American Navy wartime research into the most easily seen colour in water for application to Air Corps dinghies to aid air-sea rescue operations. Freddie comments: 'They came up with orange, which prompted me to consider using it in fly design. Black provides a solid silhouette, so I based the design on Ivens' Black-and-Peacock Spider, adding the fluorescent orange tag and the hot-orange squirrel-tail wing. At first I fished it slowly (à la Black and Peacock), but later changed to a series of short (four-inch) draws and added a lead underbody in some cases to get it well down. The colour combination certainly worked, and at the lakes where I fish the fly was soon a firm favourite.'

Hook: Standard or longshank 8–10
Tying silk: Black
Butt: Hot-orange nylon floss
Body: Fine lead wire or two layers of copper wire, with four strands of peacock herl or black chenille over
Wing: Hot-orange squirrel-tail extending to the hook bend
Hackle: Long-fibred black hen

HOUGHTON RUBY Plate 24

William Lunn was a Test river-keeper who devised a number of flies for the southern chalk-streams. Of all his dressings, three stand out above the others and are still used today. This is one. The others are Lunn's Particular and his Caperer imitation. The Houghton Ruby is an excellent female iron blue spinner imitation. I have not fished with it on its home stream, but it does kill well on the rain-fed Yorkshire rivers. I have also caught a lot of autumn grayling with it when there hasn't been an iron blue in sight.

Hook: 12–14
Tying silk: Crimson
Tail: Three fibres of a white cock hackle
Body: Rhode Island Red hackle stalk dyed crimson
Wing: Two light-blue-dun hackle tips tied spent, or sometimes semi-spent
Hackle: Rhode Island Red cock

HOUSEFLY (Pat Russell) Plate 26

See also BLUE-BOTTLE (*page 23*).

Hook: 14
Tying silk: Black
Body: Bronze peacock herl tied fat
Wing: Two small whole grey feathers tied flat across the back in a slight V-shape
Hackle: Long-fibred black cock

HOUSTON GEM Plate 18

This Scottish loch fly enjoys a high reputation.

Hook: 10–14
Tail: Red ibis or golden-pheasant tippets
Body: Black silk
Rib: Flat silver tinsel
Wing: Well-marked cock-pheasant neck feather
Hackle: Black hen

ICHNEUMON FLY Plate 20

A member of the Hymenoptera Order, most of which are terrestrial. This one species is in part aquatic, but this black-and-orange-bodied fly is rarely seen on the water. The only pattern of which I am aware goes back to Alfred Ronalds. He called it the **Orange Fly**.

Hook: 14
Body: Orange silk
Rib: Black silk

Wing: Dark starling or hen blackbird
Hackle: Very dark furnace

IMP
Plate 25

This is one of H. A. Rolt's grayling patterns which is fished wet or dry. It is as at home on any grayling stream as it is on the southern rivers for which it was devised. I have found the floating fly most effective.

Hook: 14–16
Tail: Red ibis or substitute
Tip: Flat gold tinsel
Body: Heron herl
Hackle: Black cock or hen

INVICTA
Plate 16

The Invicta is an excellent lake fly and a useful river pattern. It is fished wet just below the surface, where it is probably taken as a hatching sedge. Few lake-fishers of any experience have not caught trout on this fly. It is one of the few old flies that has survived the revolution in design of stillwater flies. James Ogden, author of *Ogden on Fly Tying*, 1879 was its creator.

Hook: 10–14

Tail: Golden-pheasant crest feather
Body: Yellow seal's fur
Rib: Gold wire through the hackle
Hackle: Natural light red, palmered along the body with blue jay at the head
Wing: Hen pheasant centre-tail tied across the back
An alternative dressing has a tail of dyed red feather-fibres trimmed square. The **Silver Invicta** and **Gold Invicta** have silver and gold tinsel bodies and ribs. The **Green Invicta** has a body of green seal's fur ribbed with gold.

INVICTA SEDGE PUPA

Dave Collyer devised this variation, purposely omitting the wings, because in his own words: 'It never seems reasonable to me that a trout should expect to find a fully-winged sedge-fly swimming about underwater!' It may not seem reasonable, but winged wet sedge patterns have always been successful.

Hook: 10
Tying silk: Olive
Abdomen: Yellow wool
Rib: Oval gold tinsel
Thorax: Mixed dark-green and brown wool, or yellow wool only
Wing-case: Oak-turkey wing strip
Beard hackle: Blue jay wing-fibres

WHITE-HACKLED INVICTA
Plate 16

According to expert Orkney fly-fisher, Stan Headley, this variation is one of Orkney's best bob-flies, but its effectiveness is not restricted to that part of the country. Stan suggests that it is a 'temperamental fly', not working for everyone, but certainly worth trying. It is fished on the bob in large sizes and is a renowned taker of big fish. It excels in coloured or peat-stained water. The hook size is 8 or 10, and the dressing is as for the standard Invicta plus a longish white hen hackle tied in front of the wing to replace the blue jay.

IRON BLUE (*Baetis niger, B. muticus*)   See EPHEMEROPTERA

These two species are common on rivers and streams throughout the country except in parts of the south-east corner of England. The colouring of these two Baetis species makes them easily distinguished from other upwinged duns. However, the differences between the two are minimal and of no significance for the angler. The nymphs are the agile-darting type. Hatches of the duns begin in April or May and continue intermittently until as late as November. These smallish duns seem to get smaller as the season progresses. They often appear when no other duns are about and can be expected even on cold, blustery days.

The spinners of both sexes are of interest to trout and grayling, and they are

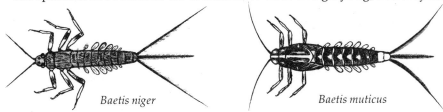

Baetis niger   Baetis muticus

likely to be encountered mainly in the latter half of the season during all the daylight hours. Both Goddard and Harris say that a mild day after a period of cold weather, when the duns might have emerged in considerable numbers, should result in a large fall of spinners. The spent females remain trapped below the surface in common with other Baetis species, and if the floating fly fails to rise fish, a sunken imitation is well worth trying.

The male dun has grey-black or blue-black wings and a grey-black abdomen with dark brown legs. The legs are dark olive and the two tails are olive-grey or black-grey. The female dun has grey-black or slightly paler wings and a dark brown-olive abdomen. The legs are olive-brown and the two tails are dark grey. The male spinner, known commonly as the jenny spinner, has transparent, colourless wings and a translucent white abdomen of which the last three segments are dark browny-orange. The two tails are white-grey and the legs are pale grey with the forelegs darker.

The female spinner, sometimes known as the little claret spinner, has transparent, colourless wings and a dark claret-brown abdomen with a paler underside. The legs are olive-grey and the two tails are pale grey.

The imitation of these species is a great killer of trout and grayling. It is of particular value to the Northern wet-fly fishers who have been copying the nymph and hatching dun for centuries with a variety of spider patterns. In addition to those dressings below, see also HOUGHTON RUBY (*page 85*), SNIPE AND PURPLE (*page 176*), WATCHETTS (*page 193*), WILLOW FLY (*page 200*), WATERHEN BLOA (*page 22*), OTTER RUBY (*page 134*), ADAMS (*page 1*), BLUE UPRIGHT (*page 23*) and GREENWELL'S GLORY (*page 77*).

IRON BLUE NYMPH

Hook: 16
Tying silk: Claret
Tail: White cock hackle fibres
Body: Mole's fur with a tip of tying silk exposed at the rear

Thotax: Mole's fur
Wing-case: Black crow or waterhen wing
Legs: Wing-case fibres tied beneath the body

87

IRON BLUE NYMPH (W. H. Lawrie)

One of two patterns suggested by Lawrie in *The Book of the Rough Stream Nymph*, 1947.

Hook: 16
Tying silk: Claret or crimson

Tail: Soft greyish-white feather-fibres
Body: Mole's fur
Thorax: Blue-black cat's fur
Legs: Very dark blue-dun hen sparsely tied

IRON BLUE FLYMPH

For fuller details see under FLYMPHS (*page 65*).

Hook: 14–16 longshank Mayfly
Tying silk: Claret or black

Tail: Dark blue-dun hackle fibres
Body: Mole's fur
Hackle: Dark blue-dun, starling or coot

IRON BLUE DUN HATCHING DUN (W. H. Lawrie)

When fished correctly, only the hackle and thorax should be on or above the surface.

Hook: 16
Tying silk: Claret
Tail: Three soft white or cream hen fibres
Body: Mole or water-rat fur

Thorax: Blue rat's fur dyed a shade of purple
Wing hackle: Medium slate-blue cock with the lower fibres trimmed away
Leg hackle: Dark blue cock with the upper fibres cut away

IRON BLUE DUN (Frank Sawyer)

Hook: 14–16
Tying silk: Purple
Tail: White cock hackle fibres

Body: Pheasant-tail herls
Hackle: Light-purple cock

IRON BLUE DUN (Pat Russell) Plate 28

Hook: 16–17
Tying silk: Crimson
Tail: Dark slate-blue cock hackle fibres
Body: Dark heron herl, leaving a tiny tip

of neon-magenta silk at the tail
Hackle: Dark slate-blue cock; two short-fibred hackles palmered from half-way down the body to the head

IRON BLUE SPINNER (FEMALE) (Richard Walker)

Hook: 14–16
Tying silk: Crimson
Tail: Six to eight long fine white goat or rabbit guard hairs
Body: Mixed magenta and chestnut-dyed

lamb's wool (1:2)
Rib: Crimson silk
Thorax: Sepia lamb's wool
Wing: Dyed slate-coloured bunches of fine hair tied spent

IRON BLUE SPINNER (MALE) (John Veniard)

Hook: 14
Tail: White cock hackle fibres
Body: White silk covered with natural

horsehair with a tip of bright red silk showing at the rear and the same exposed at the shoulder

Wing: White cock hackle-points tied spent
Hackle: One turn of white cock hackle

See also SUNK SPINNER (*page 184*) for female spinner imitation to be fished sub-surface.

IRRESISTIBLES

A series of very buoyant American dry flies, but if only trout flies lived up to their names! The larger sizes have been known to take even salmon.

IRRESISTIBLE

Hook: 12
Tail: Brown bucktail
Body: Natural grey deerhair spun and clipped
Wing: Two grizzle hackle-tips set upright
Hackle: Grizzle cock

WHITE IRRESISTIBLE   Plate 23

Tail: White cock fibres
Body: Natural grey or white deerhair spun and clipped
Wing: Two badger hackle-tips or white bucktail fibres set upright
Hackle: White cock
The **Black Irresistible** is as above except that it uses black materials and badger hackle-tip wings.

ITCHEN OLIVE   Plate 27

Gordon Mackie, the creator of this pattern, comments: 'The Itchen Olive was devised during the 1975/76 season when it was found that while trout rose every evening to pale duns, such as small spurwing and pale evening duns, they were seldom tempted by any of the standard patterns. The Itchen Olive was an immediate success, and has since accounted for hundreds of fish which would "not look at anything". It is today used widely on the Itchen and would, I'm sure, prove equally attractive to trout elsewhere which feed on "pale stuff". On the Wylye, however, where I mostly fish, the fly is not as effective, probably because it is primarily a blue-winged olive river with less pale fly during the early evening. Here, the Pheasant Tail is king.

'The beauty of the Itchen Olive is that it is easy to tie, although good-quality materials – which are essential – may not be readily available. It can be varied to represent other species, such as the medium olive, just by using different silks. Many natural flies are similar in appearance – more so than most anglers realise – so that the Itchen Olive is essentially a general-purpose fly. The fly should rise high on the surface.'

Hook: 14
Tying silk: Primrose
Tail: Four or five stiff pale-grey spade hackle fibres
Body: Thinly-dubbed medium-grey seal's fur
Rib: Tying silk
Hackle: Three or four turns of a light-grey cock hackle, stiff and springy, from a natural or photo-dyed cape. Minimum web, or two hackle feathers.

'The Itchen Olive looks quite uninteresting, and certainly not very colourful. It's meant to, because naturals are largely "dun" or grey in appearance. Size shade and posture are important, but I see no reason to add wings. I have experimented a good deal with different shades of hackle and seal's fur, as well as silks. Each is successful on occasion, but with too much alteration it ceases to be an Itchen Olive!'

IVENS' NYMPHS

Tom Ivens' book *Still Water Fly Fishing* of 1952 had a considerable impact on British reservoir fishing. This was the first authoritative work on the styles and methods of lure and nymph fishing on stillwater. The growing number of recruits to reservoir fishing were hungry for knowledge, and Ivens provided the textbook that was to be referred to and relied upon for many years afterwards. Three flies that emerged from the book have survived, the Jersey Herd, Black and Peacock Spider and this series of nymphs.

IVENS' BROWN NYMPH

Hook: 8–12
Tying silk: Brown
Body: Dark-brown ostrich herl
Rib: Oval gold tinsel

Horns: Two strands of stripped green ostrich herl, rear-facing
Head: Bronze peacock herl

IVENS' BROWN-AND-GREEN NYMPH   Plate 14

In addition to being a general nymph pattern, this is also a sedge-pupa imitation and a passable small fry imitator.

Hook: 8–10
Tying silk: Brown

Body: Olive and brown ostrich herls wound together
Rib: Oval gold tinsel
Back: Four strands of green peacock herl tied in at the head and tail, but extending beyond the bend as a tail
Head: Peacock herl

IVENS' GREEN NYMPH

Hook: 8–12
Tying silk: Green
Body: An underbody of white floss over-laid with pale-green nylon
Hackle: Brown partridge
Head: Bronze peacock herl

IVENS' GREEN-AND-YELLOW NYMPH

This is a useful sedge-pupa imitation that needs to be fished very slowly. Tom Ivens fished this without any retrieve at all, allowing it to drift round with any breeze there may be.

Hook: 10–12
Tying silk: Green
Body: Rear-half, swan herl dyed green; front-half, swan herl dyed yellow
Head: Peacock herl

JACK FROST   Plate 5

Bob Church devised this fry-imitating lure for big trout feeding on bream fry in Grafham in 1974. In addition to its original role as a bream-fry imitation, it is also an excellent general lure for use from both boat and bank. I was introduced to it during the opening week of the 1978 season when fishing Fewston reservoir. The water was as rough as the North Sea and I had caught nothing in four hours' fishing. An angler thirty yards away had caught half-a-dozen fish, so, swallowing my pride, I asked him what he was using. I was kindly supplied with my first Jack Frost, and within the hour I had my four-fish limit. It has earned a permanent place in my fly-box. Like all marabou-winged patterns, the slightest movement brings it to life, so it should be fished in steady pulls with intermittent pauses.

Hook: Longshank 6–8
Tying silk: Black
Tail: A small tag of fluorescent red wool
Body: White baby wool covered with

stretched, clear polythene
Wing: White marabou
Hackle: Generous turns of long-fibred red, and three turns of white tied rear sloping
Head: Black varnish.

JACK KETCH   Plate 12

Geoffrey Bucknall devised this still-water pattern, basing it upon the proven success of the Black-and-Peacock Spider. It is probably taken for a small beetle, with the silver tip representing the air-sac. It should be fished slowly on a long leader and it is good in deep water along a dam wall. Jack ketch was the mediaeval name

for the hangman.

Hook: 10
Tip: Flat silver tinsel
Body: Underbody of lead wire covered with mixed black, claret, blue and red seal's fur
Hackle: Three turns of long-fibred black hen

JERSEY HERD   Plate 10

A lure and fry-imitation devised by Tom Ivens. It was popular in the 1950s and 1960s, when it paved the way for many other lures. It is named after the milk-bottle top foil used in the original dressing. The dressing has been much abused by fly-tyers, but I am assured that this is Ivens' intended dressing.

Hook: Longshank 6–10
Tying silk: Black or hot-orange
Body: White floss silk covered with wide

copper-coloured tinsel or Lurex
Rib: Copper wire (optional for strength)
Tail and back: Strands of peacock herl
Hackle: Hot-orange as a beard or rear-sloping collar
Head: Peacock herl

An alternative and popular body material is gold Mylar tubing. The **Silver Herd** has a silver tinsel body; the **Red Tagged Herd** is a Silver Herd with a red wool tail; the **Yellow Herd** has a silver tinsel body and a yellow beard hackle.

JOHN STOREY   Plate 23

An excellent North Country dry fly on which, by coincidence, I caught my first trout on dry fly. It was devised by John Storey, a riverkeeper on the Rye in North Yorkshire. The revision of the wing was adapted by the creator's grandson in 1935. The original wing slanted over the body in wet-fly style. It is always fished as a floater and it is a great killer of trout and grayling on chalk-streams and rain-fed rivers. Arthur Oglesby once fished this pattern for a whole trout season to the exclusion of all other patterns, and he actually caught slightly more fish

than his average season's tally. I'm not sure what this proves, except that as a general utility fry-fly it is one on which it is hard to improve.

Hook: Down-eyed 14
Tying silk: Black
Body: Copper peacock herl
Wing: A small whole mallard breast-feather tied in a bunch sloping forward over the eye
Hackle: Dark Rhode Island Red cock

Some modern dressings incorporate a rib of red or scarlet tying silk or red DFM floss.

JOHN TITMOUSE

This variant of the John Storey was devised by Eric Horsfall Turner as a grayling fly. It was so named because it is effective when rising grayling seem merely to be 'titching' at a fly. Under these circumstances, persuading grayling to take a dry fly and hooking fish that do rise is extremely difficult. A few patterns work better than most on these occasions, and this is one of them. Its creator took more than 200 grayling on this fly in its first season, which should be proof enough of its effectiveness.

Hook: 16–18
Tying silk: Black
Tail: White hackle fibres
Body: Peacock herl
Wing: A very small mallard breast feather about 8 mm long, sloping forward over the eye
Hackle: Black cock

JUNGLE COCK   Plate 17

A lake fly in traditional style. The **Jungle Cock and Silver** is as below, except it has a silver tinsel body and rib and the option of a black or blue hackle. Both patterns are also fished as tandem lures.

Hook: 10–12
Tail: Golden-pheasant tippets
Body: Black floss.silk
Rib: Gold wire
Wing: Eyed jungle-cock or substitute
Hackle: Black cock

KATE MACLAREN   Plate 16

A Scottish loch and sea-trout fly devised by William Robertson in the 1930s. It is best on the bob when fished in a team. It is not much used beyond the Scottish Borders, but it has an excellent reputation in its homeland.

Hook: 8–12
Tying silk: Black
Tail: Golden-pheasant topping
Body: Black seal's fur with a palmered black cock hackle
Rib: Oval silver tinsel
Hackle: Red-brown cock

KE-HE   Plate 18

This lake fly, of Orkney origins, has become a standard pattern on many Scottish lochs, and in the last few seasons it has been making an appearance on some English reservoirs. In the 1930s two anglers named Kemp and Heddle (hence the name) tied the pattern to copy some black bees falling on the water. It is still popular and is probably taken for a terrestrial of some sort.

Stan Headley, an expert Orkney fly-fisher, comments: 'The Ke-He is an all-season pattern, and works well on peaty or clear waters. I prefer it on windy, bright summer days in size 10, usually on the tail. Variations on the original dressing are usually confined to the hackle colour. The **White** or **Benbecula Ke-He** is popular in the Western Isles. The **Black Ke-He** is an excellent pattern for early-season and late-season work. For late evenings, the **Orange Ke-He** is a renowned fly for use in difficult conditions, and as a taker of bigger trout.

The Ke-He seems to work no matter where in the country it is used, and visitors to the large Irish loughs would be well-advised to carry a few in largish sizes. It is also good for sea-trout in stillwater.

Hook: 8–14
Tail: Golden-pheasant tippets
Tag: Red wool
Body: Green or bronze peacock herl tied fat
Rib: Gold wire
Hackle: Medium red-brown.

KENDALL'S EMERGER (C. Kendall) — Plate 15

A spider pattern to be fished slowly during Midge hatches on stillwaters. Single colour patterns are tied in black, olive and brown. Don't underestimate this plain-looking fly; its creator took more than 100 trout on it in 1984.

Hook: Yorkshire sedge hook 8–18
Body: Fine seal's fur or wool dubbing ribbed with clear polythene
Hackle: Hen as for the body colour
Thorax: A small amount of the body dubbing in front of the hackle

KILL-DEVIL SPIDERS — Plate 19

These three Derbyshire wet flies are general imitative patterns suggestive of aquatic spiders or an assortment of terrestrials. They were once popular, but I'm not sure of their reputation today.

Hook: 14

Tip: Gold or silver tinsel
Body: Peacock herl
Hackle: Long-fibred bright medium-blue cock

The **Kill Devil Black Spider** omits the tips and has a long-fibred black hackle. The **Kill Devil Red Spider** omits the tip and has a long-fibred natural red hackle.

KILLER BUG — Plate 19

Also known as the **Grayling Bug**. Of all flies, few are more aptly named than this deadly chalk-stream grayling pattern created by Frank Sawyer. Its creator describes in his book, *Nymphs and the Trout*, how this was tied specifically to catch grayling, and how, in his own hands, it also caught salmon. Thousands of grayling and trout are caught on this each year. The dressing is so generally impressionistic that it could be mistaken for a shrimp or a pupa or larva of one sort or another. It is also one of the easiest flies to tie. The darning wool originally recommended, Chadwick's 477, has been discontinued by the manufacturers, but various beige shades work well.

Hook: 8–14
Tying silk: None
Body: An underbody of lead or fuse wire is overlaid with three layers of beige darning wool. Fine copper wire can be used to tie in the materials and finish off at the tail

KINGFISHER

A traditional lake fly. This is the tandem version.

Rear hook

Tail: Kingfisher blue feather-fibres
Body: Gold tinsel

Front hook

Body: Gold tinsel
Wing: Orange saddle hackles flanked by two strips of swan feather dyed blue
Cheeks: Jungle-cock

KITE'S IMPERIAL

Oliver Kite's version of an earlier unnamed Welsh dressing. Many still-water lures seem to shoot to fame overnight (often to disappear again equally rapidly), but the river dry fly seems to take an age before universal acceptance or recognition is achieved. Kite's Imperial was an exception to this. It was devised in 1962 and within a few years had gained a nationwide following. There are few flies which are claimed to raise fish when all else fails, but Dave Collyer puts this pattern into that category. In addition to being an excellent general dry fly, it is specifically useful as an imitation of the dark olive dun.

Hook: 14–16
Tying silk: Purple
Tail: Grey or brown hackle fibres in the early season; honey-dun fibres later
Body: Natural heron herl
Rib: Gold wire
Thorax: Heron herl doubled and re-doubled
Hackle: Honey-dun cock. Light ginger is a more readily available substitute

LACEWINGS (*Planipennia*)

These are members of the Neuroptera Order and are exclusively terrestrial. The green and brown lacewings, although similar in shape and size, are, by their colour, quite distinct from each other. The brown lacewing has a brown body and wings; the green lacewing has a green body and transparent wings. They are fairly common throughout summer, but I confess that I have never seen a trout feeding on them; nor have I ever come across them in an autopsy. However, some fly-fishers maintain that the artificial is of value and two dressings are detailed below.

BROWN LACEWING

Hook: 12–14
Tying silk: Brown
Body: Brown floss silk
Wing: Two pale-dun hackles tied flat across the back
Hackle: Light brown cock

GREEN LACEWING

Hook: 12–14
Tying silk: Bright green
Body: Bright-green floss
Wing: Two pale blue-dun hackles tied flat across the back
Hackle: Cock dyed green

LADYBIRD

Richard Walker saw fit to tie this imitation. I have yet to see a trout feeding on ladybirds and I doubt whether I shall ever add a copy of this pattern to my fly-box. But no doubt someone will tell me he has caught a limit of fat fish on an imitation when all else failed.

Hook: 14
Body: Bronze peacock herl tied fat
Wing-covers: Bright chestnut pheasant tail fibres tied over the body-length
Hackle: Black cock clipped short

LAKE OLIVE (*Cloëon simile*)   See EPHEMEROPTERA

This is a widely-distributed species similar to, but not as common as, the pond olive. The adults are medium-sized with a body length of approximately 8 mm. J. R. Harris suggests that the autumn adults are smaller than those in the spring. The main difference between these and the pond olive is that the lake olive is drabber in colour. The adults emerge between May and June and sometimes again from August to October. In the evenings a fall of spinners often stimulates interest from trout. The nymphs are the agile darting types and live among weeds in deeper water. John Goddard suggests they may favour cooler water than most Ephemeropterans, and this could account for their absence from shallower lakes.

The male dun has smoke-grey wings with pale yellow veins. The abdomen is reddish-brown with a dark olive-grey underside. The legs are olive-green and the two tails are dark grey. The female dun is similar to the male except that the tails are slightly paler and it has white wings.

The female spinner has transparent wings with faint yellow veins. The abdomen is chestnut-brown with grey-olive under. The legs are olive with the front pair olive and black, and the two tails are white with faint red rings. The male spinner is of no interest.

In addition to the patterns given, many general olive nymphs and duns would be suitable imitations. See OLIVES (*page 129*), GOLD-RIBBED HARE'S EAR (*page 72*), GOLDEN OLIVE (*page 72*), OLIVE BLOA (*page 21*), GREENWELL'S GLORY (*page 77*), ROUGH OLIVE (*page 155*), PHEASANT-TAIL SPINNER (*page 147*).

LAKE OLIVE NYMPH (John Henderson)

Hook: 12–14
Tying silk: Olive
Tail and body: Three blue game-cock's tail feather-fibres dyed light olive

Rib: Fine gold wire or yellow silk
Thorax: Dark-olive seal's fur
Hackle: Two turns of a small dun hen hackle

LAKE OLIVE DUN (Peter Lapsley)   Plate 28

Peter Lapsley recommends trimming the bottom edge off the hackle of the fly to improve its floatability.

Hook: Fine-wire 14
Tying silk: Brown

Tail: Light-dun cock hackle fibres
Body: Dark-olive condor herl
Rib: Silver wire
Hackle: Two medium blue-dun cock hackles

LAKE OLIVE SPINNER (J. R. Harris)

Hook: 12–14
Tying silk: Orange
Tail: Rusty-dun hackle fibres
Body: Deep-amber or mahogany seal's fur

Rib: Gold wire
Wing: Pale grizzle-dun hackle bunched and tied spent

LAKE OLIVE SPINNER (C. F. Walker)

Hook: Fine-wire 12–14
Tying silk: Black
Tail: Medium blue-dun cock spade fibres or saddle hackle fibres
Body: Dark-red seal's fur

Rib: Gold tinsel
Wing: Pale brassy-dun cock hackle points tied spent
Hackle: Pale-brown or honey-dun cock (may be omitted)

LARGE BROOK DUN (*Ecdyonurus torrentis*)
See EPHEMEROPTERA

A fairly widespread but localised species similar in appearance to the Late March Brown. It inhabits smaller stony streams, in contrast to the Late March Brown, which prefers larger rivers. The nymphs are the flat, stone-clinging type. The adults appear between late March and July and could be expected at any time during daylight. March Brown imitations are usually fished to represent this species.

LARGE DARK OLIVE (*Baetis rhodani*)   See EPHEMEROPTERA

Also known as the large spring olive, blue dun or early olive. This is a widespread species, usually preferring faster-flowing water. The nymph is an agile darting type and can be found clinging to rocks and stones, and, in the slower rivers, on weeds and moss. The medium- to large-sized adults appear from late February to late April, and may reappear during a spell of mild autumn weather. Consequently it is a useful grayling fly in addition to being an early-season trout fly.

In early spring the duns often stay on the water for quite a long time, drying their wings in a cold, damp atmosphere. Many northern and Scottish rivers experience prolific hatches, and even on the most unlikely days there may be a short rise period when trout take the newly-emerged duns. The female spinner, in common with other members of the Baetis genus, returns to the water and crawls below the surface to lay its eggs.

The male dun has pale grey wings with pale brown veins. The abdomen is olive-brown or olive-green, with a dark olive underside. The legs are light olive with olive-grey forelegs. The two tails are dull grey. The female dun has wings similar to the male's. The abdomen is dark olive-brown or olive-green with a paler underside. The legs are pale olive-green and the two tails are medium grey.

The female spinner, also known as the large red spinner, has transparent wings with brown veins. The abdomen is dark mahogany with a pale olive underside. The legs are dark brown-olive and the two tails are dark or olive-grey with red-brown rings. The male spinner is of no interest.

For additional patterns, see also GOLD-RIBBED HARE'S EAR (*page 72*), ROUGH OLIVE (*page 156*), EARLY OLIVE (*page 55*), DARK OLIVE BLOA (*page 21*), WATERHEN BLOA (*page 22*), GREENWELL'S GLORY (*page 77*), DOGSBODY (*page 51*), LUNN'S PARTICULAR (*page 102*), KITE'S IMPERIAL (*page 94*) and PHEASANT-TAIL SPINNER (*page 147*).

LARGE DARK OLIVE NYMPH (Taff Price)

Hook: 12
Tying silk: Yellow
Tail: Dark olive hackle fibres
Body: Mixed olive seal's fur and hare's ear fur
Rib: Gold wire

Thorax: Brown seal's fur
Wing-case: Dark olive swan or goose fibres
Legs: The end fibres of the wing-case material turned beneath the body, or olive cock fibres

LARGE DARK OLIVE DUN (Preben Torp Jacobsen)   Plate 27

The three hackles on this pattern make it a good floater. A single turn of each is sufficient, although Jacobsen ties his fuller to cope with trout-farm pollution on his home rivers of Denmark.

Hook: 12–14

Tying silk: Amber
Tail: Ginger cock hackle fibres
Body: Two natural and two heron herls dyed olive twisted together
Rib: Fine silver wire
Hackles: Three. Medium-sized pale olive and a small ginger cock wound together, with a large rusty-dun at the head

LARGE DARK OLIVE DUN (Freddie Rice)   Plate 27

Hook: 14
Tying silk: Olive
Tail: Light blue-dun hackle fibres
Body: Generous layers of tying silk covered with white moose-mane hairs dyed dark mahogany, browny-olive or dark

grey-olive, lighter in late spring and autumn
Wing: Paried slips of pale starling primaries
Hackle: Medium-olive cock

LARGE DARK OLIVE SPINNER (E. C. Coombes)

Hook: 14
Tying silk: Olive
Tail: Dark blue-dun hackle fibres
Body: Rear one-third, light-olive seal's

fur; middle third, medium-olive seal's fur; front third, light-olive seal's fur
Hackle: Light honey-dun

LARGE GREEN DUN (*Ecdyonurus insignis*)
See EPHEMEROPTERA

Although this species is not particularly rare, the trout's lack of interest in it is indicated by the paucity of artificials. The natural is found in parts of the North of England, South Wales and the West Country. The dun is fairly large with light fawn mottled wings and has a dark olive-green body with brown diagonal bands along the sides. The adults are commonest in July and August.

LARGE GREEN DUN (John Veniard)

Hook: 12–14
Tail: Dark dun cock fibres
Body: Greenish-grey seal's fur or light heron wing quill herl dyed green

Rib: Dark-brown or black tying silk
Hackle: Cock dyed green with a grizzle dyed green in front

LARGE SUMMER DUN (*Siphlonurus alternatus, S. lacustris*)
See EPHEMEROPTERA

Both species are fairly rare, but are found on stillwater in parts of Scotland, the North of England and Wales. The agile-darting nymphs of *S. lacustris* are large and brown-olive, and the large duns have grey wings, olive bodies about 14–15 mm long with pale-brown markings, and two tails. The female spinner has transparent wings with light-brown veins and a dull-green body. The adults appear mainly in July and August. *S. alternatus* prefers more alkaline water, but is similar to *S. lacustris*. The nymphs can be successfully imitated with a large olive nymph or Mayfly nymph pattern fished faster than normal, as the naturals are strong swimmers. The dun can be represented by the Dark Cahill.

LARGE SUMMER DUN NYMPH (Taff Price)

Hook: Longshank 12–14
Tying silk: Brown
Tail: Brown-olive fibres
Body: Brownish-olive seal's fur with a palmered olive hackle

Rib: Gold wire
Thorax: Mixed olive and yellow seal's fur
Wing-case: Brown feather-fibres
Hackle: One turn of dark-olive hen or cock

LARGE SUMMER DUN (C. F. Walker)

Hook: Longshank 12
Tail: Brown mallard fibres
Body: Medium grey-brown condor herl lightly stained in picric acid

Rib: Gold tinsel
Wing: A bunch of grey feather-fibres from the tip of a mallard scapular feather
Hackle: Brown-olive cock

LARGE SUMMER SPINNER (Taff Price)　　　　　Plate 26

Hook: 12
Tail: Long dark-olive fibres
Body: Light-brown polypropelene
Rib: Yellow silk or nylon

Wing: Light partridge tied spent
Hackle: None, or dark-olive clipped flat at the bottom.

LAST RESORT

This is a roach-fry imitation tied by David Train.

Hook: Longshank 4–10
Body: White acetate floss wound in a fish-shape. This is treated with solvent and flattened on the sides. When dry, it is covered with flat silver Lurex and overlaid with polythene strip. A small tuft of fluorescent red floss is tied in at either side at the shoulder
Rib: Silver wire
Wing: Twisted strands of bronze peacock herl and blue bucktail tied down at the tail
Underbody (optional): Strip of white swan feather with the rib taken over it
Head: Peacock herl

LEAD BUG

In the 1960s there was much talk of Oliver Kite's **Bare Hook Nymph**, which was no more than a bare hook with a thorax of copper wire. By presenting it accurately, and moving it in an appropriate manner, Oliver Kite took many chalk-stream trout and grayling with this unlikely pattern. The Lead Bug is the 1980s' stillwater equivalent of Kite's pattern. I don't know who devised this ugly, seemingly unattractive fly, but it has gained quite a following on some small southern, clear stillwaters. One angler was reported to have taken six double-figure Avington trout on it in one season. The bug is cast to an observed fish, with the angler aiming to drop it in front of the trout's nose. The trout's reaction is closely watched for the take. Entomologists despair!

Hook: 12
Body: Fine lead wire with a second layer for a thorax
Thorax case: Green floss

LEADHEAD

This weighted lure devised by Richard Walker should be fished in short jerks or with long pulls with pauses in between. The lure fishes upside down and so avoids becoming snagged on the bottom.

Hook: Forged 8–10 on which is pinched a BB lead shot just behind the eye

Body: Floss silk tied to just in front of the lead shot and varnished with Vycoat
Rib: Tinsel
Wing: Hairwing
Head: Lead shot painted with white plastic paint, with an eye painted on each side and varnished

Colour combinations:

Wing	Head	Body
Yellow	Light brown	Arc chrome DF wool or floss
Black	Black	Black
Grey squirrel	Brown	Red DF floss or wool
Yellow	Brown	Red DF floss or wool
Orange	Brown	Orange DF floss or wool

LECKFORD PROFESSOR   Plate 24

This southern chalk-stream dry fly was devised by Ernest Mott, a Test river-keeper. Donald Overfield records its alternative name as being **Cow's Arse**, although I am at a loss to understand why. It is described as a useful fly for 'choosy' trout. One day in 1982 I made a special point of trying it on the Dove in North Yorkshire. I tied-up three copies, which proved to be just as well, as the first two were lost among tree branches (I use only a 1½ lb b/s leader point)

before I had even covered a fish. The third fly caught three wild brown trout. It has proved its value to me on a stream far removed from the revered river for which it was developed, and I shall continue to try it on different waters.

Hook: 12–14
Body: Dark hare's ear fur
Rib: Fine flat gold tinsel
Hackles: A bright red cock hackle and a white cock hackle tied in at the rear of the shank, hiding the point of the fly

LEECHES

These are fairly common in stillwaters, where they inhabit deeper water near the lake-bed. There is little doubt that some of the black or brown lures fished slow and deep are mis-

taken for leeches. The pulsating action of marabou gives a good impression of a leech. John Veniard's Black Lure is sometimes known as the **Black Leech**.

LEPRECHAUN   Plate 7

A lure devised by Peter Wood. Because of the fluorescent green materials, it is useful when algae is about. A matuka version is commercially available. This has four cock hackles as below, but tied and ribbed in matuka-style. It is a good pattern for fishing deep on a bright, sunny day.

Hook: Longshank 6–10
Tail: Lime-green hackle fibres
Body: Fluorescent-green chenille
Rib: Silver wire
Throat hackle: Lime-green hackle fibres
Wing: Four lime-green cock hackles tied back-to-back

LIGHT OLIVE Plate 25

I tie two similar dry flies that differ only in their wing material and style that represent some of the newly-emerged lighter-coloured olive duns. Although their use has been largely confined to the northern rivers, I don't doubt their effectiveness elsewhere.

Hook: 12–14

Tying silk: Pale yellow-green or light Greenwell colour
Tail: Pale cree cock hackle fibres
Body: Tying silk
Hackle: Pale cree cock hackle
Wing: Either pale teal breast feather tip set upright or a dark teal breast feather tip tied in front of the hackle and slanting forward and clipped to size

LIGHT OLLIE Plate 26

This is a Danish pattern from Preben Torp Jacobsen. Despite its European origins, it is a useful U.K. pattern. Its creator comments: 'I tied the fly for the first time in June 1963. My intention was to create a fly imitating the most common dayflies on my home stream, the large dark olive and medium olive. It had to have the ability to float high on slightly polluted water downstream of trout-farms, and moreover to be easy to retrieve when it by accident landed among weeds and plants.

'I used the fly myself and gave it to friends, so that they could see if it worked. Fortunately, I had a detailed description of the fly in my diary, and

in 1971 friends started to ask for more flies. I tied a darker version, too, with darker hackles.

'Its name, Ollie, was given it in 1971 as a tribute to my dear friend, the late Oliver Kite, whose name among friends was "Ollie".'

Hook: 15 Mustard 72709
Tying silk: Primrose
Tail: Buff Orpington hackle fibres
Body: Four heron herls dyed in picric acid and twisted round the tying silk
Rib: Fine silver wire
Body hackle: Natural blue-dun hackle (henny cock) palmered along the body
Head hackle: Light honey-dun cock (like a Metz sandy brown)

LIGHT WOODCOCK Plate 20

A North Country wet fly, a copy of the needle flies. It is also known as the **Little Winter Brown** (See WINTER BROWN). This is an old dressing mentioned by, but probably not originating from, T. E. Pritt. It is still dressed in the original manner.

Hook: 12–14
Body: Orange tying silk sparsely dubbed with hare's ear fur
Hackle: Inside feather of a woodcock's wing
Head: Peacock herl

LITTLE MARRYAT

G. S. Marryat devised this dry fly for the southern chalk-streams. It is fished as a pale watery dun and spurwing imitation. When the pattern given is dressed with a body of peacock eye quill bleached pale brown, it is known as the **Quill Marryat**. An alternative body material is cream seal's fur, as suggested by G. E. M. Skues.

Hook: 12–14
Tail: Pale-olive guinea-fowl
Body: Australian opossum flank
Wing: Pale starling
Hackle: Pale-buff cochin cock

LOCH ORDIE Plate 18

Stan Headley, of Orkney, suggests that this pattern originated as a dapping fly, and that the wet fly evolved from the former. J. Yorston, another Orkney angler, asked the local tackle dealer, W. S. Sinclair, to tie the pattern about twenty-five years ago. Since then there has been a steady increase in the fly's popularity. Variations are endless, but Stan Headley's preferred version is given. The overall impression should be one of a brownish fly with a white hackle at the head. The hackle combinations are the choice of the fly dresser. 'It is the epitome of bob-flies' says Stan. 'Permafloted, it is almost unsinkable and skates across the surface in an irresistible fashion. I frequently fish two Permafloted Loch Ordies, a size 12 on the top and a size 10 on the tail, when fish are surface-active, and big baskets of wild brownies can be taken in this fashion. Untreated with Permaflote, it is a good general-purpose

pattern, and comes into its own in a big wave or late in the evening'.

The Loch Ordie is usually tied on size 8 to 12 hooks. Starting at the bend-end of the shank, hackle after hackle is tied in and wound on until the shank is covered, but it is always finished with a white hackle. Hackle colour is a matter of choice, but Stan Headley recommends black, very dark red/brown, dark red/brown, medium red/brown, ginger, honey-dun, all finished off with white.

The original, and now probably less frequently used, dapping fly is tied in tandem. Two hooks are tied in close tandem and thickly palmered with brown hackles (or as above), but always with a white hackle at the head. A small treble hook is whipped to nylon at the head to trail to one side, but not exceeding three-quarters of the total length of the fly. A variation is to incorporate floss silk bodies of various colours.

LONG JOHN Plate 3

Peter Thomas, creator of this pattern, describes it as 'a desperation fly, often taking fish when all else has failed. It is essentially a fly of movement, both continuous and changing'.

Hook: 8
Body: White DF floss or wool
Rib: Silver tinsel

Wing: Two very long (two or three times the hook-length) flexible cock saddle hackles, ginger, natural red, black, white, hot-orange or badger, which should be glued firmly to the shank
Throat hackle: Crimson hackle fibres on the ginger and natural red patterns
Peter Thomas has recently amended the throat hackle to an alternative one of black or white marabou.

LONG JOHN SILVER Plate 7

The lure's creator, Freddie Rice, comments: 'Many angling correspondents over the years have referred to fish using the head of a fry as the point of aim for their strike. With this in mind, I thought a large-headed fly and a deceptive appearance of length provided by long tails seemed a worthwhile experiment. A little flash in the point of aim seemed called for,

and the Long John Silver was born. The method with the leaded pattern is to allow the fly to sink to the bottom and then either slowly to retrieve it or to use a series of short rod-tip lifts to raise the muds spurts on the bottom. Either way, use a 6 lb to 8 lb leader.'

Hook: Standard or longshank 8
Tying silk: White

Tail: Four white or black and two olive ostrich herls mixed
Body: Rear half, scarlet chenille; front half, black chenille built up fatter than the rear over an optional layer of lead wire or foil
Rib: Medium silver tinsel or Lurex on the front half only

LUCKY ALPHONSE

This is an imitation of a clump of Caenis and should be fished slowly in the surface film when Caenis are about. It was devised by Richard Walker.

Hook: Longshank 12

Tying silk: Brown
Body: Natural swan herl
Hackles: Four cream cock hackles equally spaced along the shank with a little tying silk showing on either side of each

LUNN'S PARTICULAR   Plate 25

William Lunn is probably the best-remembered of all the Test's river-keepers. He produced a number of dressings, some of which are still used today. He introduced this pattern in 1917 as a copy of the medium olive and large dark olive spinners. J. W. Hills, in his book, *River Keeper*, praised Lunn, saying that he had the ability to think like a trout. He also wrote of the Lunn's Particular: 'If I had to be limited to one fly, I should choose this.' It is still a splendid fly, killing trout on both rain-fed rivers and chalk-streams.

Hook: 14–16
Tying silk: Crimson
Tail: Rhode Island Red hackle fibres
Body: Hackle-stalk of a Rhode Island Red hackle
Wing: Two medium-blue cock hackle points tied spent
Hackle: Rhode Island Red cock

LUNN'S YELLOW BOY

Another pattern from William Lunn (see LUNN'S PARTICULAR). It is a Baetis (olive) sunk-spinner imitation. See under each member of the Baetis genus for fuller details.

Hook: 14

Tying silk: Pale orange
Tail: Pale buff cock hackle fibres
Body: White hackle stalk dyed yellow or yellow seal's fur
Wing: Light buff cock hackle fibres bunched and tied in the spent position

MALLARD SERIES

An old range of fancy and imitative patterns using mallard wings. They are of proven success for lake trout and of value to the river fisherman in their smaller sizes. The combination of colours is extensive and is broadly similar to those in the GROUSE, TEAL and WOODCOCK series. The mallard wing material is taken from the small speckled brown shoulder-feathers. In all four series it is a general but flexible rule that the hackle should be the same colour as the body, and that the materials for the tail may be varied between golden-pheasant tippet fibres or crests, floss silk, wool or red ibis. As with most winged wet flies, the hackle is tied on the underside only.

MALLARD AND BLACK   Plate 17

Hook: 8–14
Tail: Golden-pheasant tippets
Body: Black seal's fur
Rib: Fine oval silver tinsel
Wing: Brown mallard
Hackle: Black hen

MALLARD AND BLUE

Body: Light-blue seal's fur
Rib: Fine oval silver tinsel
Hackle: Cock or hen dyed blue
Wing and tail: as Mallard and Black

MALLARD AND CLARET   Plate 17

This is possibly the oldest fly in the series and is a general imitative pattern. It is probably of Scottish origin. W. C. Stewart and Francis Francis both refer to similar flies. As a general lake fly, it has few peers. It kills on tiny moorland streams and on large reservoirs. Taken over a whole season, few general standby patterns give better results when fished as a top dropper. It is a fair sedge-pupa imitation and can be used to represent the nymphs or emerging sepia and claret duns. Some anglers have found it deadly in its smaller sizes when fished slowly an inch below the surface during a midge hatch. John Goddard's comment in his book, *Trout Flies of Stillwater*, is: 'the best all-rounder one is likely to find.'

Butt (optional): Green peacock herl. This is found on the mallard series only, not on the teal, grouse and woodcock patterns
Body: Claret seal's fur
Rib: Fine gold tinsel or wire
Hackle: Natural light hen
Wing and tail: As Mallard and Black
A Welsh variation has a tail of brown mallard fibres and a black hen or cock hackle.

MALLARD AND GOLD   Plate 17

Body: Flat gold tinsel
Rib: Gold wire or fine tinsel
Hackle: Black or ginger
Tail and wing: As Mallard and Black

MALLARD AND GREEN

Body: Green seal's fur
Rib: Fine oval silver tinsel
Hackle: Green hen
Tail and wing: As Mallard and Black

MALLARD AND MIXED

Body: In three sections of orange, red and fiery-brown seal's fur
Rib: Oval gold tinsel
Hackle: Dark-red cock or hen
Wing and tail: As Mallard and Black

MALLARD AND ORANGE

Body: Orange seal's fur
Rib: Oval gold tinsel
Hackle: Orange hen
Wing and tail: As Mallard and Black

MALLARD AND RED

Body: Red seal's fur
Rib: Oval gold tinsel
Hackle: Natural red hen
Wing and tail: As Mallard and Black

MALLARD, RED AND YELLOW

Body: Rear half, red seal's fur; front half, yellow seal's fur
Rib: Oval gold tinsel

Hackle: Black or orange hen
Wing and tail: As Mallard and Black

MALLARD AND SILVER

Body: Silver tinsel
Rib: Silver wire

Hackle: Black or blue hen
Wing and tail: As Mallard and Black

MALLARD AND YELLOW

Body: Yellow seal's fur
Rib: Oval gold tinsel

Hackle: Yellow hen
Wing and tail: As Mallard and Black

MALLOCH'S FAVOURITE   Plate 16

This is a traditional Scottish lake fly which is useful when the stillwater olives are about.

Hook: 12

Tail: Natural red cock hackle fibres
Body: Peacock eye quill tipped with silver
Wing: Woodcock wing
Hackle: Blue-dun hen

MARABOU-WINGED LURES   Plates 1 & 6

Marabou has become extremely popular as a winging medium for lures. Saddle hackles as streamer wings and animal hair as bucktail wings have both been in favour, but the pulsating action of marabou makes it difficult to beat. The wing works well even when a fly lure is fished slowly, giving an impression of life. Most marabou-winged lures are best fished in steady pulls, with pauses in between.

Many have individual names and they are listed separately under these. Others have no names, so I have opted for a reliable and easy-to-tie pattern from a well-known stillwater angler, Steve Parton, as an example. It is based on three colours: black, white or hot-orange. Steve describes the resultant lures as 'the deadliest bank lures for early season that I know. Bank-fishing early- or late-season are the times they really come into their own. Fast-sinking lines should be used and with four variations (white, black, hot-orange and green-lined versions) you can cover bank lure fishing from March to late May and from mid-September until the close'. The technique is initially to fish as deep as possible, and then to move up through the water to find the fish. Tandem versions are excellent general boat lures for similar periods of the season.

Hook: 3X longshank 6–10
Body: Medium black, white or hot-orange chenille
Rib: Fine oval silver tinsel
Wing: Marabou plumes to match the body colour
Cheeks (optional): Target-green fluorescent wool

MARCH BROWN (*Rithrogena germanica*)
See EPHEMEROPTERA

This was one of the first natural flies to be imitated by the fly-fisher. Indeed, Dame Juliana Berners' **Dun Fly** of 1496 could well be an imitation. Until recently the name *R. haarupi* was given to the species, but this has been changed to *R. germanica*. The natural fly is less common than popularly supposed and has a very local distribution in isolated parts of Wales, the North of England, Scotland, and, according to some authorities, in the West Country. What is more likely is that years ago before anglers began to look closely at the fly, the species was confused with the Late March Brown, which has a much wider distribution, and the two species were grouped together and jointly known as the March Brown.

The nymphs are dark bronze-green and live on smooth stones in faster-flowing water. The large-sized adults generally appear around midday and early afternoon during March and perhaps into April. They are most frequently seen at the tail of faster, broken water. Previously the March Brown was widely reported as continuing to emerge into May, but these hatches are now thought more likely to be the Late March Brown. The hatches can be prolific but irregular. In *Trout Fly Recognition*, John Goddard suggests that even when duns are in evidence, the hatching nymph is preferred by trout, and so a wet pattern is more successful. This is borne out by the many variations of the wet artificial and the scarcity of dun and spinner imitations. The reasons are considered under the Late March Brown heading.

The male dun has pale-fawn wings with heavy dark-brown veins. The abdomen is dark brown with straw-coloured rings. The legs are pale brown and the two tails are dark brown-grey. The female dun has darker wings than the male. The abdomen is a duller brown with rings similar to the male's. The legs are pale olive with darker forelegs, and the two tails are dark brown.

The female spinner, also known as the great red spinner, has transparent wings with dark veins. The abdomen is dark red-brown with straw-coloured rings. The legs are various shades of olive and the two tails are brown. The male spinner is of no interest as it dies over land and does not return to water.

LATE (or FALSE) MARCH BROWN (*Ecdyonurus venosus*)

The nymph and dun stage are similar to *R. germanica* and are found in similar types of river, but they are more widely distributed and much commoner than the March Brown. The same artificials represent both species. Some entomologists have observed the nymphs of *E. venosus* crawling ashore to make the transition from nymph to dun on rocks and stones. This is more in the manner of a stonefly than an upwinged fly. Just before the appearance of the dun, numbers of nymphs make their way shorewards, and at such times the sub-surface fly is of value. The Late March Brown is far commoner than the March Brown, but both species were known only by the latter name for centuries. This is why so many wet flies designated March Browns were developed in comparison with the few dun and spinner patterns.

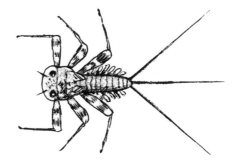

The adults emerge from April to June, and in some years in August and September. The female spinner of the species is slightly larger and has a redder body than the female spinner of *R. germanica*. The female spinners of both species can be imitated with a Cinnamon Quill or Great Red Spinner.

See also separate entry for the SILVER MARCH BROWN (*page 172*).

Many artificials purporting to represent the sub-surface March Brown may well do so, but they are so generally impressionistic that they may be taken for shrimps, water-lice or sedge-pupae.

MARCH BROWN   Plate 19

A winged wet fly.

Hook: 12–14
Tail: Partridge tail fibres
Body: Brown seal's fur or sandy hare's

ear fur
Rib: Gold wire
Wing: Brown partridge or hen pheasant
Hackle: Brown partridge

MARCH BROWN SPIDER (Roger Woolley)

Woolley was a northern fly-fisher of great experience and he listed more than 20 different March Brown dressings in his book, *Modern Trout Flies*.

Hook: 12

Tying silk: Orange
Body: Sandy hare's neck fur
Rib: Yellow silk
Wing: Speckled partridge tail tied thin
Hackle: Light-brown partridge.

MARCH BROWN SPIDER   Plate 19

Hook: 12–14
Tail: Speckled partridge tail fibres
Body: Dark hare's ear mixed with brown

or claret seal's fur
Rib: Primrose silk or silver wire
Hackle: Speckled partridge

MARCH BROWN NYMPH (John Veniard)   Plate 19

Hook: 12–14
Tail: Two strands of cock-pheasant tail fibres or brown mallard shoulder feather-fibres
Body: Cock pheasant tail
Rib: Gold wire

Thorax: Hare's ear fur
Wing-case: Woodcock wing feather-fibres
Legs: Small brown speckled partridge hackle

MARCH BROWN DUN

This is Taff Price's dressing for the male dun. The female dun imitation has a light hen-pheasant wing.

Hook: 12
Tying silk: Primrose
Tail: Cree hackle-fibres

Body: Mixed hare's ear and yellow seal's fur
Rib: Yellow silk
Wing: Dark hen-pheasant wing quill slips set upright
Hackle: Cree cock

MARCH BROWN HATCHING DUN (W. H. Lawrie)

The wings and thorax should float on the surface and the remainder should be submerged in the surface film.

Hook: 12–14
Tying silk: Yellow or orange
Tail: Three short cock-pheasant tail fibres
Body: Medium hare's ear fur

Rib: Fine gold wire
Thorax: Sepia seal's fur
Wing hackle: Dark partridge feather with the lower fibres trimmed away
Leg hackle: Dark-red cock hackle with the upper fibres cut away

MATCH HEAD

An unusual grayling fly from Harold Howarth, who praises it as both a wet fly and a floater. Although Mr Howarth rates it highly, I have used it intermittently over two seasons and have failed to catch a fish on it. The finished fly should look like a matchstick. I suppose the spent version should have a head of black tying silk!

Hook: Longshank 16
Tying silk: Pillar-box red
Body: Underbody of red tying silk
Wing: White cock feather-fibres or horsehair tied to cover the whole body in 360 degrees, making it into a 'matchstick head'. Tie in only at the head.
Head: Large mound of red tying silk

MATUKAS

An extensive series of lures originated in New Zealand. John Veniard wrote in the 1974 edition of his book, *Reservoir and Lake Flies*: 'I have yet to see a British trout angler with a Matuka in his fly-box. I find this surprising, as these patterns can be most effective in conditions when no other fly will be accepted.' The same can hardly be said today, when Matukas play an important role for the stillwater fly-fisher. No one has done more than John Veniard and Dave Collyer to publicise their worth. Perhaps the best known is Collyer's own Ace of Spades.

The Matukas are named after the bird which originally supplied the wing material. Substitutes have now been adopted. The wings are constructed by taking two round-ended feathers and placing them back to back. The lower fibres are stripped away for the length of the shank, so that the hackle-stem rests on the body, leaving a full-length back and the lower fibres beyond the bend only. The rib is taken through the upper fibres, which are then stroked rearwards. Jungle-cock eyes are sometimes added to standard patterns. These versions are known as Imperials. In addition to the dressings given, Matuka lures in a single colour are popular, e.g. all-black, all-white, all-green, etc. Matukas can all be fished fairly slowly, with frequent pauses to enliven the hackle wings.

BADGER MATUKA (Dave Collyer)   Plate 7

Hook: Longshank 6–10
Tying silk: Orange
Body: Fluorescent-orange wool
Wing: Two badger cock hackles in matuka style
Rib: Fine oval silver tinsel

Beard hackle: Hot-orange or scarlet cock
Cheeks: Jungle-cock
White chenille is a suitable body alternative, and other colours that may take your fancy.

BLACK-AND-SILVER MATUKA (Dave Collyer)

Hook: Longshank 6–8
Tying silk: Black
Body: Black chenille

Wing: Silver pheasant in matuka style
Rib: Oval silver tinsel
Beard hackle: Magenta cock hackle fibres

GREY-AND-RED MATUKA (Dave Collyer)

Hook: Standard or longshank 6
Tying silk: Grey or white
Body: Silver-grey chenille
Wing: Two white/brown hen-pheasant flank feathers
Rib: Oval silver tinsel
Beard hackle: Scarlet hackle fibres

RED QUEEN MATUKA

This is Dave Collyer's brighter version of his own Ace of Spades.

Hook: Longshank 6–10
Tying silk: Black or scarlet
Body: Bronze peacock herl
Wing: Two scarlet or crimson cock hackles in matuka style
Rib: Scarlet fluorescent floss
Overwing: Bronze mallard strip (not ribbed)
Collar: Scarlet fluorescent floss just in front of the wing
Beard hackle: White cock fibres
Head: Scarlet, with a black eye

WHITE-AND-ORANGE MATUKA

This is another Dave Collyer pattern which he says is useful when fished just below the surface.

Hook: Extra longshank 6–10
Tying silk: Black
Body: White chenille
Wing: White hen hackles in matuka style
Rib: Oval silver tinsel
Hackle: Orange and white cock hackles wound together as a rear-sloping collar.

MAYFLY (*Ephemera danica E. vulgata*)   See EPHEMEROPTERA

These two similar species are the largest of the upwinged duns. The Mayfly hatch on a river or stillwater is a feature deemed precious by all fly-fishermen. Many waters with once-prolific hatches now have few or none at all. Huge hatches still occur on some rivers, with the air thick with newly-emerged duns. Stillwater hatches have always been rarer than those on rivers. Trout feed greedily on the nymphs, duns and spinners, and the time of the Mayfly hatch on many rivers was looked upon as the 'duffer's fortnight'.

The Mayfly has been referred to in angling literature over many centuries, and the imitation of the greendrake (as the dun was often called) long taxed the fly-tying skills of our forebears. In spite of considerable attention to the Mayfly in the past, few fly-tyers placed much importance upon the nymph. G. S. Marryat was the first to do so at the end of the last century. In my opinion, Richard Walker produced the best nymph pattern yet devised. It is a great killer of trout on rivers and stillwaters and I have even caught autumn grayling on it.

The distribution of the species is widespread, although rivers and lakes having huge hatches in early June seem to be diminishing in numbers. The duns and spinners can be seen from May until the end of July. The nymphs burrow in the bottom mud and take between one and two years to mature. These large nymphs are known to leave their burrows and rise to the surface and descend again for about two weeks before the main hatch. This may happen at different places on a river over a number of evenings. The artificial nymph is well worth using in these circumstances.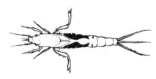

The duns usually appear in the afternoons. After

mating the female spinner (sometimes known as the grey drake or spent gnat) returns to the water, usually in the early evening to lay her eggs. The male spinner sometimes finds his way back on to the water and can be imitated by the fly-fisher. Both spinners are eagerly devoured by the trout, and the rise to the spinners can be more prolific than that to the hatching duns. Because they are the largest of the upwinged flies, they are easy to recognise.

The female dun has grey wings with a blue-green tinge and heavy black veins. They are tinged with yellow along the leading edge. The abdomen is yellow-cream with brownish markings. The legs are creamy-olive and the three tails are dark grey. The male dun has grey wings tinged with yellow and heavy brown veins. The abdomen is greyish-white with brown markings. The legs are dark brown and the three tails are dark grey.

The female spinner has transparent wings with a blue tint and brown veins. The abdomen is pale cream, the last three segments having brown streaks. The legs are dark olive-brown and the three tails are dark brown. The abdomen of the male spinner is creamy-white, with the last three segments brownish. The legs are dark olive-brown with the forelegs black-brown, and the three tails are dark brown. The transparent wings have a brown tint and heavy brownish veins. See also USD POLYSPINNERS (*page 191*).

MAYFLY NYMPH (Richard Walker)   Plate 11

Hook: Longshank 8
Tying silk: Brown
Tail: Pheasant tail fibres
Body: Optional layers of lead foil. Light yellowish-buff angora wool with two bands of pheasant tail fibres near the tail

Rib: Brown nylon thread
Thorax: As for the body, but without the ribbing. The body and thorax wool should be well picked out.
Wing-case and legs: Pheasant tail fibres, the ends turned down for legs.

MAYFLY NYMPH (John Veniard)

Hook: Longshank 10
Tail: Three strands of cock-pheasant centre tail feather
Body: Brownish-olive seal's fur
Rib: Gold wire

Thorax: Brownish-olive seal's fur
Wing-case: Dark part of a hen-pheasant's tail feather
Legs: Grey partridge breast feather

ASCENDING MAYFLY NYMPH (Roger Fogg)

Hook: 10
Body: Off-white seal's fur tied full and built up at the thorax

Hackle: French or red-legged partridge sparsely tied

SUSPENDER MAYFLY NYMPH

Devised by John Goddard and Brian Clarke as a semi-floater suspended in the surface film. See SUSPENDER MIDGE PUPA (*page 115*).

Hook: Longshank 12
Tying silk: Brown
Tail: Three tips of cream-coloured ostrich herl

Body: Mixed white, tan and yellow seal's fur (2:1:1)
Rib: Brown monocord or silk
Thorax: As for the body
Wing-case: Placed a short distance behind the eye. Ethafoam ball enclosed in a nylon mesh (ladies' tights provide a suitable material) and coloured brown

HATCHING MAYFLY NYMPH (Richard Walker)

Hook: Fine-wire longshank 10
Tying silk: Olive
Tail: Three short cock-pheasant tail fibres
Body and thorax: Four strands of Cellulite rayon floss, shades 228 and 229
Rib: Fine gold wire on body only
Wing-case: Black hen wing quill fibres

Wing: A mixture of fibres of white cock hackle dyed pale green and blue-dun, tied upright. This should be tied-in before the wing-cases, which should be taken round the outside of the wing fibres to give an emerging-nymph effect
Throat hackle: Small grouse hackle

HACKLE-POINT MAYFLY DUN (Dave Collyer)

Hook: Longshank 10
Tying silk: Olive or grey
Tail: Cock-pheasant tail fibres
Body: Varnished natural raffia
Rib: Oval gold tinsel

Wings: Two or four badger hackle tips. If four, the second set should be smaller and tied slightly pointing to the rear
Hackle: Iron blue cock

MAYFLY DUN (David Jacques)

Hook: Longshank 10
Tying silk: Red
Tail: Cock-pheasant tail fibres
Underbody: Reddish-brown floss
Overbody: Natural raffia with rings of the

underbody showing through
Hackle: Medium-olive cock tied in at the rear of the body, with a shorter-fibred light green-olive cock at the shoulder

YELLOW PARTRIDGE HACKLE MAYFLY (John Veniard)

Hook: Longshank 10
Tail: Three cock-pheasant tail fibres
Body: White floss silk

Hackle: Light yellow cock followed by a grey partridge feather dyed yellow

MAYFLY DUN   Plate 22

Hook: Longshank 10
Tying silk: Claret
Tail: Pheasant tail fibres
Body: Natural raffia with two palmered

badger cock hackles wound the opposite way
Head hackle: Cock, dyed olive

DEERSTALKER   Plate 22

Neil Patterson writes of his spinner imitation as though it were an answer to a maiden's prayer. His superlatives are probably justified. I have fished a Yorkshire stream for nine seasons through good and indifferent Mayfly hatches. Only in 1984 did I catch trout on a dun or spinner imitation on this river. Then, despite previous blanks, I rose eleven brown trout and landed seven of them – all duped by the Deerstalker.

Neil comments: 'For reasons I've never quite understood, most spin-ner patterns have hackles that hold the fly on the surface like a dun. Admittedly, some natural spinners come down on tippy-toes, wings erect. But most come down "spent" in the true sense of the word, with wings, body and tails flat out, flush with the surface film.

'To imitate the spinner correctly, you shouldn't be able to see the imitation on the surface. Which is why no spinner pattern of mine sports any feature that could possibly prevent it behaving exactly as the trout expects to see it.

'With no hackle keeping a heavy Mayfly iron from sinking straight through the film led me to use deerhair as the body material. It is hollow. By winding it in you trap little bubbles of air. This has much the same effect as strapping lifebelts along the sides.

'To give it additional floating qualities, I let the points of the deerhair fibres protrude from the back of the fly like short, stubby tails. This prevents the hook-bend pulling the fly under from the rear.'

Hook: Longshank 10
Tying silk: Brown
Tail: Pheasant tail fibres about twice the body-length
Body: White deerhair laid along the shank with the tips sticking out beyond the bend
Rib: Generous turns of tying silk, and silver wire
Hackle: Black cock wound where the thorax should be. This is trimmed for three-quarters of its length, leaving the fibres just longer than the body width. A second natural red hackle is wound through the remainder of the black hackle. These are bound into two bunches for the spent wings with figure-of-eight turns of the silk

HACKLE-POINT SPENT MAYFLY (John Veniard)

Hook: Longshank 10
Tail: Three cock-pheasant tail fibres
Body: Yellow raffia
Rib: Oval silver tinsel

Wing: Four blue-dun cock hackles (two shorter than the others), tied spent
Hackle: Light grizzle cock

MAYFLY SPINNER (John Roberts)   Plate 22

Hook: Longshank 12
Tying silk: Black
Tail: Long pheasant tail fibres
Body: White floss silk

Rib: Thick black thread or stripped black quill
Hackle: Long-fibred badger cock

PLASTAZOTE MAYFLY (C. Kendall)   Plate 22

Hook: Longshank mayfly up-eye 8
Tying silk: Dark brown
Tail: Cock pheasant centre tail fibres
Body: Plastazote cut into strips and wound

Rib: Chesnut brown floss
Wing: Teal, lightly marked, tied to lay in the spent position
Hackle: Light brown cock

MEDIUM OLIVE (*Baetis vernus, B. tenax, B. buceratus*)
See EPHEMEROPTERA

All these species are very much alike, and *Baetis vernus* is described below in detail. With the exception of *Baetis buceratus*, they are widely distributed throughout the country and are most abundant on chalk-streams. They are not found in stillwater. The nymphs are of the agile darting type, living among weeds. The medium-sized adults begin to appear in mid-May and in some places continue almost daily to the end of June, then less frequently through to October. They generally emerge in the late morning and early afternoons. The female spinners return to the water from early evening onwards.

The male dun has medium grey wings and an abdomen that is medium yellow-olive with a paler underside. The legs are pale to medium olive and the two tails are grey. The female dun has medium grey wings with a brown-olive to medium olive abdomen with a pale yellow-olive underside. The legs are pale olive and the two tails grey.

The female spinner, also known as the red spinner, has transparent wings with light brown veins. The abdomen is yellow-brown to reddish-brown, with a paler underside. The legs are grey-olive and the two tails are off-white. The male spinner is of no interest as it dies over land.

See also under OLIVE copies and the OLIVE BLOA (*page 21*), BARTON BUG (*page 11*), MISTY BLUE DUN (*page 119*), WATERHEN BLOA (*page 22*), ROUGH OLIVE (*page 156*), GREENWELL'S GLORY (*page 77*), GOLD-RIBBED HARE'S EAR (*page 72*), DOGSBODY (*page 51*), LUNN'S PARTICULAR (*page 102*), PHEASANT TAIL (*page 146*) and RED SPINNER (*page 154*).

MEDIUM OLIVE NYMPH

Hook: 14
Tail: Greenwell hackle fibres
Body: Goose shoulder herls dyed medium olive

Rib: Gold wire
Thorax: Olive seal's fur
Hackle: Short-fibred Greenwell

MEDIUM OLIVE NYMPH

A North Country pattern.

Hook: 14
Tail: Rhode Island Red cock fibres

Body: Greenish-olive wool or seal's fur
Rib: Gold wire
Hackle: Smokey blue-dun hen

MEDIUM OLIVE DUN (C. F. Walker)

Hook: 14
Tail: Pale-grey hackle fibres
Body: Two strands of condor herl, one greyish-olive, the other pale brown

Rib: Fine gold tinsel
Wing: Peroxide-bleached brownish-grey waterhen breast fibres
Hackle: Pale-olive cock

MEDIUM OLIVE DUN (Wardle)

Hook: 14
Tying silk: Medium olive
Tail: Golden-pheasant yellow breast fibres
Body: Medium-olive horsehair over olive

DFM floss and varnished
Wing: Medium-grey hackle-points tied upright
Hackle: Pale-olive cock

MERRY WIDOW

A variation on the Wulff series devised by Brenda Elphick, a professional fly-tyer. It is a useful dry fly for hot, sunny days, particularly on stillwater.

Hook: 10–16
Tying silk: Black

Tail: Calf-tail fibres dyed black
Body: Black floss
Wing: Calf-tail fibres dyed black and tied forward-slanting at 45 degrees over the eye
Hackle: Black cock tied behind the wing

A North American bucktail lure first tied in the 1930s and now popular on our reservoirs.

Hook: Longshank 6–10
Tying silk: Black
Tail: Two small bunches of red and yellow bucktail

Body: Silver Lurex or tinsel
Wing: Three bunches of bucktail, red in the centre, flanked by yellow
Throat hackle (optional): Red hackle-fibres or goathair
Head: Black varnish

MIDGES (*Chironimidae*)   See DIPTERA

Most of nearly 400 species are aquatic. They provide a substantial food source for stillwater trout and, to a lesser extent, river trout and grayling. Adults hatch on almost every day of the season, and trout may become preoccupied with the emerging pupa in the surface film. It is not uncommon for the water surface to be boiling with trout absorbed in taking the pupa, or with the backs of trout breaking through the surface as they silently pick-off pupae suspended in the film. The colour and size of the artificial and the method of fishing are important if the angler is to be successful. Midges were overlooked by generations of fly-fishers until the boom in stillwater fly-fishing ensured that greater attention was paid to stillwater fly-life. The buzzer pattern of Dr H. A. Bell (see BLAGDON BUZZER, *page 20*) and the midge patterns of others between the wars were the first patterns specifically tied to copy the natural pupa.

The larvae may vary from just a few millimetres to 25 millimetres long. Many live close to the lake-bed or are free-swimming among weeds. They are commonly called bloodworms, after the red larvae, but others are green, brown and shades in between. They are thin and worm-like and move through the water with a lashing motion. After reaching the pupal stage, they leave the lake-bed and begin the final stages of pupation, when the body may darken or change colour. They then ascend to the surface ready to emerge as adults.

Pupae vary in size and colour and often have a pronounced bend to their segmented body. They have whitish breathing filaments at the head and whitish appendages to the tail to aid swimming. The rising or emerging pupa under the surface film are of most interest to trout. The adults may emerge fairly speedily, or may take up to a couple of hours, hanging just below the surface. Their movement is slow and may be in a horizontal plane or a slow rising and sinking for short distances. Some remain static with their breathing filaments suspended from the surface film. The thorax splits and the adult emerges, leaving its pupal case behind. Calm water is favoured for a hatch and the evenings of hot sunny days often have the largest hatches.

Adults vary in size and colour. All have flat wings folded across the back. Swarms of adults are found near water or well inland. The females, returning to lay their eggs, make the buzzing noise which has resulted in the genus being termed 'buzzers'. At times, when the newly-hatched adults are being taken off the surface, the artificial should be fished motionless.

The main species, with their common names and wing-lengths, are listed below in order of emergence. Common names of species have varied over the years and are still changing as anglers find more acceptable terminology.

Common name	Wing-length	Period of emergence
Small green midge	4–6 mm	March to October
Orange/silver midge or grey boy	6.5–8 mm	April to mid-June
Black midge or duck-fly	3.5–7.5 mm	April/March and July/October
Ribbed or olive midge	6.5–7 mm	May/June and August/September
Golden dun midge	6.5–8 mm	June to August
Small brown midge	3.5–7.5 mm	Mid-June to September
Large red or ginger midge	6.6–8 mm	Mid-June to mid-September
Small red midge	4–4.5 mm	July to September
Large green midge	6.5–8 mm	Mid-July to end August

BLOODWORMS or LARVAE

See also WOBBLE-WORM, GOD-DARD'S RED-AND-GREEN LAR-VAE

I find these patterns of use fished close to the lake-bed on a sinking line in the first half of the season. If you are ever without a copy, a slim red or scarlet lure fished slowly often does the trick. Cyril Inwood once caught forty trout in a single session on a pillar-box red nymph in the absence of a closer imitation.

BLOODWORM (Geoffrey Bucknall)   Plate 12

Hook: Longshank 8
Tying silk: Red
Tail: Feather-fibres with an upward curve dyed red

Body: Feather-fibres dyed red
Rib: Oval silver tinsel
Thorax: Brown heron herl

BLOODWORM (C. Kendall)   Plate 12

The natural bloodworm has a curved segmented body and plenty of movement. This pattern has all those attributes.

Hook: Yorkshire sedge hook 8–18
Tail: Red marabou from base of the plume

Body: Optima high power gum (red floss silk on sizes 16–18) and given several coats of varnish
Thorax: Lead underbody if required. An equal mixture of red and olive seal's fur or other dubbing

BLOODWORM (Roger Fogg)   Plate 12

Hook: Sedge hook 10–12
Tying silk: Red
Body: Red tinsel underbody with a close

ribbing of red Lurex
Thorax: A small throax of red seal's fur.

MARABOU BLOODWORM (Taff Price)

This excellent, pulsating vibrant pattern is my own favourite.

Hook: Longshank 14
Tail: Red marabou
Body: Red floss

Rib: Fluorescent red silk
Head: Peacock herl

Perhaps the most simple pattern is a length of scarlet suede chenille tied in a point behind the eye of the hook and left free to wiggle on a slow retrieve.

PUPAE

Artificial pupae are well-suited to being fished either as a single fly at the end of a long leader or on all three points of a three-fly leader. They should be kept near to the surface and retrieved slowly with long, steady pulls with short pauses. A good method is to put a hatching pupa

Plate 1
LURES

Tandem Traffic Lights

Tandem White Christmas Tree

Red Baron

Badger Demon

White Tandem Marabou

Alexandra Tandem

Grafham Grey Lure

Chew and Blagdon Lure

Plate 2
LURES

Mini Dog Nobbler

Brown Dog Nob

Orange Dog Nobbler

Bed Hopper

Flashabou Pretty Dog

Black Beastie

Mini Dog Nobbler

White Bed

Plate 3
LURES

Long John

Rainbird

Roach Fry (Saville)

Popper

Perch Fry (Saville)

Squirrel and Silver

Perch Fry (Fraser)

Bullhead

Plate 4
MUDDLERS

Orange Muddler

White Muddler

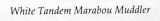

White Tandem Marabou Muddler

Black Muddler

Original Muddler

Muddlerine (treble)

Whogstopper

Spuddler

Last Resort Muddler

Plate 5
LURES

White Marabou (Carnill)

Rees Lure

Tadpole

Jack Frost

Orange Booby Nobbler

Viva

Poodle

Pink Panther

Plate 6
LURES

Black Bear's Hair

Black Magician

Black and Orange Marabou

Whiskers

Doddler

Black Marabou

Black Pulsator

Christmas Tree Pulsator

Plate 7
LURES

Long John Silver

Appetiser

Breathaliser

Chief Needabeh

Nailer

Painted Lady Streamer

Leprechaun

Badger Matuka

Olive Matuka

Yellow Matuka

Ace of Spades

Zuluka

Plate 8
LURES

White Baby Doll

Pink Baby Doll

Green-Backed Baby Doll

Black and Red Baby Doll

Baby Deer

Glowdoll

Nell Gwynne

Undertaker

Brown Trout Streamer

Orange Bucktail

Golden Anna

Silver Anna

Plate 9
LURES

Polystickle

Sinfoil's Fry

Epsom Salts

Easy-Tied Trout Snack

Roach Fry (Kendall)

GJ Fingerling

Tom's Terror

Parrot

Whisky Fly

Mrs Palmer

Sweeney Todd

Fireball

Bowler Hat

Mickey Finn

Church Fry

Goldie

Banded Squirrel Bucktail

Black Ghost

Jersey Herd

Missionary

Dawn and Dusk Lure

Dambuster

Wormfly

Fuzzy Wuzzy

Plate 11
NYMPHS

Mayfly Nymph (Walker)

Wiggle Nymph (Goddard)

Crane-Fly Larva (Price)

Twitchett Nymph

Water Tiger

Black Booby Nymph

Woolly Worm

Green and Orange Nymph

Green DF Partridge

Cased Caddis (Carnill)

Stickfly (Harris)

Caddis Larva (Fogg)

PT Nymph

Black PT Nymph

PT Nymph (Church)

Ombudsman

Alder Larva (Carnill)

Plate 12
BEETLES, NYMPHS, MIDGE PUPAE

Green and White Chomper

Black Chomper

Water Cricket

Corixa (Fogg)

Plastazote Corixa

Silver Corixa (Fogg)

Jack Ketch

Hot Pants

Snail (Church)

Tadpolly

Persuader

Red Larva (Goddard)

Bloodworm (Bucknall)

Bloodworm (Kendall)

Wobble Worm

Bloodworm (Fogg)

Hatching Midge Pupa
(Goddard)

Hatching Midge Pup
(Goddard)

Suspender Midge Pupa

Midge Pupa (Roberts)

Midge Pupa (Fogg)

Midge Pupa (Roberts)

Midge Pupa (Fogg)

Midge Pupa (Fogg)

Midge Pupa (Fogg)

Plate 13
SEDGES

Latex Sedge Pupa (Fogg)

Latex Sedge Pupa (Fogg)

Hatching Sedge Pupa (Roberts)

Buff Buzzer

Sedge Pupa (Kendall)

Sedge Pupa

Shredge

Longhorn

Green Peter

Fiery-Brown Sedge (Carnill)

Sienna Sedge

Yellow Sedge Pupa

Turkey Yellow

Turkey Green

Sedge Pupa (Goddard)

Sedge Pupa (Goddard)

Plate 14
NYMPHS

Something and Nothing

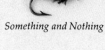

Something and Nothing

Something and Nothing

Red Spot Shrimp (Patterson)

Phantom Larva (Russell)

Phantom Midge Pupa (Lapsley)

Orange Wonderbug

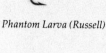

Gerroff

Mating Shrimp (Goddard

Damsel Nymph (Lapsley)

Damsel Nymph (Lapsley)

Damsel Nymph (Kendall

Chenille Grub

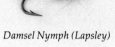

Chenille Grub

Caterpillar

Palmer Nymph (Voss Bark)

Aylott's Orange

Fuzzy Brown Nymph

Rat-Tailed Maggot

Ivens Green & Brown

Green Lurex Nymph

Endrick Spider

Cove Nymph

Barrie Welham Nymph

Plate 15
NYMPHS

Claret Nymph (Henderson)

Orange Nymph (Cove)

Orange Nymph (Price)

Caenis Nymph (Carnill)

White Nymph (Fogg)

White Nymph (Wallace)

Brown Collyer Nymph

Green Collyer Nymph

B-WO Nymph (Jacobsen)

Stonefly Nymph

Brown Stonefly Nymph (Fogg)

Sepia Nymph

Black Duckfly (Carnill)

Blae and Black Buzzer (Carnill)

Mosquito Pupa (Collyer)

Medium Olive (Carnill)

Large Ginger (Carnill)

Polyrib Buzzer (Carnill)

Kendall's Emerger

Footballer

Bowtie Buzzer

Grey Goose Nymph

Pheasant Tail Nymph
(Sawyer)

SS Nymph

Plate 16
TRADITIONAL WET FLIES

Claret Pennell

Kate MacLaren

Pennell's Black and Silʋ

Grouse and Yellow

Teal, Blue and Silver

Malloch's Favourite

Campbell's Fancy

Wingless Wickham's Fancy

Freeman's Fancy

Burleigh

Silver March Brown

Spider

Claret Bumble

Dunkeld

White-Hackled Invicte

Silver Invicta

Gold Invicta

Standard Invicta

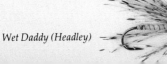

Wet Daddy (Headley)

Fiery Brown

Plate 17
TRADITIONAL WINGED WET FLIES

Professor

Cinnamon & Gold

Golden Olive

Jungle Cock

Mallard and Black

Mallard and Claret

Mallard and Gold

Woodcock and Green

Woodcock and Hare's Ear

Grouse and Claret

Connemara Black

Peter Ross

Watson's Fancy

Blae and Black

Royal Coachman

Colonel Downman's Fancy

Butcher

Teal-Winged Butcher

Bloody Butcher

Kingfisher Butcher

Plate 18
LAKE FLIES AND MINI-LURES

Blue Zulu

Zulu

Houghton Gem

Hardy's Favourite

Bibio

Soldier Palmer

Parmachene Belle

Cardinal

Blood Fly

Airy Fairy

Twitcher

Doobry

Ke-He (Headley)

Harray Horror

Loch Ordie

Mini-Whisky

Mini-Appetiser

Black Joe

Mini-Muddler

Mrs Simp

Plate 19

RIVER WET FLIES, NYMPHS AND BUGS

Coch y Bondhu

Killer Bug

Dove Bug

Early Olive Nymph (Bucknall)

Sunk Spinner (Paterson)

PVC Nymph

Hatching Olive Nymph
(Goddard)

Hatching Olive (Bucknall)

Amber Spinner (Clegg)

Black Kill Devil Spider

Priest

Spurwing Nymph (Waites)

Woodcock and Green

March Brown Nymph

Winged March Brown

March Brown Spider

Starling Bloa

Greenwell Nymph

Olive Bloa

Snipe Bloa

Plate 20
RIVER WET FLIES

Badger Palmer

Snipe and Gold

Clyde Sandfly

Red Tag

Rolt's Witch

White Witch

Grayling Witch

Bradshaw's Fancy

Partridge and Mole

Light Watchet

Dark Watchet (Pritt)

Red Dotterel

Yellow Dotterel

Orange Dotterel

Ichneumon Fly

Light Woodcock

Fog Black

Plate 21
RIVER WET FLIES

Black and Blae

Black Spider (Perry)

Black Spider (Stewart)

Honey Bumble

Yellow Bumble

Purple Bumble

February Red (Fogg)

Brown Owl

Dark Bloa

Dark Needle

Dun Spider

Waterhen Bloa

Hare's Lug and Plover
(Stewart Style)

Hare's Lug and Plover

Winter Brown

Partridge and Blue

Partridge and Orange

Snipe and Purple

Plate 22
MAYFLIES, DAPPLING FLIES AND SPECIALS

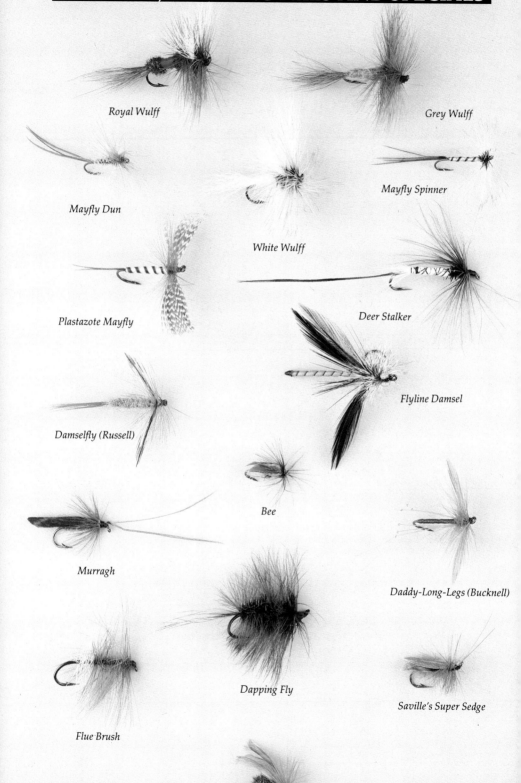

Royal Wulff

Grey Wulff

Mayfly Dun

Mayfly Spinner

White Wulff

Plastazote Mayfly

Deer Stalker

Flyline Damsel

Damselfly (Russell)

Bee

Murragh

Daddy-Long-Legs (Bucknell)

Dapping Fly

Saville's Super Sedge

Flue Brush

Hoolet Moth

Plate 23
DRY FLIES

White Irresistible   Adams

Soldier Beetle   Dogsbody   John Storey

Beacon Beige   Beacon Beige Variant (Fogg)

Ermine Moth

Grayling Steel Blue   Goddard's Last Hope (light)   Goddard's Last Hope (dark)

Coachman   Hacklepoint Coachman   Great Red Sedge (Collyer)

Grey Spinner   Herefordshire Alder

Plate 24
DRY FLIES

Blue Upright

Driffield Dun

Adult Stonefly (Veniard)

Leckford Professor

Wickham's Fancy

Greenwell's Glory

Rat-faced MacDougall

Furnace

Claret Spinner

Ginger Quill

Ginger Spinner

Houghton Ruby

Governor

Barton Bug

Hi C Pale Watery

Hi C Badger

Plate 25
DRY FLIES

Grizzly Palmer

Whitmore's Fancy

Silver Badger

Red Badger

Double Badger

Badger Palmer (Fogg)

Dark Hendrikson

Light Cahill

Pheasant Tail

Blagdon Green Midge

Sanctuary

Lunn's Particular

Green Wizard

Imp

Grayling Fiddler

Light Olive (Roberts)

Light Olive (Roberts)

Plate 26
DRY FLIES

Large Summer Spinner (Price)

Light Ollie

Funnel Dun (hackled)

Funnel Dun (winged)

Funnel Spinner

Black Bi-Visible

Badger Bi-Visible

Housefly (Russell)

Grizzle Mink

Great Red Spinner

Little Red Sedge

Walker's Red Sedge

G and H Sedge

*Golden-Eyed Gauzewing
(Price)*

Brown Silverhorn

Black Ant

Plate 27
DRY FLIES

Orange Otter

Barret's Bane

Misty Blue Dun

Enigma

Enigma II (Russell)

Itchen Olive (Mackie)

Yellow May Dun (Roberts)

Sturdy's Fancy

Treacle Parkin

Large Dark Olive (Rice)

Large Dark Olive (Jacobsen)

Hawthorn Fly (Jacobsen)

Gravel Bed (Fogg)

Black Pensioner

Light Pensioner

Tup's Pensioner

Plate 28
DRY FLIES

Cree Duster

Amber Spinner (Fogg)

No. 3 Para

Iron Blue Dun (Russell)

Grannom (Russell)

Orange Quill

Tup's Indispensable

Parody

Knotted Black Midge (Roberts)

Reed Smut Nymph (Jacobsen)

Simulium (Jacobsen)

Lake Olive Dun (Lapsley)

Black Gnat (Rice)

Pale Watery Dun (Rice)

Grey Duster

Blue-Winged Olive (Righyni)

Sherry Spinner (Rice)

pattern on the top dropper and to fish with ordinary pupa imitations further down the leader. Takes are often gentle, and the leader needs to be watched carefully. In a ripple or rough water this may be impossible if the flies are some distance away. The best solution is to put a dry Sedge on the top dropper and use this as an indicator. The natural pupae have to make the journey to the surface from the bottom, and even when none is near the surface, deeply-fished imitations are effective.

Some of the patterns may be listed in only one colour, as their creator suggested, but there is no reason why they should not be tied in other colours to represent a variety of natural midges. The creators of some of the patterns have stipulated that the body should go round the bend of the hook to imitate the natural. Other fly-tyers have omitted this. It is a matter of choice whether the body extends round the bend, but most fly-fishers prefer the more natural-looking artificial. Tail filaments, if used, should be kept fairly short. The breathing tubes may be tied in a single bunch sticking out of the top of the thorax, or more realistically in two bunches with figure-of-eight turns of the tying thread. Caddis or sedge hooks are useful for pupa imitations.

There is no doubt that the imitation of midge-pupae has been pushed to the extreme in fly-tyers' attempts to match the natural's appearance. A number of experienced stillwater anglers are reverting to simpler patterns. That expert nymph-fisher, Arthur Cove, has said that he never uses the 'traditional buzzer' imitations nowadays. He merely ties simple spider patterns in buzzer colours. Cove's patterns have a floss-silk body with a silver rib and a small black hen hackle for those to be fished well below the surface, or with a cock hackle for those to be fished just below the surface film. Perhaps half the answer lies in the addage that 'It's not what you fish, but how you fish it'.

HATCHING BUZZER PUPA (Dave Collyer)

The use of deerhair in this and other patterns makes them extremely buoyant and avoids the need to have large additions to the head of the fly as in the case of the Suspender patterns.

Hook: 6–12
Tying silk: Black, olive or brown
Body: Floss silk or feather-fibres in black, claret, gold, dark olive, orange or scarlet
Rib: Flat tinsel, gold, copper or silver Lurex
Thorax: Deerhair spun on and trimmed.

HATCHING MIDGE PUPA (John Goddard)   Plate 12

Hook: 10–14
Tying silk: As for body colour
Tail: White fluorescent wool tied well round the bend
Body: Marabou silk or fluorescent wool of an appropriate colour
Rib: Silver Lurex
Overbody: A strip of opaque PVC wound over
Thorax: Turkey dyed brown or peacock herl
Head filaments: White fluorescent wool

SUSPENDER HATCHING MIDGE PUPA   Plate 12

Devised by John Goddard as a means of enabling the pupa to hang beneath the surface film. It is adapted from an American idea from *Nymph Fishing for Larger Trout*, by Charles E. Brooks. Almost any midge-pupa pattern can be adapted to this method of suspension.

Hook: 10–14
Tying silk: To match the body colour
Tail: White fluorescent wool (optional) tied well round the bend
Body: Seal's fur of an appropriate colour

Rib: Fine silver wire or Lurex
Thorax: Turkey fibres dyed brown or peacock herl
Head: A small ball of Ethafoam wrapped in a nylon mesh. Ladies' tights provide a suitable material

MIDGE PUPA (Richard Walker)

Hook: 10–18
Tail and breathing filaments: White cock hackle fibres
Body: Coloured silk or floss taken just around the bend
Rib: White cock hackle stalk or fine silver thread

Thorax: Dyed swan herl for the orange and green pupae; sepia turkey fibres for the black and olive pupae, or peacock herl. The head is finished off so that the breathing filaments stick up at almost 90 degrees with the final turns of the thorax materials in front of the filaments.

MIDGE PUPA (Roger Fogg)   Plate 12

Unimpressed by 'ultra-realism' in pupae imitations, Roger Fogg suggests that colour and profile are the main factors influencing a feeding trout and has dressed a series of simple patterns which 'you may be assured will catch as many fish as any others'. In addition to the patterns given, which are for use just below the surface, he has had success with weighted pupal imitations which are allowed to sink to the bottom and are retrieved in long draws. The lead-foil weight is wrapped round the shank beneath the thorax. Some fly-tyers prefer pupal imitations with breathing filaments and tail; others deem them unnecessary. I confess to preferring flies with breathing filaments, but Roger Fogg says that their absence on his patterns has not apparently affected their efficiency.

Hook: 10–16 sedge hook
Abdomen: Marabou floss silk in black, brown, various greens, dark red, dull orange, extending half-way round the bend
Rib: Fine copper wire
Thorax: Seal's fur tied fairly fat and matching the body colour

MIDGE PUPA   Plate 12

This is representative of many modern traditional buzzer dressings.

Hook: 10–14
Tying silk: As for the body colour
Tail and breathing filaments: Fluorescent white wool or white Dollybody

Body: Tying silk or floss silk of appropriate colours
Rib: Silver wire
Thorax: Peacock herl on the black and the green versions; mixed orange and brown seal's fur on the orange version

POLY-RIB C PUPA (Bob Carnill)   Plate 15

The black version is detailed below. Others include olive, claret, brown, etc.

Hook: Sedge hook or standard 10–14
Tying silk: Black
Tail: Electron-white DRF floss
Body: Swan, goose or heron herl dyed black

Rib: Pre-stretched heavy-duty clear polythene or PVC wound on so that the body material shows through the rib. Seven or eight turns are adequate
Thorax: Mole's fur dyed black
Thorax cover: Body material
Wing stubs: Two quill-like fibres from the

narrow side of white primary swan feathers tied in at the rear underside of the thorax and rear-facing.
Breathing filaments: A short length of white nylon baby wool tied in horizontally at the eye and clipped short.

See also BLAGDON BUZZER (*page 20*), BOW-TIE BUZZER (*page 26*), FOOTBALLER (*page 66*), and PHANTOM MIDGE (*page 145*).

ADULT MIDGES

ADULT BUZZERS (Bob Carnill)

Bob Carnill comments: 'First and foremost, all the Adult Buzzers are wet flies, i.e. to be fished in or below the surface film. They are designed primarily to imitate the dead, dying, drowned or drowning mature fly. However, having said that, they can be made to simulate a freshly-hatched adult struggling to gain "lift-off". This is achieved by fishing the fly on the top dropper and dibbling it back to the boat, half-in and half-out of the water.

'I have seven Adult Buzzers, one for each major month of the trout-fishing season. Even though each has its own specific month, each can effectively overlap the first and last days – or even weeks – of the months on either side of the one allotted. For example, April is the allotted month for the *Black Duck Fly Adult Buzzer*, but it is often fished with great success during the last days of March, and often well into May. So as you can see, there are no cast-iron rules.

'Here then are the seven Adult Buzzers and their respective months: **Blae and Black**, March: **Black Duck Fly**, April; **Grey Boy**, May; **Medium Olive**, June; **Large Ginger**, July; **Beige and Ginger**, August; **Large Dark Olive**, September. The first Adult Buzzer I ever tried was the Blae and Black. It was tied in 1964 with spring trout on Ullswater in mind, and it proved so effective that the other six followed in their turn in ensuing years.

'My best trout to date on the Adult Buzzer was a 4 lb 12 oz brownie (hen fish) from Rutland Water. I have had lots in the 2–3 lb bracket. Adult Buzzers are particularly effective during a rise to egg-laying females. This can occur at any time of the day depending on the time of year, but early-morning and late-evening are usually the best times.'

ADULT MIDGE (Richard Walker)

Body: Dyed feather-fibres tied slightly fatter at the thorax
Wing: Two short white hackle points
Hackle: Long-fibred cock

Body colours	Hook size	Body rib	Thorax colours
Black	10–16	White hackle-stalk	Black
Green	12–16	White hackle-stalk	Green
Orange	12–16	White hackle-stalk	Crimson
Olive/brown	12	White hackle-stalk dyed yellow	Crimson

BLAGDON GREEN MIDGE   Plate 25

Green midges can be expected at any time during the six months of the trout season. This particular dressing goes back probably to the 1920s, but sadly it is one with which I have no success. However, others must find it of use, as a number of reputable fly-tyers offer it. Courtney Williams suggests that as a river fly it is a good aphis or caterpillar imitation.

Hook: 14–16
Body: Emerald-green wool
Hackle: White cock hackle

OLIVE MIDGE CLUMP (J. R. Harris)

Other midge colours can be tied with materials dyed in appropriate colours.

Hook: Fine-wire 8
Body: Pale-olive swan herl or seal's fur
Hackle: Three or four stiff cuckoo saddle or neck hackles dyed olive and palmered down the body
Rib: Gold wire

BLACK DUCK FLY (ADULT BUZZER) (Bob Carnill)   Plate 15

Hook: 12–14 standard or sedge hook
Tying silk: Well-waxed black Gossamer
Body: Goose, swan or heron herl dyed black
Wing: Very light iron blue dun cock hackle points, rear-facing from the back of the thorax on a flat horizontal plane and divided in a semi-spent position
Thorax: Mole's fur dyed black
Thorax cover: A web of body herl
Hackle: Sparsely-tied black hen.

LARGE GINGER (ADULT BUZZER) (Bob Carnill)   Plate 15

Hook: 10 standard or sedge hook
Tying silk: Waxed orange or golden-olive Gossamer
Body: Hot-orange swan herl
Rib: Close turns of stripped peacock eye quill dyed ginger
Wing: As for previous pattern
Thorax: Any light beige-brown under-fur; not seal's fur
Thorax cover: Hen secondary feather-fibres dyed ginger-orange
Hackle: Sparsely-tied pale ginger or honey hen

MEDIUM OLIVE (ADULT BUZZER) (Bob Carnill)   Plate 15

Hook: 10 standard or sedge hook
Tying silk: Light or medium-olive Gossamer
Body: Medium-olive goose, swan or heron herl
Wing: As for previous pattern
Thorax: Mole's fur dyed medium-olive
Thorax cover: A web of body herl
Hackle: Sparsely-tied medium to light-olive hen hackle

KNOTTED MIDGE (John Veniard)   Plate 28

An imitation to represent the mating pair.

Hook: 14–16
Tying silk: Black
Body: Black floss or silk
Hackles: Black cock at both ends of the body.

MINI LURES   Plate 18

Most stillwater lures are tied on longshank hooks and are consequently a fairly large offering to a fish. On many occasions small lures prove attractive or are necessary. Some smaller fisheries insist on a maximum hook-size. Many smaller attractor flies of the traditional design are moderately effective, but now small or mini-versions of the large reservoir lures are popular. A dressing is tied on a standard size 8 or 10 hook and fished in the manner appropriate to the pattern. Mini-versions of most of the popular lures are available commercially.

MINNOWS

These small fish are a source of food for both river and lake trout. See also under FRY (*page 64*) and MUDDLER MINNOW (*page 123*).

MINNOW

A floating pattern to be fished close to the surface.

Hook: Extra longshank 6–8
Tying silk: White
Body: Minnow-shaped plastazote with painted yellow eyes with black centres. Red spots on the body
Back: Large bunch of medium-olive marabou tied in at the head and rear with a tail trailing behind

HAIRY MINNOW (Taff Price)

Hook: Longshank 8–10
Tail: Red DFM wool
Body: Flat silver tinsel
Rib: Oval silver tinsel
Wing: White bucktail with dark-green bucktail over
Underbody wing: White bucktail extending to the tail and a small tuft of red bucktail at the throat
Head: Black with a painted white eye and black centre

MYLAR MINNOW (Sid Brock)

Hook: Longshank 10–14
Tying silk: Black
Underbody: Wool or floss
Body: Mylar tubing with the inner core removed and the outer tube pushed over the shank
Back and tail: Peacock herl
Head: Black tying silk varnished, with a painted eye each side

MISSIONARY   Plate 10

This was originally devised by J. J. Dunn for the big trout on Blagdon and other reservoirs much earlier this century. A more recent variation by Dick Shrive is popular. Rainbow trout often take it on the drop. The flat wing is an essential feature, so that the fly seems to flutter or swing gently left and right as it sinks. This movement sometimes seems very attractive to fish.

Hook: Longshank 6–10
Tying silk: Black
Tail: Dark ginger or scarlet cock hackle fibres
Body: White chenille
Rib: Flat silver tinsel or Lurex
Wing: A single grey mallard or teal breast feather tied on flat and extending just beyond the bend
Throat hackle: As for the tail. White hackle fibres are sometimes used.
The version tied with a hot-orange tail and hackle is called the **Orange Missionary**.

MISTY BLUE DUN   Plate 27

Devised by Tony Waites, head-keeper for the Driffield Anglers' Club, which fishes the delightful Yorkshire chalkstream, the Driffield Beck, this is an imitation of the medium olive dun.

Hook: 14
Tying silk: Yellow

119

Tail: Three long fibres from a light blue-dun cock hackle
Body: Yellow tying silk
Rib: A strand of natural heron herl so closely wound that the tying silk just shows through
Hackle: A light brown and light blue-dun cock wound together

MITES

These aquatic creatures are a source of trout food, but most fly-fishers imitate them only occasionally, perhaps when the examination of trouts' stomach contents revealed a high percentage of them. They probably quickly disintegrate in a trout's stomach, and consequently do not figure prominently in stomach contents. Most water-mites are bright red, but others are green, yellow or blue. They live in large colonies in mud on lake-beds and in weeds. They are small, varying between 2 and 6 mm (¼-inch) and are difficult to imitate. Richard Walker has suggested this pattern which he says can be improved upon by painting the hook vermilion.

Hook: 16–18
Tying silk: Vermilion
Body: Small ball-shaped white feather-fibres dyed vermilion
Hackle: One turn of cock hackle dyed vermilion

MULTI-MITE (Taff Price)

Hook: Longshank fine-wire 12–14
Body: Three small buttons of dubbed orange, green or red DFM wool and seal's fur mix
Hackles: Any short sparse hen hackle tied in front of the three small bodies

MONTREAL

A North American lure which is highly praised by Dave Collyer. He writes in *Fly Dressing II* that this and the bucktail Cahill are 'possibly the most effective hairwing American patterns that I have used in the U.K.'

Hook: 8–12
Tying silk: Black

Body: Claret floss
Rib: Flat gold tinsel
Tail: Scarlet cock hackle fibres
Wing: Brown squirrel-tail
Beard hackle: Claret cock hackle
An alternative version has a scarlet mohair body and ginger cock hackle.

MOSQUITO   See DIPTERA

The thirty species of mosquito have been largely overlooked as trout flies, possibly because they resemble to some extent the midges and phantom midge. Trout take much less interest in them than the other two insects, but they are well worth trying on a shaded part of a lake on a hot sunny day, or in the evening of such a day. The larvae are free-swimming and the pupae are similar to the midge-pupae except that they lack the white breathing spiracles at the head. The pupa pattern should be fished slowly under the surface film and twitched occasionally. A twenty-yard cast should take half-an-hour to be retrieved. It takes a lot of faith to fish in such a fashion!

MOSQUITO LARVA (Taff Price)

Hook: 12–14
Body: Grey silk

Rib: Black Terylene or silk
Hackle: White or blue-dun clipped short.

MOSQUITO PUPA (Dave Collyer)

Plate 15

Hook: 12
Tying silk: Black, taken well round the bend

Body: Stripped peacock eye quill
Thorax: Mole or muskrat fur in a ball shape

MOSQUITO ADULT (Taff Price)

Hook: 14–16
Body: Thinly-dubbed grey polypropylene
Rib: Black silk

Wing: Two small grizzle hackles tied spent
Hackle: Blue-dun

MOTHS (*Lepidoptera*)

Most moths are not aquatic, but some find their way on to river and lake surfaces by accident. However, one family of moths is aquatic. Only the adult winged moths are of any interest. Some of the smaller aquatic moths are at first glance taken for sedges, and a small sedge pattern will imitate these. The brown china moth is one of the larger and more common aquatic species. It is about 16 mm long and dark brown.

Terrestrial moths vary in size and colour from white to grey to brown and shades in between. The adults skitter across the surface, creating quite a disturbance. As a late-evening/dusk/night fly, a floating moth can be deadly in lake margins or on rivers. The white artificial has the added advantage of being easy to see in failing light. A moth fished on the last few casts of the evening has on more than one occasion saved me a blank. See also COACHMAN (*page 39*) and GREY DUSTER (*page 79*).

ERMINE MOTH

Plate 23

An imitation of the lighter-coloured moths devised by the Reverend Edward Powell.

Hook: 12–14
Tail: Orange wool divided into a V-shape
Body: White rabbit's fur on any white wool or fur
Rib: Black thread
Hackle: Grey partridge.
An additional white hackle can be added behind the partridge hackle to aid flotation.

HEATHER MOTH

A Scottish loch pattern to be fished on the bob.

Hook: 8–12
Tail: Barred teal feather-fibres
Tip (optional): Silver tinsel

Body: Grey or white fur or dubbed wool
Rib: Flat silver tinsel
Hackle: Palmered grizzle or grey-dun or badger hackle.

HOOLET MOTH (Geoffrey Bucknall)

Plate 22

The origin of this fly's name probably lies in 'hoolet', the old Scottish name for an owl. In original patterns the wing feather from that bird was used, but in Geoffrey Bucknall's version woodcock is preferred. The cork underbody makes the pattern very buoyant for fishing in a wave.

Hook: 8–10
Tying silk: Black

Body: An underbody of cork strip wound on to the shank with bronze peacock herl over

Wing: Woodcock wing feather tied low over the body, either rolled or flat

Hackle: Two natural red cock hackles

ORANGE UNDERWING (Geoffrey Bucknall)

Hook: 6–8

Butt: Orange fluorescent wool for about a quarter of the body

Body: Brown wool or herl over a sliver of cork

Wing: 25 mm (1-inch) brown-owl pri-mary feather, rolled and tied on flat

Hackle: Long-fibred natural red cock tied in front of the wings

The **Yellow Underwing** has a fluorescent yellow butt.

MRS PALMER   Plate 9

A lure devised by Richard Walker in 1973. It works better than most in dirty water and is best fished fairly slowly.

Hook: Longshank 6–8

Tying silk: Black

Body: White fluorescent wool taken to within 6 mm (¼-inch) of the eye; then three or four turns of arc-chrome fluorescent wool to within 3 mm of the eye

Rib: Fine flat silver tinsel over the white wool body only

Wing: Pale yellow goathair about twice the hook-length

Beard hackle: White cock hackle fibres

Cheeks: Jungle-cock

MRS SIMPSON   Plate 18

This stillwater fly from New Zealand is, apart from the Matukas, the only pattern from that country to have gained general acceptance in the U.K. The number of paired cock-pheasant rump feathers for the wing can be reduced on the smaller sizes.

Hook: Longshank 8–12

Tying silk: Black

Tail: Black squirrel-tail fibres

Body: Red, yellow or green chenille

Wing: Up to six pairs of green cock-pheasant rump feathers tied in alongside the body; largest at the front, the smallest at the rear.

Head: Tying silk varnished black

MUDDLERS

The original Muddler Minnow was devised by Don Gapen for fishing in Northern Ontario, and the dressing was published in 1953 in Al McClane's *The Practical Fly Fisherman*. Nottingham tackle-dealer, Tom Saville, introduced it into the U.K. in the mid 1960s. Many variations have been devised to represent various fry or small fish. They are excellent lures and can be deadly when fished in a wave or as a fry-imitation. This is arguably the most successful fly pattern to cross the Atlantic in our direction. Other lures can be adapted to the Muddler-style. See also FIRE-BALL (*page 64*) for a variation on the Muddler theme.

The heads on all these patterns, unless otherwise stated, are constructed by natural deer-body hair spun on the shank and clipped to a ball-shape. The original pattern had a few long hairs trailing underneath as a hackle. All patterns should use Naples tying silk or stronger, as the construction calls for the silk to be held taut under some strain. The shape of the head can be varied according to preference. Ball- or cone-shaped is popular. Some patterns are tied with a pointed cylindrical head.

See under WHOGSTOPPER (*page 199*) for a pattern that has a head at each end of the shank.

BLACK MUDDLER Plate 4

Hook: Longshank 6–10
Tying silk: Black
Body: Black floss or black chenille
Rib: Gold or silver tinsel
Tail (optional): Orange DRF floss

Wing: Black bucktail or squirrel
Hackle (optional): Black cock tied as a throat
Head: Natural deerhair spun and clipped

FOAM-HEADED MUDDLER

Any of the Muddler dressings can be tied with a plastic foam head instead of the usual deerhair. Eyes can be painted on if desired. The result is a buoyant pattern that will stay just below the surface.

LAST RESORT MUDDLER (R. Kendall) Plate 4

I have had good reports of this lure when jumped across the surface in a heavy wave.

Hook: Longshank 6
Tail: Marabou plumes, yellow, orange or lime

Body: White or DFM lime chenille
Wing: Marabou plumes, yellow, orange or lime but a different colour to the tail
Head: White deerhair hardly clipped, merely tidied up

MARABOU-WINGED MUDDLER Plate 4

Many lures are no more than hybrids between two or more proven patterns. This is one, utilising the attractive action of marabou in conjunction with the rounded deerhair head. Yellow, black and white versions are available commercially, tied as single-hook lures or in tandem.

Hook: Longshank 6–10
Tying silk: To match the overall colour
Body: Floss or fine chenille
Rib: Silver oval tinsel

Wing: Marabou plumes extending well beyond the rear of the hook in the same colour as the body
Throat or underwing: Marabou plume extending only to the rear of the hook
Head: Deerhair dyed as the body and wing colour, spun and clipped to shape
The tandem version has as the front hook a longshank or standard-length hook dressed as above. The rear hook omits the underwing and the Muddler head and instead has a head of peacock herl.

MUDDLER MINNOW Plates 4 & 18

The original dressing.

Hook: Longshank 4–12
Tying silk: Brown
Tail: A folded slip of oak-turkey wing feather
Body: Flat gold tinsel

Wing: Grey squirrel fibres between two matched mottled oak-turkey wing sections
Head: Deerhair spun and clipped to a ball-shape, leaving a few long fibres trailing to the rear as a hackle

ORANGE MUDDLER (Taff Price) Plate 4

Useful in dirty water conditions or when trout are feeding on daphnia.

Hook: Longshank 6–10
Body: Gold tinsel

Rib: Gold wire
Wing: Orange bucktail
Head: Deerhair spun and clipped, with some hairs unclipped as a collar

SCULPIN MUDDLER

A bullhead imitation.

Hook: Longshank 4–8
Body: Optional underbody of lead wire. Buff seal's fur tapering to the front, finishing about one-third of the way from the eye
Rib: Oval gold tinsel
Wing: Light red squirrel-tail fibres tied half-way along the shank, with two cree cock hackles tied in horizontally on the bare shank. Over the cree hackle roots are tied in three small well-marked hen-pheasant body feathers, one on either side of the roots and the other on top of the shank to flare out to imitate the large fins of the bullhead

TEXAS ROSE MUDDLER

Hook: Longshank: 6–10
Body: Orange or yellow wool or floss
Rib: Silver or gold tinsel
Wing: Bucktail dyed primrose
Head: Deerhair spun and trimmed in a bullet-shape

WHISKY MUDDLER

A Muddler variation of the Whisky Fly.

Hook: Longshank 6–8
Tying silk: Scarlet fluorescent floss
Butt: Tying silk
Body: Silver or gold Mylar
Rib: Tying silk
Wing: Oak-turkey wing sections and calf-tail dyed orange
Head: Deerhair spun and clipped

WHITE MUDDLER   Plate 4

Hook: Longshank 6–10
Tying silk: Black or white
Tail: White swan fibres
Body: Silver tinsel
Rib: Oval silver tinsel
Wing: White swan
Head: White deerhair spun and clipped in a bullet-shape, with longer fibres trailing to the rear

MUDDLERINE   Plate 4

Midlands reservoir expert, Steve Parton, has explained how this dressing came about. He had been sea-trout fishing on the Dovey with two friends and they had had success with a Muddler with a severely barbered head (they had twenty-five sea-trout over 3 lb to two rods in one night). Steve decided to experiment with a Muddler dressing on an elverine rig. Twenty-one sewin in two nights was the initial result. Later it had its trial on Rutland where it was cast to six fish. All six were hooked and landed (an unusual-enough feature when Muddler fishing), and since then Steve has used only the standard Muddler dressed on an elverine rig. There is no doubt that the treble hook enables better hooking. Below are Steve's two methods for constructing the elverine rig.

'The trouble inherent in an elverine rig of either the single- or double-shank varieties is that the treble hook can flop about on the end of the shank. This prevents guaranteed repeatable presentation, as there is a better-than-sporting chance that the rig will foul itself in casting. There are two ways of curing this tendency. The first is:

'Insert the treble in the vice ensuring that the eye of the hook is horizontal. Tie-in at the eye, take 6 inches of 12 lb nylon and loop it round one leg of the treble. Pull tight with your right hand and take several turns of thread over the hook and nylon ends until it is fairly secure. Then whip-down the treble shank until interference with the points makes it difficult and return to the eye, where you whip-finish and varnish the whole thread-covered shank.

'Take the treble and nylon ends out of the vice and assemble the treble to the elverine shank, taking care to get the shank in right side round. Insert the flat end of the shank nearest the hook loop into a vice set horizontal and tie-in eye. Arrange the nylon ends one on either side of the shank and whip down to the loop and back again. Cut off surplus, whip-finish and varnish. Take the assembled rig out of the vice and pull to straighten the assemblage. Give all the whippings another two coats of varnish and allow to dry before tying a Muddler dressing on the rig.

'The second method is:
Tie-in a tinsel body on the treble, varnish and allow to dry. Dress the shank separately. Slide a piece of clear plastic tubing of appropriate size in bore over the shank of the treble and cut it off dead-level with the eye. Assemble the treble to shank and close shank. Slide tubing back up to treble to go over and hold the joint in position.

'The major advantage of method two is that it allows you to change the treble in the event of a point being broken. The trouble that can happen is that the shank is prone to work-harden and break off without warning. This could be a thorough annoyance should it happen when you've a big fish on!'

MURK-MEISTER

This is a useful lure for fisheries where the water becomes thick with mud or algae. The materials and style of dressing ensure maximum visibility and a disturbance trout will detect. The method of fishing is with short, quick pulls, with pauses between the pulls. The pattern was devised by Richard Aylott.

Hook: Longshank 6–10
Tying silk: Hot-orange
Tail: White fluorescent wool
Bodies: Two bodies each of arc-chrome wool eased out and dubbed on the silk and built up fat
Hackles: Two, one in the centre of the body, the other at the shoulder, both stiff ginger cock.

MURRAGH   Plate 22

This Irish loch fly is a wet imitation of the great red sedge (see SEDGES, *page 157*). I have seen a number of dressings for this pattern, all of which differ only in their body colour. No doubt different species of sedge are copied with different body colours.

Hook: Longshank or standard 8–10
Body: Brown, claret or grey seal's fur
Rib: Gold wire
Wing: Brown mottled turkey tied long
Collar hackle: Natural red cock
Antennae (optional): Two cock-pheasant tail fibres

MYLAR FRY

A simple but effective fry-imitating lure.

Hook: Longshank 8
Tail: Green marabou

Body: Silver Mylar tubing with the centre core removed
Head: Tying silk varnished black and with a painted eye

A bucktail lure popular at many of the Midlands reservoirs, and particularly at Rutland. It needs to be fished slowly near the surface. It is good in a wave, and sometimes effective when sedges are hatching.

Hook: Longshank 6–10

Tying silk: Black
Tail: Red cock hackle fibres or hair fibres
Body: Gold Lurex or tinsel
Rib: Gold wire
Wing: Bright-red skunk or goathair with an overwing of brown hair
Throat hackle: Deep-brown cock fibres

NEEDLE-FLIES (*Leuctra fusca, L. hippopus*)

These two species of stonefly, almost indistinguishable from each other, are widely-distributed throughout the country in rain-fed rivers and chalk-streams, preferring rivers with a stony bottom. They are similar in overall appearance to the willow fly, although much smaller. They are dark brown, slim-bodied flies. Their size varies between 5–9 mm. *L. hippopus* is an early species, appearing from February to April; *L. fusca* appears from August to October. For general details, see STONEFLIES (*page 180*). See also WINTER BROWN (*page 200*) and LIGHT WOODCOCK (*page 100*).

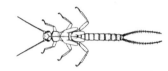

NEEDLE-FLY (John Veniard)

A floating pattern.

Hook: 14
Body: Medium-olive tying silk with dirty-yellow fur dubbed at the tail

Wing: Two small blue-dun cock hackle tips tied low over the back
Hackle: Medium-grizzle blue-dun cock

DARK NEEDLE

Plate 21

An old North Country wet pattern.

Hook: 14
Body: Orange silk
Hackle: Dark-brown owl's wing feather
Head: Peacock herl

Another old dressing bearing this name has a claret silk body and a starling wing for the hackle. The **Light Needle** has an orange silk body and is hackled with the flank feather of a young starling.

DARK SPANISH NEEDLE (Taff Price)

Hook: 14
Tying silk: Brown
Body: Thinly-spun orange and brown seal's fur

Wing: Thin dark-brown hen wing quill tied flat across the back
Hackle: Brown cock-pheasant hackle

LIGHT SPANISH NEEDLE (Taff Price)

A wet pattern.

Hook: 14–16

Body: Crimson silk
Hackle: Inside of a jack snipe wing

The original and best-known member of this series of stillwater lures is the Dog Nobbler, devised and popularised by Trevor Housby in the early 1980s. The success of the series is due to the pulsating action of the marabou herl tail in conjunction with the weighted head, which causes the lure to dive head-first when there is a pause in the retrieve. Fished in a sink-and-draw fashion, they can be extremely effective. Like some other exceptionally killing patterns, it has been banned on some smaller stillwaters. It is a fairly offensive-looking lure in its larger sizes; even its name does little to appease those who frown on the use of such lures.

The Nobbler's extensive 'ironmongery' has caused some concern about trends in fly-dressing. I hesitate to mention that I have seen tandem versions. But Nobblers catch fish and there is a place for them on some fisheries. Every 'dog' has its day, and a new and imaginatively created lure is blazoned across the pages of the angling press the Nobblers and their variations seem to be the lures of the 1980s. Other similar lures have been developed; all are based upon the marabou herl tail or wing and a weighted head or body and have equally outlandish names.

DOG NOBBLER

Plate 2

Hook: Longshank 4–12
Underbody: Lead-wire or foil strips along the shank or just at the shoulder; or a large split-shot pinched on and glued to the shank at the shoulder
Overbody: Coloured chenille
Rib (optional): Silver wire
Tail: A thick bunch of marabou herl tied long
Head (optional): Peacock herl
Eye: Painted on the split shot

The colour variations are infinite: White, yellow, green, black, pink, orange, and others are all used, and in their fluorescent alternatives. Most patterns are tied with the tail the same colour as the body, but two-colour Nobblers are also used. Black-and-green and white-and-orange are popular. **Mini-Nobblers**, sometimes called **Frog Nobblers** are tied on size 8 or 10 standard-length hooks. Another variation which is attractive is the **Palmered-body Nobbler**. The longshanked lure has a split-shot head with painted eye and a palmered badger hackle over the body which is ribbed with silver wire. The **Booby Nobbler** is an unweighted Nobbler with the inclusion of two foam beads trapped in a stocking-mesh behind the eye. This makes the lure very buoyant. Further details of this are in the section headed BOOBIES. Many other lures have been 'nobbled' and tied in this style. The following lures are all commercially available in Nobbler form: Appetizer, Jack Frost, Missionary, Sweeny Todd. The basic colours of the original lure are tied with Nobbler materials. For example:

SWEENY TODD NOBBLER

Hook: Longshank 8
Underbody: Lead foil or wire near the head
Overbody: Black chenille for the rear two-thirds; front one-third, neon magenta fluorescent floss or wool
Rib: Silver wire
Tail: Black marabou plume
Hackle: Scarlet cock as a rear-facing collar

Head: Peacock herl

In 1984 a fly-tyer, Sid Knight, successfully patented the name and dressing of the Dog Nobbler as tied and named by Trevor Housby. It was a sad day for fly-fishermen when that happened; an attempt to corner the market or create a monopoly was seen to have been given legal approval. Voices of disapproval were heard, and the situation was roundly condemned by the fishing-tackle trade and by fly-fishermen across the country. Sid Knight's reason for his action was that it was to 'prevent the commercial exploitation of inferior products'.

My opinion is that the Dog Nobbler is an easy fly to tie; there is little to tie incorrectly. There are many similar lures or variations of the Nobbler and all are efficient trout lures. Would the fly-fishing world be any better off if Frank Sawyer, Canon Greenwell and James Wright, William Lunn, Richard Walker and many others had all patented their own dressings and named flies? Trout-fishers the world over would be considerably worse off.

However, what is undeniable is that Sid Knight ties flies of high quality. He sent me the Dog and Mini Nobblers used in the illustrations, and I have only the highest praise for the workmanship.

The Nobbler concept and dressing is not as new as we are led to believe. Peter Mackenzie-Philps pointed out in an article in *Trout, Rod and Line* that as long ago as 1941 a similar fly was being used in the U.S.A. for jigging through holes in iced-over lakes for perch and other fish. The lure, called a **Goggle-Eye Ice Fly**, had a marabou herl tail, a lead-shot head and a floss-silk body. One thing that is beyond doubt is that the combination of a marabou herl tail and a leaded head is a killing one.

NO-HACKLE FLIES

The dressing of floating flies without the use of hackles was publicised after considerable research by two Americans, Carl Richards and Douglas Swisher, in their book *Selective Trout*, published in the U.S.A. in 1971. Their belief is that the body and wings of the fly are the stimulus to a trout, and to a lesser extent the hackle, this being so for the smaller sizes. After experimenting with natural dubbed fur, they dressed many patterns with polypropylene fibres as a greater aid to flotation. All the flies were dressed on fine-wire hooks, and to help them land right way up, the bunches of tail fibres were widely spread by being tied on either side of the shank and divided by tying-in more body fibres at the bend of the hook, forcing the tail fibres apart. Two patterns are listed below.

NO-HACKLE BLUE-WINGED OLIVE DUN

Hook: 14–18
Tail: Light-grey cock hackle fibres
Body: Medium-olive, or medium-olive and medium-brown rabbit's fur mixed

Wing: A bunch of light or medium-grey hen hackle-fibres set upright or in a V-shape.

NO-HACKLE QUILL GORDON

Hook: 12–14
Tail: Ginger cock fibres
Body: Mixed pale-yellow and dark-brown rabbit's fur
Wing: Dark-grey duck quill fibres set

upright or in a V-shape
These two patterns can be tied with bodies of polypropylene fibres of appropriate colour.

NO 3 PARA   Plate 28

This Parachute-style dry fly was devised by Pat Russell for both river and stillwater to catch those trout that rise only once and are not motivated into doing so again. Its creator knows of no better fly (save his own Enigma) for bringing unco-operative fish to the surface. Pat Russell wrote in a letter to me: 'Last year I met American Harry Solomon and found that he and others had come to the conclusion that if one can hold a nymph-like body in the surface film, as happens with the No 3 Para, you're in with a treble chance'. The fly was devised after the Falklands war, when the No 3 Parachute Brigade fought so bravely, and it was named in their honour.

Hook: 14–16
Tying silk: Scarlet
Tail: Rhode Island Red hackle fibres
Body: Rhode Island Red hackle stalk and silk
Hackle: Barred badger and cream cock

OAK FLY   See DIPTERA

This is a member of the Diptera Order, a flat-winged terrestrial fly so named because it is often seen resting on tree trunks. It has a fairly large body about 12 mm (½-inch) long which is orangey-yellow. Our forefathers valued it as an angler's fly and it is mentioned in Charles Cotton's addition to *The Compleat Angler*, and possibly even earlier, as the fifteenth-century **Tandy Fly** of Dame Juliana Berners was thought by G. E. M. Skues to be an oak-fly imitation.

Hook: 12–14
Tying silk: Orange
Body: Orange floss
Rib: Black silk or stripped peacock quill
Wing: Woodcock wing tied flat over the back
Hackle: Furnace cock

OLIVES   See EPHEMEROPTERA

Before a more detailed classification was generally accepted among anglers, all the Baetis species, with the exception of the iron blue and pale wateries, were grouped together and referred to as olive duns. Therefore many old patterns bearing this name could represent one or more of the Baetis genus. The patterns below could represent many of the different olives, depending upon the shades of the materials used and the hook sizes. For natural-history details and more specific patterns see under BLUE-WINGED OLIVE (*page 23*), LAKE OLIVE (*page 94*), LARGE DARK OLIVE (*page 96*), DARK OLIVE (*page 48*), MEDIUM OLIVE (*page 111*), OLIVE UPRIGHT (*page 130*), POND OLIVE (*page 150*) and SMALL DARK OLIVE (*page 173*). In addition, see also the artificial flies: USD OLIVE (*page 190*), WATERHEN BLOA (*page 22*), ROUGH OLIVE (*page 156*), GOLD-RIBBED HARE'S EAR (*page 72*), GREENWELL'S GLORY (*page 77*), OLIVE BLOA (*page 21*), DARK OLIVE BLOA (*page 21*), DOGSBODY (*page 51*), KITE'S IMPERIAL (*page 94*), PHEASANT-TAIL SPINNER (*page 146*), LUNN'S PARTICULAR (*page 102*), SUNK SPINNER (*page 184*) and LIGHT OLIVE (*page 100*).

HATCHING OLIVE NYMPH (Geoffrey Bucknall)   Plate 19

To be fished as a floater.
Hook: 12–14
Tail: A slim strip of light-olive goose feather-fibres

Body: Light-olive goose feather-fibres
Rib: Fine gold tinsel
Thorax: A knob of dark-olive seal's fur
Wing-case: Dark wing feather

HATCHING OLIVE NYMPH (John Goddard)   Plate 19

To be fished in the surface film.
Hook: 12–16

Tying silk: Brown
Body: Olive-green condor herl with three

tips for the tail
Rib: Silver Lurex
Overbody: A strip of PVC dyed olive over the body and rib
Thorax: Dark pheasant tail fibres; later in the season, peacock herl
Wing-cases: Dark pheasant tail fibres doubled and redoubled
Hackle: Pale honey-dun tied in front of the thorax

OLIVE DUN (Cliff Henry)

This is described in John Goddard's book, *Trout Flies of Stillwater*, as being 'an exceptionally good one', with particular reference to the imitation of the stillwater olives.

Hook: 16

Tying silk: Green
Tail: Grey-blue hackle fibres
Body: Light-olive hen hackle stalk
Wing: Mallard duck quill feather
Hackle: Pale gingery orange

OLIVE QUILL

This is better known as a river dry fly, but Bob Church recommends it fished wet on stillwaters.

Hook: 12–16
Tail: Medium-olive cock fibres

Body: Peacock quill dyed olive
Wing (optional): Medium starling wing feather
Hackle: Medium-olive cock

OLIVE SPINNER (John Veniard)

Hook: 14
Tail: Medium-olive cock fibres
Body: Yellow tying silk covered with horsehair

Rib: Gold wire
Wing: Hackle tips or hackle fibres of medium blue-dun cock tied spent
Hackle: Medium-olive cock

OLIVE SUN NYMPH

A stillwater nymph pattern devised by Richard Aylott. Richard Walker wrote that he found it useful in bright sunshine. It should be fished just below the surface on a long leader and cast, if possible, into the path of a cruising fish.

Hook: 12–14
Tying silk: Pale green
Tail: Small golden-pheasant topping
Body: Green-yellow fluorescent floss tied thinly
Rib: Fine gold thread
Head: Bronze peacock herl

OLIVE UPRIGHT (*Rhithrogena semicolorata*)
See EPHEMEROPTERA

This fly occurs in the western half of the U.K., Scotland, the north-west and West of England, and Wales. Its nymphs are similar to those of the March Brown, clinging to stones on faster-flowing rivers. The adults are fairly large and have dark blue-grey wings, a grey-olive body and two tails, and are similar to the slightly smaller blue-winged olive. They appear between late April and July, hatching in large numbers in the evenings or in the afternoons if the weather is cool. The spinner is sometimes known as the yellow upright. The male spinners have yellowish wings and bodies and the females are a duller olive-yellow. The spinners can be copied with a Pheasant Tail with a rusty-dun hackle.

OLIVE UPRIGHT DUN

Hook: 12–14
Tail: Light to medium-olive cock hackle fibres
Body: Peacock quill dyed olive
Hackle: Light to medium-olive cock

OMBUDSMAN Plate 11

Brian Clarke designed this pattern in the early 1970s, when doing the research which eventually led to his book, *The Pursuit of Stillwater Trout*. He writes that he was 'seeking to represent a wide range of bottom-living creepy-crawlies which trout consume: caddis larvae, alder larvae and the like from the world of the real; and a conceptual range of bugs which should exist, even if they don't. In short, I was seeking to design something which looked like the kinds of food items which trout were accustomed to seeing – and to feeding upon.

'The Ombudsman, as originally designed, when cast and wet, does not keep the sleek shape of the dry finished article in the fly-tying vice. It becomes somewhat ragamuffin and bedraggled. But a sharp jerk when it has been allowed to sink to the fishing depth, and the steady motion of the retrieve, will bring the feather-fibres back into profile which is sufficiently appealing to the trout to cause them to take the confection.

'I designed the Ombudsman to be fished slowly along the bottom from the end of a long leader attached to a floating line. But it is fished by some from a sinking line (an unappealing method for me); and it will also take fish when fished close to the surface where, presumably, trout take it for some form of ascending pupa.

'I called the fly the Ombudsman after much public discussion of the role of a government-appointed individual whose job it was to act as adjudicator in alleged cases of abuse or misuse of executive power. He was presented, it seemed to me, as someone who would be all things to all men. My fly was intended to be many things to many fish. Poetic licence took care of the rest.

'I took my first fish ever from Rutland Water – on the introductory Press Day – on the Ombudsman. It was on the same day that I also took on the fly – although a different one – the first pike in Rutland Water. Up to that fateful moment, great play had been made by Water Authority officials on the "miracle" they had achieved in bringing this big lake to the status of a major trout fishery without pike finding their way into it. Big lake, but, in the light of events, small miracle!'

Hook: Longshank 8–10
Body: Underbody of one or two layers of copper wire with an overbody of bronze peacock herl to within 6 mm (¼-inch) of the eye
Rib (optional): Copper wire
Wing: Any large dark-brown mottled wing feather tied as a roof close over the body and extending to a point 6–12 mm beyond the bend
Hackle: Soft brown cock tied in front of the wing
Head: Thick brown silk tied over the wing roots

ORANGE JOHN

A stillwater pattern devised by John Ketley, a former captain of the English fly-fishing team. It is a wet sedge fly to be fished on the top dropper in traditional loch-style towards the end of the season. As a bob fly it can be fished dry, skittering along the surface during the retrieve.

Hook: 10
Tying silk: Brown or orange
Body: Hot-orange seal's fur with a palmered light-brown hackle

Rib: Goldfingering through the body hackle
Wing: Hen pheasant
Hackle: Honey-cock wound as a collar

ORANGE LURES

In addition to those detailed below, other orange lures can be found under WHISKY FLY (*page 196*), NOBBLERS (*page 127*) and MUDDLERS (*page 122*).

When the water temperature is high during July and August, or when rainbows are gorging themselves on daphnia, then one of the most successful tactics is to strip an orange lure fast in the top few feet of water. Sometimes almost any orange lure works well, but perhaps the best are the Orange Bucktail and the Whisky Fly. There are times when orange lures and nymphs take trout and patterns of other colours fail. Bob Church termed this annual event at Grafham as 'orange madness'.

The success of the orange lure is notable when the water temperature is high and large amounts of blue-green algae come to the surface. The orange colour of the lures is poorly reflected beyond a few feet down, and in water thick with algae trout are likely to see the lure colour as blue-grey, or at eight or ten feet possibly even as black. Small fish darting about will be seen as the same colour. A cynic or a purist may scorn bright-orange lures, but there are times when trout certainly don't see them as orange.

ORANGE BUCKTAIL (Taff Price)   Plate 8

Hook: Longshank 8–10
Body: Oval gold tinsel
Wing: Orange bucktail

Head: Black with a painted white eye and black pupil

ORANGE STREAMER (Taff Price)

Hook: Longshank 6–10
Body: Orange floss
Rib: Oval gold tinsel
Wing: Two hot-orange cock hackles

tied back-to-back with two cock badger hackles one either side
Cheek: Jungle-cock about a quarter the wing length

ORANGE TANDEM LURE (R. French)

Rear hook

Tail: Pale-orange DFM wool
Body: Gold or silver Lurex
Rib: Fine oval gold or silver tinsel
Wing: Orange bucktail

Front hook

Body and rib: As for rear hook
Thorax: Pale-orange DFM wool
Beard hackle: Hot-orange cock
Wing: Orange bucktail at the shoulder and at the tail of the front hook
Head: Black with painted eye

ORANGE NYMPHS   Plate 15

The first of these stillwater patterns was created by Arthur Cove and is recommended to be fished on a bright, sunny day. It has a reputation

132

for catching trout when snails are on the surface.

Hook: 10–12
Body: Orange seal's fur or synthetic substitute
Rib: Flat gold tinsel
Thorax: As for the body, but more pronounced
Wing-case: Pheasant tail fibres over the thorax

A second pattern has been devised by Taff Price, who recommends it as useful when trout are feeding on daphnia. The story goes that Taff was fruitlessly fishing and trying any fly in his box. Well down the list he tried a Partridge and Orange, an old North Country wet fly. He caught a trout and its stomach contents showed that it was full of strawberry-jam-coloured daphnia. The orange nymph was devised as a result.

Hook: 12–14
Tying silk: Orange
Body: Orange seal's fur
Rib: Gold wire
Back: Swan fibres dyed deep orange (optional to varnish)
Antennae: Two or three of the orange swan fibres extending forward over the eye

ORANGE OTTER   Plate 27

This is a grayling dry fly devised by the Reverend Edward Powell, who said that it was the only fly he knew to bring grayling up from the bottom when they were not feeding on the surface. Courtney Williams records contemporary comments on the pattern as 'Phenomenal . . . devastating . . . one hell of a fly'. My own comment on the fly is that I have caught grayling on it, but not with outstanding success.

Hook: 12–16
Tail: Natural red cock fibres
Body: Orange seal's fur (otter substitute) tied in two halves
Hackle: Natural red cock in the middle of the body

ORANGE QUILL   Plate 28

Despite its unlikely appearance, this is a blue-winged olive and general olive copy. It was popularised by G. E. M. Skues, who did not invent the fly, but who discovered its effectiveness for the b.-w.o. It is a useful evening pattern. I've had success with it as a late-season trout fly and as an early-season grayling fly, when I've found it, on occasion, to be exceptional.

Hook: 12–14
Tail: Orange hackle fibres
Body: Quill dyed pale orange
Wing: Rusty-dun hackle points
Hackle: Orange cock

Other dressings have a pale starling wing and a natural light red cock hackle or a medium ginger cock hackle.

ORANGE SPINNER

A G.E.M. Skues pattern which he fished as a blue-winged olive spinner imitation. See also USD POLYSPINNER (*page 191*).

Hook: 14

Tying silk: Orange
Tail: Honey-dun hackle fibres
Body: Medium-olive seal's fur
Rib: Fine gold wire
Hackle: Rusty-dun or blue-dun cock

OTTER RUBY

An iron blue dun imitation tied by Jim Nice in the late 1950s.

Hook: 14–18
Tying silk: Brown or claret

Tail: Fibres of the hackle used
Body: Condor herl dyed magenta
Rib (optional): Fine gold wire
Hackle: Iron-blue or brownish-black cock

OVERFIELD'S NO-NAME NYMPH

Donald Overfield is probably this country's leading angling historian. This is his general impressionist nymph that represents a number of naturals when it is dressed in different-coloured materials.

Hook: 12–14
Tail: Pheasant tail or condor herl tips
Abdomen: Tapered tying silk with a strip of cock hackle (which has been stripped along one side) glued along either side
Rib: Gold or silver wire
Back: Stretched clear PVC
Wing-case: Suitable-coloured feather-fibres
Legs: Six legs of heron herl or pheasant tail fibres

PAINTED LADY STREAMER   Plate 7

A Taff Price lure which he recommends should be fished at dusk.

Hook: Longshank 4–8
Tail: Spotted guinea-fowl body feather-fibres dyed blue
Body: Black floss tied thin and tapering to the rear
Rib: Flat silver tinsel or Lurex
Wing: Four black cock hackles
Cheek: Jungle-cock
Hackle: Long-fibred magenta as a beard
Head: Black tying silk

PALE EVENING DUN (*Procloëon bifidum*)
See EPHEMEROPTERA

A fairly widely-distributed species of upwinged dun, but occurring quite locally. The nymphs are the agile darting type and prefer slower-moving water. John Goddard points out that the dun often appears at the same time as the blue-winged olive and often trout will rise to the pale evening dun in preference to the b.-w.o. It has been undervalued as a fly pattern and the absence of artificials reflects this.

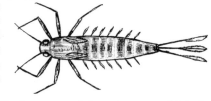

The pale evening dun is easy to identify because of the absence of hind-wings, which makes the species unique among river duns. In the past it may have been included under the general heading of 'pale watery', but the pale evening dun is slightly larger and paler than the one species we term the pale watery. It appears in the evenings of July and August. The dun is pale coloured and the male has distinctive yellow eyes. The spinner is of doubtful value to the fly-fisher as it is likely that the female returns to the water only after dark. For other patterns, see LUNN'S YELLOW BOY (a pale version) (*page 102*) and PALE WATERY (a pale version) (*page 135*).

PALE EVENING FLYMPH   See FLYMPHS

Hook: 14–16 longshank Mayfly
Tying silk: Primrose or white
Tail: Pale honey-dun hackle fibres

Body: Creamy-red fox fur
Hackle: Pale honey-dun

PALE EVENING DUN (Oliver Kite)

Hook: 14–16
Tying silk: White
Tail: Cream cock fibres

Body: Grey goose herls, doubled and redoubled at the thorax
Hackle: Cream cock

PALE EVENING DUN (John Veniard)

Hook: 14
Tail: Pale honey-dun fibres
Body: Pale yellow seal's fur

Wing: Starling wing
Hackle: Pale honey-dun cock

PALE WATERY (*Baetis fuscatus*)   See EPHEMEROPTERA

The term pale watery was once collectively applied to this and three other species, the small dark olive, small spurwing and large spurwing, and possibly to the pale evening dun, but these are now considered separately. The distribution is good in the South of England, parts of Wales and the North and on other alkaline waters. The smallish adults appear from late May to late October. I have found the duns greedily taken by grayling as well as trout. The nymph is an agile-darting type preferring to live among weed-beds. The duns hatch during the day, but the appearance of the female spinner is mainly in the evening.

The male dun has medium- or pale-grey wings and a pale greyish-olive body, of which the last two segments are pale yellow. The legs are light-olive and the two tails grey. The yellow eyes of the male help to identify it, but might also help to confuse it with the pale evening dun.

The female dun has pale-grey wings and a pale grey-olive abdomen, with the last two segments yellow-olive. The legs are pale-olive and the two tails grey. The female spinner, sometimes called the golden spinner, has transparent wings and a medium golden-brown abdomen, of which the last three segments are darker. The legs are pale watery and the two tails grey-white. The male spinner is of no interest as it does not return to the water.

For other patterns see POULT BLOA (*page 21*), HI C PALE WATERY (*page 84*), DAILY DUN (*page 45*), GODDARD'S LAST HOPE (*page 71*), USD PARADUNS (*page 190*), GREY GOOSE NYMPH (*page 79*), LITTLE MARRYAT (*page 100*), ENIGMA (*page 57*), TUP'S INDISPENSABLE (*page 188*), PHEASANT TAIL (*page 146*) and LUNN'S PARTICULAR (*page 102*).

PALE WATERY NYMPH (Frank Sawyer)

Hook: 14
Tying silk: None
Tail: Four or five ginger cock fibres
Body: Fawn-pink darning wool and un-

varnished copper wire wound together over an optional layer of copper wire
Thorax: Wood-pigeon primary feather

PALE WATERY NYMPH (Alistair Howman)

Hook: 12–14
Body: Grey nylon

Wing-case and legs: White ostrich herl

HATCHING PALE WATERY DUN (W. H. Lawrie)

Only the legs and thorax should float on the surface.

Hook: 16
Tying silk: Primrose
Tail: Blue hen hackle fibres
Body: Pale-blue cat's fur, thinly spun
Rib: Fine gold wire

Thorax: Blue cat's fur mixed with primrose worsted
Wing hackle: Pale-blue cock with the lower fibres cut away
Leg hackle: Grey or henny cock with the upper fibres cut away

PALE WATERY DUN (Richard Walker)

Recommended also as a chalk-stream grayling fly.

Hook: 16
Tying silk: Primrose
Tail: Fibres of the hackle used
Body: Swan secondary herl tinted the palest greenish-grey with a few turns of tying silk built up and exposed at the rear.

A drop of clear cellulose should be added to the tip to give it an amber tint
Wing (optional): Honey-dun hackle fibres set upright; or bleached starling wing
Hackle: Honey-dun or deeply-tinted cream cock

PALE WATERY DUN (Freddie Rice)   Plate 28

Hook: 14–16
Tying silk: Light yellow
Tail: Light blue-dun or pale honey-dun hackle fibres
Tip: Unwaxed tying silk

Body: Two or three herls: light-grey heron, white swan or goose wing, palest olive
Hackle: Palest olive or pale honey-dun cock

PALE WATERY SPINNER (John Veniard)

Hook: 14–16
Tail: Pale golden-yellow cock fibres
Body: Pale-yellow tying silk covered with natural horsehair

Wing: Pale blue-dun hackle points tied spent
Hackle: Pale golden-yellow cock

PALE WATERY SPINNER (G. E. M. Skues)

Hook: 14–16
Tying silk: Pale orange
Tail: Honey-dun hackle fibres
Body: Light-cream seal's fur or dubbed

wool
Hackle: Pale-blue cock tied in bunched spent-wing fashion

PALMERS

The palmer-style of dressing trout flies, of winding the hackle along the length of the body, goes back to the time of Berners in the fifteenth century and was commonplace there-after. Five patterns are mentioned in Thomas Barker's *Art of Angling* of 1651 which 'will serve all the year long, morning and evening'. Thomas Best, writing in the *Art of Angling*, 1813, wrote: 'The angler should always try the Palmers first, when he fishes a river he is unaccustomed to; even in that which he constantly uses, without he knows what fly is on the water, and should never be changed til he does.'

The great value of the palmered hackle on both the wet and floating fly is that it gives the fly an impression of movement and life, and what has been termed a "buzz" effect. Scores of different palmers have been developed over the centuries and many still remain today because of their trout-killing qualities. They are used on both river and stillwater, and they can be used to represent a hatching or floating sedge, a floating moth, a caterpillar and, when fished in the surface film in the appropriate colours, a variety of natural hatching duns. The palmers have always been written about in glowing terms, and I have no doubt about their effectiveness today, despite the trend towards more accurate and complex dressings.

AMBER PALMER (Roger Fogg)

An emerging sedge pattern to be fished just below the surface.

Hook: 10–12
Body: Amber seal's fur
Rib: Oval gold tinsel
Hackle: Palmered red-brown or ginger hen

BADGER PALMER (Roger Fogg)   Plate 25

Hook: 10–16
Tying silk: Brown
Body: Mixed hare's ear fur and blue rabbit's or mole's fur
Rib: Brown silk
Hackle: Palmered badger cock

BLACK PALMER

Fished as a floater or as a wet fly. It represents a number of insects, midges, terrestrials, beetles and sedges, and is a reliable pattern to try at any time. A nondescript black fly is a good standby to keep in any fly-box.

Hook: 12–16
Body: Black ostrich herl
Rib: Gold wire
Hackle: Palmered black cock. An option is to trim the body hackle and have an additional hackle at the head

BROWN PALMER

A useful sedge pattern when fished just below the surface.

Hook: 10–14
Tag (optional): Green DFM silk
Body: Dark-brown floss or seal's fur
Rib: Gold tinsel
Hackle: Palmered red-brown cock

GREEN PALMER

This can be tied with an optional lead underbody and fished deep where it might be taken for a dragonfly larva.

Hook: 6–12
Body: Green seal's fur
Rib: Fine gold thread
Hackle: Palmered cock dyed green

GREY PALMER

Hook: 10–12
Body: Grey seal's fur

Rib: Flat gold tinsel
Hackle: Palmered badger cock

GRIZZLY PALMER

Plate 25

Hook: 8–12
Body: Black seal's fur

Rib: Flat gold tinsel
Hackle: Palmered grizzle

MOTTLED PALMER (Roger Fogg)

A floating pattern to represent the grannom or other mottled-winged sedge.

Hook: 10–14
Tying silk: Black
Tag: Green DFM silk

Body: Twisted mottled turkey tail feather-fibres wound along the body, or hare's ear
Rib: Oval gold tinsel
Body hackle: Palmered coch-y-bondhu or Greenwell cock
Head hackle: Dark-brown cock

PINK PALMER

Pink has been a colour rather neglected by fly-tyers until recently. This stillwater pattern has been suggested as a useful top dropper when others are failing.

Hook: 12
Tail: Pink or white hackle-fibres
Body: Fluorescent-pink seal's fur
Rib: Silver wire or fine oval silver tinsel
Hackle: Palmered pink or white hackle

RED PALMER

A very old pattern, similar to the lake fly, the Soldier Palmer. It has a reputation as a dry fly in some parts of the country. Harry Powell, the famous Usk fly-dresser, tied a long-hackled floating variant known as **Whiskers**. The traditional dressing is given below.

Hook: 8–12
Tying silk: Red
Body: Red seal's fur or wool
Rib: Gold tinsel
Hackle: Palmered natural red cock

SOLDIER PALMER

Plate 18

There is little doubt that the obscure origins of this pattern go back many centuries. One suggestion has been that the name came from the English army redcoats. It has become an excellent lake and reservoir fly, used throughout the British Isles. It is best fished on the top dropper, but it also fishes well deeper. It is probably taken for a sedge-pupa, but when fished deeper it could well represent a shrimp. Many variations have been tied, some using fluorescent red/orange seal's fur for the body, or adding a fluorescent wool tag.

Hook: 10–12
Body: Scarlet seal's fur or wool
Rib: Flat gold tinsel or gold wire
Hackle: Palmered bright chestnut cock

WHITE PALMER

A light-coloured moth imitation.

Hook: 10–14
Tying silk: Ash-coloured

Body: Grubby-white seal's fur
Rib: Pale-coloured silk
Hackle: Palmered dirty-white cock

PALMER NYMPH
Plate 14

Many palmered nymphs are known simply by their colour (see PALMERS). This pattern was devised by Conrad Voss Bark, author of *Fly-Fishing for Lake Trout*, 1972. It should be fished deep or just below the surface. Movement through the water enlivens the body hackle and gives an impression of life. It was originally tied as a general pattern for Two Lakes fishery in Hampshire and its inspiration came from the Bumble patterns of T. C. Kingsmill Moore. Mr Voss Bark has amended his original dressing to the one below.

Hook: 8–12
Tail: Very short folded pheasant topping
Underbody: Yellow seal's fur, thinly dubbed
Rib: Thin gold wire
Body hackle: Short-fibred olive-green hackle palmered down the body; about three turns
Head hackle: Three turns of a short-fibred dark-red cock hackle

PAPOOSE

A Dave Collyer lure which he describes as being an offspring of the CHIEF NEEDABEH (*page 36*). It should be stripped fast close to the surface on bright sunny days.

Hook: 8–10
Tying silk: Black
Tip: Oval silver tinsel

Body: Scarlet floss
Rib: Oval silver tinsel
Wing: Eight married strips of goose feather
Cheeks: Jungle-cock
Beard hackle: Scarlet and yellow cock fibres

PARACHUTE NYMPH

The nymph pattern below was devised by Davy Wotton to hang in the surface film or to sink very slowly. Most nymphs can be so adapted by tying in a large sparsely-dressed hackle at the head. This is wound in the normal way and not in the Parachute style described in the glossary.

Hook: 10–16
Tail: Green cock-pheasant tail-fibres
Body: Cock-pheasant tail herl dyed green
Rib: Very fine silver wire
Thorax: Mixed brown and medium-olive seal's fur
Wing-case: Cock-pheasant centre tail fibres
Hackle: Long-fibred grizzle

PARMACHEENE BELLE
Plate 18

An American lake fly named after Parmacheene lake. By American standards this is a very old pattern, devised in the 1870s, but it is still catching trout both in the States and the U.K. A dry version is fished in the States, but I have not heard of its use here.

Hook: 6–12
Tail: Red and white duck fibres

Butt (optional): Black ostrich herl
Body: Yellow floss or wool
Rib: Flat gold tinsel
Wing: White duck or swan with a strip of red ibis substitute on each side. The ibis substitute should be half the width of the duck or swan fibres

Beard hackle: A mixture of scarlet and white cock

The original pattern had no butt and was ribbed with silver tinsel.

PARODY   Plate 28

Other than a mention in my previous book, I doubt whether this fly has been considered by many anglers. It is an excellent dry fly for late-season trout and autumn grayling. I don't think it is taken as a copy of any particular natural fly, but I have caught dozens of fish on it from northern rivers.

Hook: 14
Tag: Yellow wool or floss
Body: Mixed orange and claret seal's fur (2:1)
Rib: Fine gold tinsel
Hackle: Grizzle cock

PARROT   Plate 9

Trevor Housby devised this series of lures and small fish imitators. They are particularly good when fished deep on sinking lines. No doubt their visibility has much to do with their success. I am told they are excellent for sea-trout, too.

Hook: Longshank 6
Body: Silver Mylar tubing tied in at the end of the shank with the ends frayed for the tail. The body is flattened to give a fish-belly shape underneath
Wing: Coloured Fish-hair with silver Mylar strips as an overwing, both extending to just beyond the tail. Recommended colours for the Fish-hair are white, red, black, green, orange, blue
Head: Black tying silk

PARTRIDGE AND BLACK

This is a different fly from those in the PARTRIDGE SERIES (*this page*). It is a popular wet fly on the Clyde and its tributaries. I am not sure what it is taken for, but trout autopsies always produce a range of black or dark-coloured insects or other food items. This pattern is probably sufficiently generally imitative to be mistaken for any one of a number of edible sub-surface creatures.

Hook: 14
Body: Black floss or tying silk
Wing: Marbled partridge tail feather
Hackle: Black hen

PARTRIDGE SERIES

A series of spider-type wet flies of ancient origin devised for rough-stream fishing. Some have made the transition to stillwater. All have a partridge hackle. They are also known by the reversal of their names e.g. Blue Partridge.

PARTRIDGE AND BLUE   Plate 21

This is quite possibly a gravel-bed imitation. I tie a similar dressing to the one below that omits the dubbed body. The Partridge and Blue is not a popular fly, but I have reason to remember it with affection. It once saved a fruitless April day on the Nidd when, cast upstream over likely lies, it caught eight brown trout in about forty minutes. The dressing given is T. E. Pritt's.

Hook: 14
Body: Blue tying silk lightly dubbed with lead-coloured lamb's wool
Hackle: Partridge back feather.

PARTRIDGE AND CLARET

W. H. Lawrie describes this as a killing spring fly on the Tweed and other Scottish Border rivers.

Hook: 12–14

Body: Claret worsted or claret seal's fur
Rib: Fine gold wire
Hackle: Dark partridge

PARTRIDGE AND GREEN

This is a suitable grannom imitation. See under SEDGES (*page 157*).

Hook: 12–14

Body: Bright-green tying silk
Hackle: Dark partridge rump feather.

PARTRIDGE AND HARE'S EAR

A Welsh wet fly.

Hook: 12–14
Body: Hare's ear fur

Rib: Gold wire
Hackle: Dark partridge

PARTRIDGE AND MOLE   Plate 20

A Welsh wet fly.

Hook: 14
Tail: Dark partridge fibres

Body: Mole's fur
Rib: Silver wire
Hackle: Dark partridge

PARTRIDGE AND ORANGE   Plate 21

The best-known of the series. It is usually fished as a river wet fly, but I have heard of its use as a floater. It is probably taken for a stonefly. As a North Country trout and grayling pattern, it is one of the best flies one could choose, and it is one of my favourites for a three-fly leader. The pattern with a gold tinsel rib is one of Reg Righyni's favourite grayling flies. Although I have never caught a trout on it as a lake fly, others have. It should do well when daphnia are about, when orange-bodied flies are the best bet. Richard Walker caught an 18 lb rainbow trout on a pattern on a wide-gape size 8 or 10 hook tied with a short floss-silk body.

Hook: 12–16
Body: Orange silk
Rib (optional): Gold tinsel or wire
Hackle: Dark partridge

PARTRIDGE AND ORANGE (Thomas Clegg)

Hook: 14–16
Tying silk: Yellow
Body: Orange DFM floss

Rib: Brown Naples silk
Hackle: Grey partridge

PARTRIDGE AND PEACOCK SPIDER

A Welsh wet pattern.

Hook: 12–14

Body: Peacock herl
Hackle: Dark partridge

PARTRIDGE AND RED

Hook: 12–16
Body: Wine-red silk

Hackle: Dark partridge

PARTRIDGE AND SILVER

A useful early-season fly.

Hook: 12–14

Body: Silver tinsel
Hackle: Dark partridge

PARTRIDGE AND YELLOW

A good early-season fly, probably giving the best results in the evening from April to June.

Hook: 12–16

Body: Yellow silk
Rib: Fine gold wire
Hackle: Light-grey partridge back feather

PARTRIDGE GLORY

A West Country pattern. I use a similar fly that has a gold wire rib. It certainly looks nicer, but I wouldn't like to say whether or not that influences the fish.

Hook: 14
Body: Medium-brown floss
Hackle: Dark partridge

PEARLY

A successful lure which in its various colours can be fished at all depths throughout the season. It should generally be fished slowly or with a medium retrieve, although later in the season it is sometimes necessary to fish it fast. It was devised by Syd Brock, who suggests that the appropriate colours are black, white, yellow or orange.

Hook: Longshank 8–10
Tail: Cock fibres the same as the body colour
Body: Coloured wool, see text
Wing: Marabou plume of the body colour
Head: Pearl or bead painted in the same colour with an added eye each side; glued to the shank behind the hook eye

PEARLY NOBBLER

A Syd Brock variation of his own Pearly on the theme of the Dog Nobbler. It can be tied in the same variety of colours as the Pearly.

Hook: Longshank 6–10

Tail: A bunch of yellow marabou
Body: Black chenille, or to match the tail
Head: A black bead fixed with glue behind the eye, with a painted eye

PENNELLS

A series of now-standard general stillwater patterns devised in the last century by H. Cholmondeley Pennell. They are also useful river wet flies. In addition to the two listed below there are the less-frequently-used brown, yellow and green variations tied with similar materials dyed as appropriate. The Pennells are best fished as bob-flies. The smaller sizes are probably taken for variety of natural flies, but particularly midges. Thickly-hackled versions are used for dapping. Pennells are also occasionally tied in tandem to be fished as deeply sunk lures.

PENNELL'S BLACK   Plate 16

Hook: 8–14
Tip: Oval silver tinsel
Tail: Golden-pheasant crest and tippet fibres
Body: Black floss silk
Rib: Oval silver tinsel
Hackle: Long-fibred black cock

PENNELL'S CLARET   Plate 16

Hook: 8–14
Tail: Golden-pheasant tippet and crest fibres
Body: Claret seal's fur
Rib: Fine gold tinsel
Hackle: Long-fibred furnace cock

PENSIONERS

A series of Parachute-style dry flies devised by Peter Mackenzie-Philps. They were originally tied for an elderly angler with failing eyesight who needed a highly visible dry fly. For further details of the Parachute style, see glossary.

BLACK PENSIONER   Plate 27

This is a fair imitation of any dark floating fly.
Hook: 12
Tail: Black cock fibres
Body: Black dyed cock-pheasant centre tail fibres
Rib: Fine gold wire
Wing: White mink tail hair tied upright
Hackle: Black cock in Parachute style

LIGHT PENSIONER   Plate 27

This does best when olives are about.
Hook: 12
Tail: Greenwell cock fibres
Body: Hare's fur
Rib: Fine gold wire
Wing: White mink tail hair tied upright
Hackle: Greenwell cock in Parachute style

TUP'S PENSIONER   Plate 27

A variant of the Tup's Indispensable dressed in Pensioner style.
Hook: 12
Tail: Blue-dun cock fibres
Body: Shrimp-pink bug fur or seal's fur
Rib: Fine gold wire
Wing: White mink tail hair tied upright
Hackle: Blue-dun in Parachute style

PEPPER'S OWN

Tony Pepper devised this dry fly for the trout and grayling in the rivers of his native Yorkshire. It has gained a popular following after it appeared in a number of magazines and Richard Walker mentioned it in one of his books. The two hackles ensure that the fly rides well, even on rough water.

Hook: 14–15
Tying silk: Purple
Tail: Three strands of cock pheasant centre tail herl tied to twice the body length

Body: Wound strands of cock pheasant centre tail herl
Rib: Red silk
Hackles: Red cock with a honey grizzle cock nearest the eye

PERCH FRY

Many larger stillwaters contain great quantities of perch and the fry appear frequently in the trout's diet. The imitation should be fished in the manner of a small fish. For other patterns see FRY and CHURCH FRY.

PERCH FRY (Gordon Fraser) Plate 3

This is the best-looking imitation I have come across.

Hook: Longshank 2–4
Body: Six to eight bunches of goathair dyed golden-olive tied on top and under the shank. The underside hair should be shorter than that on top. All the whippings should be soaked in varnish. The body is trimmed to a general fish outline and given perch stripes with black or dark-olive indelible felt-pens
Head: A bowl-shaped Muddler head of deerhair

A **Roach Fry** imitation can be tied by using white goathair for the body with touches of red.

PERCH FRY TANDEM (Tom Saville) Plate 3

Front hook
Body: Embossed gold tinsel
Wing: Two cree hackles tied outside two olive cock hackles back to back over both hooks with jungle-cock cheeks
Beard hackle: Hot-orange cock

Rear hook
Tail: Golden-pheasant tippets
Body: Embossed gold tinsel

PERSUADER Plate 12

In *Trout Flies of Stillwater*, John Goddard describes how he wanted a nondescript stillwater pattern that had '. . . to be fairly large, in order to attract the attentions of a trout from a reasonable distance; to have an attractive colour or colour combinations; to have a succulent body; and, finally, at least loosely resemble some of the more common forms of food on which trout feed'. It can be fished slow and deep or faster nearer the surface. It is a fly with which I have consistently caught dozens of trout each season and one I would never be without. If I were to be limited to half a dozen stillwater patterns, the Persuader would certainly be close to the top of the list.

Hook: 8–10
Tying silk: Orange
Body: Five strands of white ostrich herl
Rib: Round silver tinsel
Thorax: Orange seal's fur
Wing-case: Three strands of dark-brown turkey herl from the tail feather

Reputed to be one of the best traditional lake and sea-trout flies ever devised. It dates from the turn of the century and is named after its creator, who adapted it from the **Teal and Red**. In addition to being a fancy fly, it is a good small fry-imitator which should be fished on the point of the leader.

Hook: 8–14
Tail: Golden-pheasant tippets
Body: Rear half, silver tinsel; front half, red seal's fur
Rib: Oval silver tinsel
Wing: Barred teal breast feather-fibres
Hackle: Black cock or hen

PHANTOM MIDGE (*Chaoborus*)   See DIPTERA and MIDGES

A different group of species from the chironimids, the commoner midges, and confined largely to stillwaters. The overall length of the adult is about 7 mm and it is pale green or off-white depending upon the sex. The pale green female returns to the water's edge to lay her eggs about dusk. The main difference between these and the chironimids, with which they are often confused, is that the wings of the phantom midge at rest cover all the abdomen, while the chironimid's wings leave a few segments exposed at the rear.

The larvae are almost transparent but for four blackish air-bladders. The body length is between 12–16 mm. The larvae tend to lie horizontally in the water and move exceptionally quickly. The pupae are about the same length, with a semi-transparent body and a large thorax that turns orangey-brown with maturity. The pupae hang upright in the water for about four days, at various depths according to John Goddard, and rise to the surface for the transformation into the winged adult only just before emerging. For a fuller account of their life-cycle I recommend *The Development of Modern Stillwater Fishing*, by David Jacques.

PHANTOM LARVA (Peter Gathercole)

Hook: Silvered longshank 14
Underbody: Brown tying silk tied in at the rear and front of the shank to represent the swim-bladders

Body: Transparent polythene strip 6 mm (¼-inch) wide wound over the underbody and tapering to the rear
Hackle: Short-fibred white or badger cock

PHANTOM LARVA (Pat Russell)   Plate 14

Pat Russell first tied this pattern because of the scarcity of any other imitations. He comments that the artificial 'is not far removed from a bare hook!' He sent a couple of examples to Tom Chapman, the keeper at Peckham's Copse, and related this story to me in a letter: 'Now, his wife, June, was wanting Tom to show her how to fish, but Tom appeared to be busy or had other excuses. At last, spotting the Phantom Larva flies still unused on the mantelpiece,

June decided on a "Do-it-yourself" approach. With a fly tied to Tom's rod, she wandered out to make her first cast over water. As soon as she retrieved she found she had a fish on and landed it. Things were quiet for the other rods, and this aroused their interest, especially as they knew that June had never fished before. When after unhooking and despatching she cast out again and caught a second fish, rods descended on her and asked for the magic formula. The fly's reputation was made!'

Pat Russell made a later improvement to the pattern by using spade-end hooks tied to nylon and taking the body of the fly a short way up the nylon.

Hook: 16
Body: Grey fluorescent floss wound from the eye to just short of the barb. The air-bladders are marked with indelible felt-tip pens. One is marked on top of the bend, the other behind the eye. All this is covered with clear varnish

PHANTOM MIDGE LARVA (Peter Lapsley)   Plate 14

Peter Lapsley comments: 'This pattern works as well as it does as much because it is something the fish have never seen before as because they take it for a natural phantom larva, which would be virtually impossible to imitate on a hook.' It looks to me more like a pupal imitation.

Hook: Straight-eyed 14–16
Tying silk: Brown
Body: Pale-yellow floss silk
Rib: Fine silver tinsel
Thorax: Rusty-coloured pheasant tail fibres in a small lump behind the eye

PHANTOM MIDGE PUPA (Peter Gathercole)

Hook: 14
Tail: A bunch of white feather-fibres clipped square
Body: White floss covered with clear polythene and ribbed with silver wire
Thorax: Amber seal's fur
Wing-case: Light-brown feather-fibres
Head: White feathers as used for the tail

PHANTOM PUPA (John Goddard)   Plate 11

Hook: 16
Tying silk: Brown
Body: White marabou silk
Rib: Narrow silver Lurex

Thorax: Two strands of orange marabou silk
All the body and thorax are then covered with a strip of clear PVC.

ADULT PHANTOM MIDGE (John Goddard)

Hook: 14
Tying silk: Orange
Body: Grey condor herl
Rib: PVC dyed olive

Wing: White hackle points tied spent
Hackle: Honey cock tied in well back from the eye

PHEASANT TAIL   Plate 25

The floating Pheasant Tail is one of the best dry flies ever devised. It has been attributed to Payne Collier (about 1901). As a general imitative pattern, few flies come close to competing with it. A number of 'one-fly only' men have opted for this. It is probably taken mainly for the spinners of the blue-winged olive, iron blue, pale watery and medium olives. The original patterns were not winged, but later variations, tied specifically to represent spinners, have wings added. It can also be fished wet, but is rarely so used.

I have seen a number of commercially-dressed patterns bearing this name with a plain brown cock hackle. These may be variations of the original, but they are not *bona fide* Pheasant Tails after Payne Collier. They may carry the pheasant-tail fibre body, but the important hackle has been changed and therefore the name of the pattern should be changed, too. The dressing with

146

one of the hackles given below is a splendid fly. Accept nothing less.

See also USD POLYSPINNERS (*page 191*). The PHEASANT-TAIL NYMPH is considered under a separate entry (*this page*).

Hook: 12–14
Tail: Honey-dun hackle fibres
Body: Cock-pheasant tail fibres

Rib: Gold wire
Hackle: Honey-dun cock

An alternative hackle is a bright-blue or rusty-dun hackle. A spinner pattern can be tied with hackle fibre or hackle tip wings tied horizontally either side of the shoulder. The wing-colour should be of the natural fly to be imitated. This version can be fished dry or in the surface film.

WHITE-WINGED PHEASANT TAIL (Dave Collyer)

Described by its creator as a hybrid between a Hackle-point Coachman and a Pheasant Tail.

Hook: 14–16
Tying silk: Brown

Tail: Tips of the body material
Body: Cock-pheasant tail fibres wound over a wet varnished shank
Wing: White cock hackle tips
Hackle: Ginger cock

PHEASANT-TAIL SPINNER (M. Riesco)

Hook: 12–14
Tail: Blue-dun hackle fibres
Body: Cock-pheasant tail fibres

Wing: Light blue-dun cock hackle points tied spent
Hackle: Golden-dun cock

PHEASANT-TAIL NYMPHS

This name is given to a series of nymphs with cock pheasant-tail fibres as their body material. Many different variations have developed around the one theme. Other patterns are listed under COVE NYMPH (*page 43*) and TWITCHETT NYMPH (*page 190*). All are nondescript patterns that are probably taken for a wide range of food sources depending upon the dressings and the manner and depth at which they are fished. They are reliable as general stand-by patterns for the point of a leader during the early season, or fished close to weedbeds in their smaller sizes later in the season. The larger sizes may even be mistaken for small fish when retrieved in the appropriate style.

Bob Church tied a pattern similar to that given below, with a hackle or legs of pheasant-tail fibre tips and a prominent thorax of fluorescent lime-green material. It is useful in dirty water. A second pattern with a fluorescent-orange thorax is better in bright clear-water conditions.

LEADED PHEASANT-TAIL NYMPH (Bob Carnill)

Bob Carnill comments: 'This pattern is a good all-rounder for both river and stillwater trout. It can be fished as a bottom-crawler (particularly the leaded version), or as a free-swimming nymph anywhere between the bottom and the surface. Its overall shape simulates many of the larger nymphs, such as the diving beetle larvae, damosel nymphs and even the Mayfly nymph. On the Derbyshire Derwent, the Pheasant Tail Nymph is my number one fish-catcher. I fish it from the start of the season, right through to the end of the Mayfly. It performs well when used with any accepted wet-fly technique – upstream nymph, across-the-stream, and down-and-across – even in sizes as large as 8 longshank.

147

'It is important to take fur used for the thorax from between the eyes of a wild rabbit's mask. A small amount of the drab under-fur should be mixed in with the guard-hairs. This greatly improves the dubbing properties of the material and adds a little bulk.'

Hook: Longshank 8–14
Tying silk: Waxed brown Gossamer or Naples for larger sizes
Tail: Six or seven cock-pheasant tail fibres

Rib: Heavy copper wire
Thorax: Lead wire covered with rabbit's mask fur in a prominent thorax
Thorax cover: A broad web of unmarked cock-pheasant centre tail fibres

To represent a range of nymphs, larvae and aquatic beetles, and for use in a variety of water conditions, the thorax can be tied with fluorescent or ordinary seal's fur dyed green, orange, sepia, yellow or red.

BLACK PHEASANT TAIL   Plate 11

A general nymph pattern. Useful when black midge-pupae might be expected.

Hook: 10–12

Tail, body and thorax cover: Pheasant tail fibres dyed black
Rib: Silver wire
Thorax: Black seal's fur

SAWYER'S PHEASANT TAIL NYMPH   Plate 15

Frank Sawyer's best-known and most popular pattern. It is an impressionist nymph and works well when used to represent the nymphs of the large and small dark olives, iron blue, sepia and claret duns. It is a great killer of trout and grayling on rivers and lakes. Sawyer would have fished it in the induced-take style. On rivers, the fly should ideally be cast upstream to a visible fish and, as the nymph drifts down towards the fish, the rod-tip should be raised, causing the nymph to rise in the water and inducing the fish to take it.

This is easier said than done. Sawyer must have had a sixth-sense. I usually "guestimate" where the nymph is in relation to the fish, raise the rod-tip and watch the fish. If it moves forwards, upwards or side-ways, I strike. I've found the nymph

effective on the northern rivers, where one is rarely able to see the individual fish. I cast the nymph into likely lies and watch for takes on the leader in the usual manner.

On stillwater, it is an excellent general pattern and a good imitation of the sepia and claret nymphs. It is an easy fly to tie – an aspect not unusual among many of the better patterns; the good ones are often the simplest.

Hook: 12–16
Tying silk: None
Tail: Three cock-pheasant tail fibres
Underbody: Copper wire with a hump for the thorax
Overbody: Pheasant tail fibres wound on with the copper wire and tied fatter at the thorax
Wing-case: Pheasant tail fibres doubled and redoubled

PINK PANTHER   Plate 5

Shocking-pink or blancmange-pink trout flies have no natural counter-part, and precisely because the colour is so outrageous, it has been avoid-ed by fly-dressers. I think Peter Mackenzie-Philps was the first to tie a

pink version of the Baby Doll, but few other patterns have incorporated pink as the major colour. In 1983 Gordon Fraser devised some fluor-escent-pink flies to try on those occa-sions when nothing else works.

Perhaps the 'shock factor' was the key, but the flies seemed to spark off aggression in the trout, resulting in fish being taken and the flies being hailed as successful. The Pink Panther described below uses marabou plumes. The pattern is one of many on a basic theme. The colour is the major departure. See also Pink Palmer under PALMERS (*page 136*).

Hook: Longshank or standard 6–8
Tying silk: Pink
Tail: Fluorescent-pink marabou plume
Body: Optional underbody of lead wire. Fluorescent-pink seal's fur
Rib: Flat silver tinsel

PINK SPINNER

Devised by John Goddard as an imitation of the large spurwing female spinner.

Hook: 14–15
Tail: White or cream hackle fibres
Body: Pink Cellulite floss No 29

Rib: Orange DFM filament
Wing: Two small pale blue-dun cock hackle tips or hackle fibre bunches tied spent
Hackle: Two turns of pale blue-dun cock

POACHER

A lake and river fly devised by Angus Robertson for sea-trout and, in its smaller sizes, for brown trout. It is fished also as a beetle copy.

Hook: 6–12
Tail: Golden-pheasant red body feather fibres

Body: Rear-third, golden-coloured floss or seal's fur; front two-thirds, peacock herl tapering to the rear
Rib: Fine oval gold tinsel
Hackle: Red or black cock tied bushy.

POLYSTICKLE   Plate 9

A small-fish and fry imitator to be fished fairly fast. It catches trout throughout the season, but does best in late August and September. It was developed in the mid 1960s by Richard Walker as the **Sticklefly**, but Ken Sinfoil incorporated the polythene body to produce this dressing. It fishes well jerked along high in the water like a wounded fish. Richard Walker suggested that a longshank size 12 white polythene version would kill well during a Caenis hatch. The tandem version is known as the **Multistickle**.

Hook: Longshank 6–8
Tying silk: Black
Body: Black tying silk is wound on the rear three-quarters of a silvered hook in open spirals and crimson floss silk is wound on the front quarter before the body is built up with turns of clear polythene or PVC in a fish-shape
Back and tail: Brown, orange, yellow or buff dampened Raffene
Beard hackle: Red or hot-orange hackle fibres
Head: Varnished tying silk with an optional eye painted on
The **Black Polystickle** has a black Raffene back and tail, a red cock hackle and a black silk rib.
The **Green Polystickle** has a dark green Raffene back and tail, a beard hackle of bronze mallard flank feather-fibres and a black silk rib.
The **White Polystickle** has a white Raffene back and tail, a fluorescent white underbody, a white cock beard hackle and a black silk rib.
The **Peter Ross Polystickle** is as for the original pattern, but with a back and tail of teal flank feather-fibres.

POND OLIVE (*Cloëon dipterum*)   See EPHEMEROPTERA

Although this is primarily a stillwater species, it is sometimes found on slow-moving rivers. It is widely distributed and it is probably the most important upwinged fly for the stillwater fly-fisher. The small mottled brown olive-coloured nymphs are agile darters and live among weed-beds in the shallow lake margins. The nymph is more important than the dun, and the emerging dun in the surface film is taken in preference to the floating adult. The adults are similar to the medium olives, but generally darker and without hindwings. The olive-brown body sometimes has reddish markings. The wings are darkish grey and the two tails are black-ringed.

The medium-sized duns appear from May to late June, although it is reported that a second generation appears in September during some years. These are smaller than the earlier adults. John Goddard says the size of the duns has a wide variation, probably more so than any other upwinged species. The beautiful female spinner (also known as the apricot spinner because of its overall colouring) is readily taken by trout. The spinners often return to the water at dusk and trout take them with little disturbance, in a manner quite different from the slashing rise to sedges.

For other suitable imitations see GOLD-RIBBED HARE'S EAR (*page 72*), GREENWELL'S GLORY (*page 77*), ROUGH OLIVE (*page 156*), LARGE DARK OLIVE (*page 96*), OLIVE BLOA (*page 21*), S.S. NYMPH (*page 179*), PVC NYMPH (*page 152*), GREY DUSTER (*page 79*), OLIVES (*page 129*) and LAKE OLIVE (*page 94*).

POND OLIVE NYMPH (C. F. Walker)

Hook: 14–16
Tail: Speckled brown feather fibres
Body: Mixed brown and ginger seal's fur with a rib of pale brown condor herl for the gills
Rib: Silver tinsel
Thorax: Dark-brown seal's fur
Hackle: Medium honey-dun

POND OLIVE DUN (Taff Price)

Hook: 14 or Yorkshire Flybody hook
Tying silk: Olive
Tail: Blue-dun fibres
Body: Swan or goose herl dyed olive
Rib: Brown silk
Wing: Bunched blue-dun hackle fibres tied upright
Hackle: Olive cock

POND OLIVE SPINNER (John Goddard)

To be fished in the surface film.

Hook: 12–14
Tying silk: Orange
Tail: Pale badger cock fibres
Body: Condor herl dyed apricot and covered with pale-olive PVC
Wing: Pale-blue hackle tips tied spent
Hackle: Dark honey-dun cock fibres tied under each wing, replacing the traditional hackle style

POND OLIVE SPINNER

Hook: Fine-wire 14
Tying silk: Olive
Tail: Pale-grey speckled partridge breast feather

Body: Stripped orange peacock herl
Rib: Waxed scarlet tying silk
Hackle: Four or five turns of very pale

blue-dun cock hackle with one turn of a hot-orange cock in front. The hackles are bunched in the spent position

POODLE
Plate 5

John Wadham devised this lure in 1978. It has caught thousands of trout, including, in the hands of its creator, brown trout to 7½ lb. Bob Carnill summed up the Poodle as: 'The nymph-fisherman's lure' because it is worked very slowly or simply left to drift around in the wind to be slowly retrieved only when the line has blown parallel to the reservoir bank. The pulsating marabou allows the lure to be fished slowly. The Poodle has a reputation for taking fish already feeding on daphnia.

Hook: Longshank 6–10
Tying silk: Black
Tail: Black marabou or Arctic fox
Tip (optional): Two or three turns of DRF signal-green wool
Body: Black chenille. Optional lead underbody
Wing/body plumes: Four or five small shuttlecocks of black marabou tied along the top of the shank. As each one is tied in another turn of the body chenille is wound on. The result is a sort of marabou matuka

POPPERS
Plate 3

These unusual-looking 'flies' have been adapted from the North American bass lures. In the U.K. they are used for sea-trout and reservoir trout. They are fished high in a surface wave, where the disturbance they cause seems attractive to the fish. The Popper should be fished on a single-fly leader or on the top dropper of a two- or three-fly leader. If the Popper is not taken, a following trout will often take one of the lower flies.

Hook: Special popper hook 4–6

Body: A reverse bullet-shape cork is slotted on to the front of the shank with the eye of the hook coming out of the lower edge of the front flat face of the body. This can be painted as desired, with or without eyes
Tail: Four long cock hackles tied two each side of the shank with the curve of the hackle outwards. These can be colour-matched or contrasted with the body
Hackle: A cock hackle is wound over the tail roots behind the body, the same colour as or contrasting with the tail

PRETTY-PRETTY

A Tom Ivens lure which he recommended should be fished fast.

Hook: 4–8
Tip: Silver tinsel
Tail: Small golden-pheasant topping

Body: Peacock herl and green ostrich herl twisted together
Rib: Oval silver tinsel
Wing: Orange-yellow goathair
Hackle: Hen dyed green as a beard

PRIEST
Plate 19

An excellent fancy fly for grayling which is mainly fished wet. I have found it better than most in a slightly discoloured water. No doubt the brightness of its dressing contributes to its success under these circumstances. On the occasions I have

fished it dry, I've been able to attract only fairly small fish.

Hook: 14
Tail: Red ibis or red wool tag
Body: Flat silver tinsel
Rib: Oval silver wire
Hackle: Badger hen

PROFESSOR Plate 17

A stillwater fly named after Professor John Wilson of some 140 years ago. It is of Scottish origin, but it is still used on Sassenach waters. It is used for sea-trout in its larger sizes. A streamer lure is listed by John Veniard; it has a collar hackle of brown cock, a wing of a pair of grizzle hackles and a black-varnished head.

Hook: 6–10
Tail: Long red ibis fibres or substitute
Body: Yellow tying silk or floss
Rib: Gold or silver tinsel or wire
Wing: Grey mallard flank feather
Hackle: Ginger cock

PULSATORS

These lures are Chris Kendall's improvement on the standard marabou lure. Chris comments: 'the standard dressing for the marabou lure does not utilise the full movement potential of marabou. Certainly, the wing moves freely but a chenille or tinsel body is rigid by comparison.

The solution I came up with was to dress the wing around the head as opposed to on top of it. Unfortunately this arrangement gave the effect of three or four wings as the marabou bunched up. After more experimentation the lure gained a long collar hackle and the wing was dressed more heavily. Dressed in this way it has a rippling and pulsating action which enables the lure to be fished ultra-slow when need be.'

Black, white and orange lures are all effective as are a number of **Pulsator** variants of other lures: **Viva, Jack Frost** and **Christmas Tree** (plate 6). The wings on these variants must be tied in two tiers, to avoid masking the tag completely. The first (longer) wing is made from herl from the top of the plume, the shorter wing is made from the denser herl nearer the base.

BLACK PULSATOR (C. Kendall) Plate 6

Hook: Longshank 4–10
Body: Black chenille
Rib: Oval silver tinsel
Wing: Black marabou tied all around the body. Use about one plume
Hackle: Long-fibred black cock as a rear-sloping collar
Head: Black varnished tying silk

PURPLE DUN (*Paraleptophlebia cincta*)   See EPHEMEROPTERA

This upwinged dun is restricted to the West and North of England on small faster or larger medium-paced rivers where the hatches can be prolific. The nymphs prefer weed-beds. The medium-sized dun is similar to the iron blue dun, with a purple-tinged dark brown body and black-grey wings. The most obvious difference between the two is that the purple dun has three tails and the iron blue only two. The duns appear throughout the day from May to August. Because of the similarity, artificials copying the iron blue dun are often adequate as the angler's imitation. Specific patterns are:

PURPLE DUN (John Veniard)

A winged wet fly.

Hook: 14
Tail: Dark-brown hen fibres
Body: Purple seal's fur
Wing: Starling wing
Hackle: Dark-brown hen

PVC NYMPH
Plate 19

John Goddard recommends this pattern for any of the olive nymphs. The PVC body gives a translucent effect. The fly is equally effective on rivers and stillwaters, wherever olives are found. Its creator suggests that it is best fished in stillwaters in sink-and-draw fashion on a very long leader. It is particularly good when fished close to weed-beds where the natural olive nymphs abound.

Hook: 12–16
Tying silk: Brown

Tail: Golden-pheasant tips dyed olive-green
Underbody and thorax: Copper wire
Overbody and thorax: Three strands of olive or olive-brown condor herl. The body (not the thorax) is covered with a PVC strip 3 mm (⅛-inch) wide and over-lapped.
Wing-pads: Two or three strands of dark pheasant-tail herl

John Goddard suggests that a narrow silver Lurex rib added beneath the PVC simulates air-bubbles trapped beneath the skin.

RAINBIRD
Plate 3

This Freddie Rice lure should be fished very slowly along the bottom of weedy lakes. The use of the keel-hook means that a minimum amount of weed is picked up by the hook-point.

Hook: Cranked-shank keel-hook 8

Tying silk: Black
Body: Black floss
Rib: Flat gold tinsel
Wing: Hot-orange squirrel-tail
Head: Scarlet fluorescent wool with peacock sword fibres wound in front

RAT-FACED MACDOUGALL
Plate 24

A highly buoyant North American rough-water dry fly. The deerhair body makes the fly very hard to sink.

Hook: 10–12

Tail: Deerhair or ginger hackle fibres
Body: Spun and clipped deerhair
Wing: Two grizzle hackle points
Hackle: Ginger cock

RED BARON
Plate 1

A Steve Parton lure which he describes as 'An anti-daphnia summer-time boat tandem', which pretty well sums it up. It should be fished to 15 feet deep in daphnia Clouds, but only in conditions of bright sunlight. One usually associates orange lures with daphnia, but Steve suggests that this is a good pattern to which to change when trout go off a tandem hot-orange lure. Rear hook and front hook are dressed the same.

Tails: Target-green fluorescent wool
Bodies: Fluorescent-red chenille
Ribs: Fine oval silver tinsel
Wings: Fluorescent-red or pink marabou with cheeks of target-green fluorescent wool over

RED QUILL

This southern chalk-stream pattern was one of F. M. Halford's favourites. He described it as 'The sheet anchor of the dry-fly fisherman on a strange river'. Few today would praise it that highly, but it is still a useful pattern. In Halford's day it was probably fished only as a floater, but it seems that it is also fished wet. This is probably how the pattern originated, as it is attributed to Thomas Rushworth in about 1803. It is usually fished as an imitation of the blue-winged olive, but some sources have suggested it as a representation of the claret dun. See also HI C RED QUILL (*page 84*).

Hook: 14

Tail: Bright natural red cock fibres
Body: Peacock quill dyed reddish-brown
Wing: Medium starling wing
Hackle: Bright red cock

Other dressings omit the wings and have a hackle of pale blue-dun cock, or replace the wing with one of a bunch of pale blue cock hackle fibres tied upright.

RED SPIDER

This is one of W. C. Stewart's trio of wet flies which he fished in a team on the Scottish rivers of the last century and with which he killed thousands of trout. The other two patterns are the **Black Spider** and **Dun Spider**. The semi-palmered hen hackle is important, giving the impression of life and movement so necessary in an artificial wet fly.

Hook: 14–16
Body: Yellow tying silk
Hackle: Feather from the outside of a landrail, or a small red hen hackle palmered half-way down the body

RED SPINNER

The Red Spinner is the name given to a female olive spinner, more particularly to the female medium olive spinner and the small dark olive spinner. The large red spinner is the name given to the female large dark olive spinner. See also HI C RED SPINNER (*page 84*), USD POLY-SPINNER (*page 191*) and GREAT RED SPINNER (*page 75*).

RED SPINNER (Jim Nice)

Hook: 14–18
Tying silk: Pale-brown or red
Tail: Blue-dun or ginger cock fibres
Body: Scarlet DFM floss

Rib: Brown silk
Hackle: Red cock wound through a blue-dun cock

RED SPINNER (J. R. Harris)

Hook: 14
Tail: Red cock hackle fibres
Body: Brown-red or claret seal's fur
Rib: Gold wire
Wing: Two blue-dun or rusty-dun hackle

points tied upright and sloping backwards slightly and separated
Hackle: Natural red cock, two turns at most

RED TAG   Plate 20

Probably the best-known grayling fly, and deservedly so, because it catches thousands of grayling each autumn. According to Courtney Williams it originated in Worcestershire around 1850 and was known as the **Worcester Gem**. It seems likely that it was invented by a man named Flyn, but it was popularised by F. M. Walbran, the author. On some days grayling will take only an artificial fly with some red in the dressing, and on these occasions few, if any, flies are better than a Red Tag. A tip from Reg Righyni on the tying of the tag of the dry fly is worth remembering. He ties the tag on the long side initially; if the grayling are well on take, the longer tag helps the fly to float correctly. If the fish are choosy, the tag can be clipped shorter. The fly can be fished both wet and dry. See also BADGER RED TAG (*page 10*) and TREACLE PARKIN (*page 187*) for similar flies.

Some Yorkshire grayling-fishers use a pattern with a lime-green tag. It is known as the **Green Tag**. The tie with a crimson tag is known as the **Crimson Tag**, and that with a white floss or wool tag is the **White Tag**. The **Gold Tag**, which has a tip of gold tinsel, was once a popular fly.

Hook: 12–16
Tag: Scarlet or bright red wool
Body: Peacock herl
Hackle: Natural red cock or hen

REES' LURE (Trevor Rees) — Plate 5

Black and green is a killing combination for a trout lure. This one devised by Trevor Rees of South Wales also uses a weighted diving head.

Hook: Longshank 6–12
Tying silk: Black
Tail: DFM lime green wool
Body: Bronze peacock herl with a few turns of DFM lime green wool behind the wing roots
Wing: Black marabou with black squirrel over
Throat hackle: Black cock
Eyes: Two silver chain beads

ROACH FRY (Tom Saville) — Plate 3

Hook: Longshank 6
Tail: Bright-red hackle fibres
Body: Embossed silver tinsel
Wing: Olive-green hackles tied back-to-back
Cheeks: Jungle-cock
Hackle: Blue-dun cock as a beard
Head: Black tying silk

ROACH FRY (C. Kendall) — Plate 9

A buoyant imitation for fishing just below the surface. Other species of fish can be imitated by varying the colours. See also **Perch Fry** (*page 144*) and **Fry** (*page 64*).

Hook: Longshank 6–8
Tying silk: Black
Tail: Two scarlet red hackles clipped into a tail shape
Body: Ethafoam cut into strips and wound on, pearl nylon tube slipped over it
Back: Pale blue raffene. When this is tied in at the rear the whipping can be white varnished
Hackle: Scarlet red cock fibres bunched either side of the lower half of the body
Head: Black varnish with painted red eyes and black pupils

ROGER'S FANCY

Roger Woolley was an excellent fly-tyer and he wrote two good books on the subject, *Modern Trout Fly Dressing*, 1932, and *The Fly Fisher's Flies*, 1938. This is one of his patterns for grayling, to be fished mainly as a floater. Woolley was a keen grayling fisher and contributed to *The Grayling*, originally written by Richard Lake. He was a fly-tyer for sixty-one years. For much of that time he was tying professionally, yet he never used a vice.

Hook: 14–16
Tail: Red floss
Body: Pale-blue heron herl
Rib: Silver wire
Hackle: Pale-blue hen
Head: Short red floss sloping forward over the eye

ROUGH OLIVE

Dressings under this heading may be general imitations of any of the olives. By varying the dressing, the shades of the materials and the hook-sizes, all the olives can be copied with a Rough Olive from March to October.

ROUGH OLIVE NYMPH

Hook: 14
Body: Brown-olive heron herl with the tips used for the tail
Rib: Gold wire
Wing-case: Dark starling wing fibres
Hackle: Brown-olive hen with a darker centre

ROUGH OLIVE (Terry Griffiths)

Hook: 14
Tail: Dark-olive cock fibres
Body: Dark-olive goose herl
Rib: Gold wire
Wing: Pale starling wing
Hackle: Dark-olive cock

ROUGH OLIVE (M. Riesco)

Hook: 12–14
Tail: Blue-dun fibres
Body: Olive seal's fur
Rib: Gold wire
Hackle: Olive badger cock

RUBE WOOD

This North American lake fly is one of many now used on our stillwaters. It is similar to Dick Shrive's version of the Missionary. It is recommended to be fished fairly fast just below the surface.

Hook: 6–12
Tying silk: Black
Tail: Teal breast-fibres
Tag: Orange or scarlet wool tied small
Body: White chenille or suede chenille
Wing: Mallard or teal flank feather
Beard hackle: Natural red-brown cock

RUBY

A Syd Brock lure. The scarlet colour is unusual, but in *Stillwater Flies – How and when to fish them*, its creator writes: 'I have had outstanding results with this lure fished on a slow-sink line when all other lures have failed.' It should be fished with a long leader and retrieved in short, smooth pulls.

Hook: Longshank 6–10
Tying silk: Black
Tail: Scarlet cock hackle fibres
Body: Stretched scarlet plastic tape
Wing: Four cock hackles dyed scarlet
Cheeks: Golden-pheasant tippets either side
Throat hackle: Scarlet cock hackle fibres

SANCTUARY   Plate 25

This trout and grayling fly was devised by Dr Sanctuary, of Scarborough, in the 1880s. I've found it an excellent fly in September and October. It is not so popular today, but I have found it reliable on northern streams. Dr Sanctuary seemed to know what he was doing when it came to grayling. He is credited with a 4½ lb specimen from the Wylye.

Hook: 14
Body: Dark hare's ear fur
Rib: Flat gold tinsel
Hackle: Coch-y-bondhu

More than 190 species of sedge exist on rivers and stillwaters in the U.K., but, according to J. R. Harris, only 40–50 are of interest to the fly-fisher. Many species are nocturnal; others appear during the day and evening. All year round the sedge or caddis larvae are a source of food for trout and grayling feeding off river- or lake-bed, and pupae and adults are taken from spring to autumn. Every fly-fisher ought to be familiar with the life-cycle of this important group of flies.

Most sedges are referred to by fly-fishers merely by their general appearance, i.e. a 'dark-brown sedge', or a 'light sedge', or a 'small grey sedge', etc, and few fly-fishers bother to determine exactly which species is which. This is in complete contrast to the attitude towards the Ephemeroptera, which most fly-fishers aspire to name and imitate accurately. The truth is that on most occasions artificials of approximate size, shape and colour are sufficient to represent most species, be they sedges or upwinged duns.

After hatching, the grub-like larva goes in search of sand, small stones, sticks or vegetation with which to build its case, though some species are free-swimming. The interior of the case is lined with a silken material produced by the larva. The finished case is well camouflaged, probably being made from materials from the river-bed on which it rests. The caddis moves by sticking its head, thorax and legs out of the case and dragging it along. The cased caddis, surrounded by stones and sand, hardly seems an attractive meal to a trout, but the larvae are avidly devoured wherever they are found. The stomach contents of a 1 lb trout from Bewl Bridge reservoir in Kent contained more than forty cased larvae, most between 15 and 25 mm long.

Copying the natural with an artificial presents no problems, although it is difficult to fish the larva imitation on a river as the natural larva is frequently static on the river-bed, and when it does move it does so slowly. However, the stillwater angler can copy the larva by moving his imitation slowly across the bottom on the end of a long leader. In addition to patterns given below, see also WORMFLY (*page 203*) and STICKFLY (*page 180*).

Some caddis are vegetarians, but others eat all types of water insects, including the Ephemeroptera nymphs so important to the fly-fisher. On some stretches of the Test where caddis abound, the quantity of upwinged duns and their nymphs is significantly lower than on those stretches with fewer caddis.

After about eleven months, the larva seals its case, but still allows water to flow through. The case is attached to rocks or stones to prevent it being washed away as the larva begins to change to its pupal stage. The larva spins a silken cocoon inside the case and the wings and legs begin to form. Some weeks or months later the pupa emerges by chewing its way through the case wall to swim to the surface. The pupa is broadly similar to the adult in colour and size. The change from pupa to adult takes place on the surface or on rocks or vegetation at the water's edge, and the emerging adult is free to fly away. Those flies appearing on fast-flowing water emerge fairly quickly; those on stillwaters emerge more slowly.

It is when the pupa leaves the case and ascends to the surface to emerge as an adult that the trout become most interested. Free of its case, the pupa rising to the surface becomes an attractive target for a feeding fish, and the fly-fisher can easily copy the emerging fly below or actually in the surface film. If sedges are hatching, then whatever is the surface interest in them, the sub-surface interest in the pupae will be greater. For every rise to the newly-emerged adult, perhaps half a dozen pupae are intercepted.

The pupa is well copied by any of the pupa or hatching-sedge patterns given. One of the best is Steve Parton's Sienna Sedge, which has always caught fish for me whenever there has been a hatch of sedge of any type. Special sedge-pupa hooks with a curved shank are worth experimenting with. Some of the pupae imitations listed could well be improved by dressing them on these hooks.

Most adult sedges are pale-coloured on hatching, but reaching their full colouring only after some hours. After mating, the female lays her eggs on plants at the waterside or, depending on the species, drops her eggs in flight over the water, deposits them on the surface, or crawls down to the river or lake bed to lay them in the sand or mud.

The adult sedge is easily recognisable. Most species are fairly large (the female is generally larger than the male), and all have large wings which rest roof-like beyond the length of the body. The four wings are covered in tiny hairs. Prominent features are the large antennae on the head of the fly. Most adults are a shade of brown, although some are black or greyish.

The greatest hatch is in the evening, but some sedges appear throughout the day. Commonest are the caperer, great red sedge, silver sedge and cinnamon sedge. Just a few artificials are sufficient to represent the adults of a number of species. But such is the importance of the natural fly that many artificials have been devised, and this is reflected in the number I have included. Many species have huge stillwater hatches, and the boom in this branch of fly-fishing has meant that many new patterns have been tied. Pick a few patterns that you can tie and with which you can catch fish and stick with them.

Almost any big, bushy fly will catch fish at times, especially when darkness is falling. It is usually sufficient simply to match the natural with an imitation conforming to approximate size, outline and colour. Palmer-bodied flies create most disturbance on the surface. They can be fished by retrieving them in short bursts of varying speeds, or they can be left motionless. Some newly-hatched sedges skitter across the surface before they take flight. The trout's interest is quickly aroused. A sedge pattern tied to the top dropper with other flies fished sub-surface is often an effective tactic in choppy water.

Below is an alphabetical list of the more important natural sedges and some of the patterns that represent them. Imitations of a more general appearance are listed later.

BLACK SEDGE (T. Thomas)

The natural fry is long and slim with black wings and antennae. The wing length is between 11 and 12 mm. The adults appear during the day from June to September. The black sedge is widely distributed, but usually confined to larger rivers.

Hook: 10–14
Body: Black wool or chenille
Wing: Black moosehair tied flat and clipped square
Hackle: Black cock tied in reverse so that it slopes foward

COMMON SPECIES OF SEDGE AND THEIR CHARACTERISTICS

Common name	Scientific name	Stillwater or river	Type of case	Period of emergence	Size of adult	General appearance
Great red sedge	Phryganea striata, P. grandis	Both	Vegetation; in a spiral	Evenings; May–July	20–27 mm	Fairly common; mottled reddish-brown wings with a centre black bar
Caperer	Halesus radiatus, H. digitatus	Both	Vegetation	Evenings; Aug–Nov	20–23 mm	Common; mottled yellow-brown wings; orange-brown body and legs
Large cinnamon sedge	Potamophylax latipennis	Both	Gravel/sand; curved	Evenings; June–Sept	18–19 mm	Fairly common; similar to caperer
Mottled sedge	Glyphotaelius pellucidus	Both	Vegetation	May–Sept	17 mm	Cream to yellow-brown wings with brown patches
Brown sedge	Anabolia nervosa	Both	Sand/sticks	Evenings; Aug–Oct	11–16 mm	Medium brown; emerges via reeds, etc
Cinnamon sedge	Linnephilus lunatus	Both	Vegetation	Daylight; June–Oct	14–15 mm	Slim appearance; cinnamon brown wings and black markings
Grey or silver sedge	Odontocerum albicorne	River	Sand; slightly curved	June–Sept	13–18 mm	Silver-grey wings
Welshman's Button	Sericostoma personatum	Both	Fine sand; slightly curved	Daytime; June–Aug	12–15 mm	Dark brown wings, grey-black body; mated female has a dark brown egg-ball
Black sedge	Athripsodes nigronervosus	Both	Fine sand; slightly curved	Daytime; June–Sept	11–13 mm	Long, slim black wings and antennae
Grey flag	Hydropsyche instablis, H. pellucidula	River	Silken web between stones	Daytime	10–12 mm	Grey wings with blackish markings
Medium sedge	Goëra pilosa	Both	Small stones	Daytime; May–June	10–12 mm	Very hairy species; greyish-yellow to darker yellow wings
Sand fly	Rhyacophila dorsalis	River	Free-swimming	Daytime; April–Oct	Variable	Wings are various shades of brown
Marbled sedge	Hydropsyche contubernalis	River	Free-swimming	Evening	11–12 mm	Marbled-brown patches on a greenish wing; body orangey
Grannom	Brachycentrus subnubilus	River	Cylindrical or square-sectioned when young	Daytime; April–June	9–11 mm	Fawn-grey wings; mated female has green egg-sac at rear
Small silver sedge	Lepidostoma hirtum	Both	Vegetation in a square section	Evening; May–June	9 mm	Grey or grey-brown; mated female has green egg-sac at rear
Brown silverhorn	Athripsodes cinerus	Both	Sand/vegetation; slightly curved	Daytime; June–Aug	8–10 mm	Brownish with black markings; antennae curve back over body in flight
Black silverhorn	Mystacides azurea, M. nigra, Athripsodes aterrimus	Both	Sand/vegetation; slightly curved	Daytime; June–Aug	8–9 mm	Black with antennae which curve over the body in flight
Longhorn	Ocetis lacustris, O. ochracea	Still-water	Sand; curved and tapered	Daytime	7–13 mm	Very common; greyish-yellow or fawn wings with long antennae
Grouse-wing	Mystacides longicornis	Both	Fine sand; slightly curved	Evening; June–Sept	8–9 mm	Slim with greyish-yellow wings with three grey-brown bands; long antennae
Small red sedge	Tinodes waeneri	Both	Sand/vegetation; long, often curved	Evening, May–Oct	8 mm	Reddish or yellowish-brown wings
Small yellow sedge	Psychomyia pusilla	River	—	Evenings	5–6 mm	Very common; brown-yellow wings

BROWN SEDGE

A widely-distributed and common species usually appearing in the evenings from August to October. The adult emerges by crawling up weed-stalks and does not emerge in open water. The colour is medium brown and the wing length varies between 11 and 16 mm. The caddis case is made from sand and small sticks.

LARGE BROWN SEDGE (Richard Walker)

Hook: Longshank 10
Tying silk: Orange
Tag: Yellow fluorescent wool or floss
Body: Mahogany-brown ostrich herl tied very fine
Wing: Light-brown cock fibres
Hackle: Light-brown cock

LITTLE BROWN SEDGE (Taff Price)

Hook: 14
Tying silk: Orange
Body: Cinnamon turkey tail fibres and gold wire twisted together
Hackle: Palmered natural red-game with a second hackle tied at the shoulder
Wing: Two natural game hackle tips tied over the body

BLACK SILVERHORN SEDGE

All the silverhorns are common. The larvae usually build their cases of sand and frequently construct them with a slight curve. They prefer stillwater or slow-moving rivers. The daytime-hatching adults appear from June to August. They are all black. The wings are 8–9 mm long and the long antennae curve back over the body in flight. A suitable imitation is the Black Sedge.

BROWN SILVERHORN SEDGE

The notes for the Black Silverhorn apply also to this species, except that the wings are 8–10 mm long and are brownish with black markings.

CAPERER

A widely distributed and common species. Hatches are generally in the evening and can be expected on open water from late August to November. The adult is large with a wing of 20–23 mm. The wings are mottled yellowish-brown and the body is orangey-brown. The fly's importance, particularly on the southern chalk-streams, is reflected in the excellence of the pattern devised by William Lunn, a Test river-keeper whose imitation is used country-wide. The artificial is useful both on river and lake. The species is similar to the large cinnamon sedge.

CAPERER (William Lunn)

Also known as the Welshman's Button.

Hook: 12–14
Body: Four or five strands of dark turkey tail fibres with a centre-band of two swan fibres dyed yellow
Wing: Coot's wing dyed chocolate-brown
Hackles: Medium Rhode Island Red with a black cock in front, or wound together

160

Adults often appear during the day and early evening and are fairly common throughout the country from June until October. They are slim with cinnamon-brown wings with black markings. The wings are about 14 mm long and sometimes may appear as a deep yellow rather than brown. The large cinnamon sedge (*P. latipennis*) is so like the caperer that it need not be considered separately. The **Cinnamon and Gold** is a useful wet fly when the cinnamon sedges are hatching. The **Yellow Sedge pupa** of Steve Parton is a good imitation of any yellow-bodied sedge-pupae, but it was tied specifically to represent the pupa of the cinnamon sedge. It should be fished as a point fly and retrieved slowly.

Hook: 14–16
Body: Swan herl dyed Naples yellow with a thin back of stretched halved black marabou silk
Rib: Yellow nylon rod-whipping thread wound over the back
Thorax: Mixed chestnut seal's fur and brown mink
Wing-stubs: Goose fibres dyed sepia
Wing-case: A scrap of dark-brown feather
Hackle: Very sparse red-game

The method of tying needs a little explanation: Tie in the body herl, ribbing and marabou silk. Thinly wind on the body herl, tie down and tie in the stretched black marabou floss silk and rib in the counter direction. Tie in the scrap wing-case feather with three turns towards the eye and wind back. Cut off the scrap. Dub and wind half the thorax only. Make two small wings by a folded single slip and tie in flat either side of the hook. Dub and wind the remainder of the thorax. Take one or two turns of the hackle and rake back and lock down with thread. Pull over the wing-case, tie down and whip-finish.

CINNAMON SEDGE (Richard Walker)

Hook: Longshank 10
Tying silk: Hot-orange
Tag: Yellow fluorescent floss

Body: Buff ostrich herl
Wing: Barred buff cock hackle fibres
Hackle: Ginger or natural red cock

GRANNOM

An early-season species common in most parts of the country. It first appears in April and continues until June. It is confined to rivers, where the larvae live in weed-beds. The adults emerge during the day, often around noon, with possibly a later hatch. They are 9–11 mm long and have fawn-grey wings. The mated female is easily distinguishable by the green egg-sac carried at the tail of her abdomen.

GRANNOM (Pat Russell)   Plate 28

Hook: 14
Tying silk: Green
Tip: Fluorescent-green wool
Body: Natural heron herl

Wing: Blue-dun cock fibres clipped level with the bend
Hackle: Ginger cock

GRANNOM (David Jacques)

This pattern is tied in reverse. The wings and the hackle are at the bend and the egg-sac is at the eye. David Jacques devoted much of his book *Fisherman's Fly*, 1965, to this species, and it is from there that the dressing is taken.

Hook: 14
Tying silk: Green
Body: Dark hare's ear fur with a ball of green wool at the tip

Wing: Hen-pheasant wing sloping well back
Hackle: Rusty-dun cock

GREAT RED SEDGE

The two species that share this name are widely distributed on rivers and stillwaters. They are the largest of this country's sedges, with a wing length 20–27 mm. The larvae are also large and, according to J. R. Harris, are known to kill even small fish. The adults hatch in the evening in open water and are commonest from late May to July. The wings are mottled reddish-brown with some lighter markings and a blackish bar down the centre.

GREAT RED SEDGE (Dave Collyer) Plate 23

Hook: 6–10
Tying silk: Brown
Tail: Red cock hackle fibres
Body: Grey mole's fur with a palmered dark-red cock hackle

Rib: Gold wire
Wing: Brown speckled hen's wing tied rear-sloping as far as the bend
Hackle: Dark red cock

GROUSE-WING SEDGE

A common stillwater sedge which rarely appears on rivers. The flies hatch in the evenings of June to September. They are slim and have greyish-yellow wings with three grey-brown bands. The antennae are about twice the length of the wings.

GROUSE-WING PUPA (Richard Walker)

Hook: 14
Body: Sheep's wool dyed green and dubbed on light brown silk
Rib: Very fine gold thread

Hackle: Small well-marked grouse
Horns: Two blackish pheasant tail fibres about twice the hook-length tied rear-slanting

GROUSE WING (Richard Walker)

Hook: Longshank 12
Tying silk: Black
Tag: White fluorescent wool or floss tied small

Body: Ostrich herl or swan dyed chocolate
Wing: Grouse wing or tail fibres, or dark sepia and brown speckled turkey fibres
Hackle: Dark furnace

GREY FLAG

A reasonably common species almost confined to flowing water. The adults usually hatch on open water during the day. The wings are about 11 mm long and are grey with blackish markings. The larvae do not build cases, but rest between stones and spin a silken web tunnel around themselves.

GREY SEDGE (John Veniard)

Hook: 12
Body: Grey seal's fur
Rib: Silver wire

Wing: Grey squirrel-tail fibres
Hackle: Grizzle cock

GREY or SILVER SEDGE

Usually found on fast-flowing water. The larvae build their cases with a light curve and use mainly sand as the material. The adults appear from June to September and are large with silvery-grey wings 13–18 mm long.

SILVER SEDGE (Taff Price)

Hook: 12–14
Tying silk: Grey
Body: White or grey floss
Rib: Silver wire

Hackle: Palmered ginger with a second ginger hackle at the head
Wing: Coot or grey duck tied over the back

LONGHORNS

These two species are daylight-hatching and are important to the stillwater angler. They have long antennae and slim, narrow wings 7–13 mm long. The wing colour varies from greyish-yellow to pale fawn, and the body is greyish-green. The imitation below, from Richard Walker, can be tied in various colour combinations to represent different sedge species. It can be fished either slowly in the surface film or with a steady retrieve in the top two or three feet.

Hook: 8–12
Body: Rear two-thirds, amber or pale blue-green ostrich herl; front one-third, sepia or chestnut ostrich herl; all tied fat
Rib: Gold thread over the rear section
Hackle: Brown partridge tied rear-slanting
Horns: Two pheasant tail fibres twice the hook-length tied on top of the hook, rear-facing at about 45 degrees

MARBLED SEDGE

This early-evening species is found mainly on rivers. The wings have a marbled appearance with brownish patches on a brownish-green wing. The body is greenish with orangey-brown legs which make the species easily recognisable.

MEDIUM SEDGE

A daytime species appearing in May and June. It is medium-sized with broad wings, about 11 mm long, that are greyish-yellow to a darker yellow. It is one of the hairier species.

SAND-FLY

This early-season sedge first appears in April and continues throughout the season until autumn. It is a daytime species but often difficult to identify because of variations in colour and size. Some wings are sandy coloured; others may be mid- or very dark brown. It is not to be confused with the Clyde sandfly, a localised name for the gravel bed.

SAND-FLY (Taff Price)

Hook: 14
Tag: Two turns of gold wire
Body: Ginger or sandy hare's fur

Wing: Starling wing
Hackle: Light-coloured natural red or ginger cock

SILVER SEDGE

One of the smaller species. It has a wing length of about 9 mm and is generally grey or grey-brown. The female carries a green egg-sac at her rear after mating. The adults appear from May to August in rather localised areas throughout the country, usually preferring rivers to lakes. A suitable imitation is found under the Grey or Silver Sedge above.

SMALL RED SEDGE

A common species appearing from May to October. It is an evening-hatching fly and the wings are reddish-brown and about 8 mm long. It can be copied with any of the small red sedge patterns, particularly the Little Red Sedge of G. E. M. Skues.

SMALL YELLOW SEDGE

A common sedge and the smallest that interests trout. It hatches in the evenings and can be distinguished by its 5–6 mm browny-yellow wings.

WELSHMAN'S BUTTON

F. M. Halford named this species thus and in so doing caused confusion with the beetle of the same name. It is widely distributed on rivers and less frequently on lakes. The adults hatch from early May to July during the day and evening. The wing-length is 12–15 mm and is chestnut-brown with golden hairs. The female often carries a large brown egg-sac as her abdomen. William Lunn's Caperer is a good imitation, as is Skues' Little Red Sedge.

Listed below are various assorted sedge imitations: Larvae in their cases, pupae and adult dressings, and many nondescript general patterns representing two or more species.

SEDGE LARVAE

Some of these caddis cases look very realistic. I've no doubt that they catch trout, but I prefer the fur-and-feather alternatives. See also STICKFLY (*page 180*) and WORMFLY (*page 203*).

CADDIS LARVA (Brian Clarke)

Hook: Longshank 8–10
Body: Pheasant tail fibres or bronze or sandy-coloured peacock herl

Rib: Copper wire
Hackle: Honey-coloured hen
Head: Yellow or fawn wool

CASED CADDIS (Bob Carnill) Plate 11

Hook: Extra longshank 8–12
Body: An underbody of black Gossamer silk and lead wire and an overbody of two-toned fur from the leading edge of a hare's ear. This represents the case.
Abdomen: Tied between the body and hackle. White swan or goose herl to represent the larva
Rib: Silver wire over the abdomen
Hackle: Black hen sparsely tied at 90 degrees to the shank
Head: Large. Tying silk varnished black

PHEASANT-TAIL CADDIS LARVA (Roger Fogg) Plate 11

Hook: Longshank 8–14
Tying silk: Black
Body: Lead-foil strips wound over with hare's ear fur and roughly covered with open turns of pheasant tail fibres and peacock herl
Rib: Tying silk or copper wire for strength
Shoulder: Dirty wool wound in between body and hackle to represent the larva
Hackle: Any dark hackle clipped short
Head: Black or brown tying silk

SAND CADDIS (Taff Price)

Hook: Longshank 10–12
Body: A copper- or lead-wire underbody with a second layer of floss silk, leaving enough of the shank clear for the hackle to be tied in later. Coat the body in a water-resistant adhesive and completely cover with sand.
Hackle: A single turn of brown hackle when the body is dry

A **Twig Caddis** and a **Gravel Caddis** can be dressed by replacing the sand with small twigs and vegetation and with very small stones.

SEDGE PUPAE or HATCHING WET PATTERNS

In addition to the patterns listed, see also BROWN-AND-YELLOW NYMPH (*page 128*), AMBER NYMPH (*page 4*), ALL ROUNDER (*page 3*), PALMERS (*page 136*), INVICTA (*page 125*), WHOGSTOPPER (*page 199*), GREEN PETER (*page 77*), MURROUGH (*page 125*) and TURKEY GREEN/YELLOW (*page 189*).

DIVING CADDIS (Gary LaFontaine)

Hook: 8–16
Body: Dubbed Sparkle Yarn; colour to match the natural
Wing: A soft wing of partridge or mallard breast-fibres, the tips of which should extend beyond the hook-bend. A second wing of about 30 filaments of clear Sparkle Yarn is tied in at about 45 degrees over the first wing. This should be longer than the first wing
Hackle: Rear-facing brown cock

FIERY-BROWN SEDGE (Bob Carnill) Plate 13

This should be fished wet at any position on the leader. It is reputedly extremely effective as a single point-fly cast to rising fish. Bob Carnill comments: 'There are occasions when trout drown adult sedges sitting on the surface. They do this by rising from directly below the fly and slapping it down with their tails. When this happens, a leaded Fiery Brown cast into the boil of a "slap-down" rise, allowed to sink, and then drawn out of it, can produce very exciting results.'

Hook: 8–12
Tying silk: Brown Gossamer

Body: Fiery-brown seal's fur
Rib: Gold tinsel
Wing: Two layers, single folded dark bronze mallard tied low and extending beyond the bend
Hackle: Rich-brown hen wound as a collar

HATCHING SEDGE-PUPA (John Roberts) — Plate 13

I was inspired to dress this after using Stan Headley's **Twitcher** under other circumstances. I thought that an emerging sedge-pupa imitation could make good use of a spun deerhair head. This buoyant pattern will hang in the surface film in the manner of the natural sedge preparing to break through on to the surface. It can be fished static, in twitches, or in slow, steady pulls. On some patterns I tie in a few turns of fine lead wire at the rear of the shank before tying in the body material. This ensures that the fly hangs vertically.

The addition of further turns of lead wire allows the fly to be fished below the top inch of water but still remain fairly buoyant.

Hook: 10–12 sedge hook
Tying silk: To match the body colour
Body: Orange, green, brown or beige seal's fur
Rib: Fine gold tinsel or wire
Hackle: Brown partridge tied as a rear-sloping collar
Head: Natural deerhair spun in Muddler style and roughly trimmed. The fibres should not be densely packed, nor trimmed all to the same length

HATCHING SEDGE-PUPA (John Goddard and Brian Clarke)

May be weighted if desired.
Hook: 12
Tying silk: Orange
Body: Medium-olive seal's fur
Rib: Silver wire
Wing: Grey mallard wing quill sections sloping back below the body, tied in alongside the thorax

Antennae: Two brown mallard fibres tied in at the thorax and sloping backwards over the body
Thorax: Medium-olive seal's fur
Legs: Grey partridge hackle dyed green as a throat only

An orange version is tied with orange seal's fur and a brown partridge hackle.

LATEX PUPA (Roger Fogg) — Plate 13

The fluorescent floss under the translucent overbody makes this into an excellent pupal imitation. Trout are often willing to take fur-and-feather flies, but on occasions they need something a little out of the ordinary. This might be the answer. One cynic summed it up as: 'more suited to being fished below a float for grayling!' There is the look of the maggot about it, but that comment came from a fishless angler after the orange pattern had taken three trout to 3¼ lb from under his nose. Roger Fogg fishes it sink-and-draw, with the most successful sizes 12 and 14. It was originally tied for river fishing in much smaller sizes.

Roger relates its history thus: 'In 1978 I was having a great deal of trouble trying to catch trout on a still pool on a river. It was during a hot spell and the fish were taking something very small but obviously succulent. The creatures in question turned out to be the pupae of tiny sedges, probably members of the *Hydroptilidae*. Such sedges have long been regarded as too small for the angler to copy in Britain, although the Americans have developed micro-caddis patterns. The pupae were mainly pale green and pale orange-amber. Conventional dressings failed, so I tried small fluorescent latex imitations on size 18 and 20 hooks. They worked a treat.'

The pattern below is the green version. The body of the orange version has orange latex over fluorescent orange wool.

Hook: 12–20 caddis hook

Tying silk: Brown
Body: An underbody of fluorescent lime-green floss covered with natural cream-coloured latex. The latex strip should be ribbed under tension from the bend with the tension released towards the thorax. This produces the tapered body
Thorax: Chestnut-brown ostrich herl
Hackle: Chestnut-brown hen

LONGHORNS (Richard Walker) — Plate 13

These pupal imitations are useful when the adults are hatching, but not being taken by trout. The variety of body colours of the artificial ensures that a wide variety of naturals can be represented by the one pattern. They are best fished sink-and-draw, the speed of which can vary from very slow to fairly fast.

Hook: 10–12

Tying silk: Pale yellow
Body: Rear two-thirds, amber or pale sea-green wool; front one-third, sepia or chestnut wool
Rib: Fine gold thread on the rear section only
Hackle: Two turns of short brown partridge
Horns: Two strands of pheasant tail fibres slanting at 45 degrees over the back and about twice the hook-length

SEDGE-PUPA — Plate 13

Hook: 10–14
Body: An underbody of brown or white tying silk overlaid with clear, colourless

nylon monofilament tapering to the rear
Hackle: Partridge hackle tied rear-sloping
Head: Peacock herl

SEDGE-PUPA (C. Kendall) — Plate 13

Chris Kendall dresses four different sedges in this style. Collectively, they cover most of the species one comes across in the UK. The four colour variations are ginger, green-bodied, silver-grey and cinnamon.

Hook: Yorkshire sedge hook 8–14
Abdomen: Antron and seal's fur mixed 50/50, colour as above, ribbed with clear polythene

Breathers: Two bronze mallard fibres tied from rear of thorax facing backwards
Legs: Dyed partridge in colours to match body
Wing cases and shellback: Dyed white duck fibres to match body colour. The wing cases are tied either side of the shank
Thorax: As for the abdomen without the rib

SEDGE-PUPA (John Goddard) — Plate 13

A paern which its creator describes as 'one of my best stillwater patterns'. It is fished deep or in midwater and retrieved at a steady pace with occasional pauses.

Hook: Longshank wide-gape 10–12
Tying silk: Brown
Body: Choice of orange, cream, dark-brown or olive seal's fur. The orange and

olive can be lightly covered with fluorescent material of the same colour
Rib: Fine silver Lurex
Thorax: Three dark-brown condor herls
Wing-case: Four light-brown condor herls doubled and redoubled
Hackle: Two turns of rusty-hen or honey-hen

SHORTHORNS (Richard Walker)

A small pupa imitation to represent the black and brown silverhorns and the grouse-wing pupae.

Hook: 12–14
Tying silk: Dark brown
Abdomen: Very dark olive-brown feather-fibre

Rib: Pale-yellow tying silk
Thorax: Greeny-yellow or orange fluorescent wool tied fat
Wing-case: A single strip of black Lurex
Hackle: Brown partridge tied in two bunches on the lower side of the body, rear-facing

SIENNA SEDGE   Plate 13

One of Steve Parton's dressings which he describes as an excellent point or dropper fly when brown-bodied sedges are on the water. It is also possibly an imitation of a brown or ginger-bodied hatching midge-pupa. It can be fished also as a dry fly.

Hook: 8–14
Tying silk: Black

Body: Sienna seal's fur with a palmered red-game hackle
Rib: Fine oval gold tinsel through the body hackle
Throat hackle: Red-game
Wing: Cock-pheasant secondary feather. Cinnamon or reddish variations are preferred. As an alternative, use the side tail-feathers. The wing should be tied narrow and extend to the bend

ADULT SEDGES

Most of these are general patterns used to copy one or more species.

DARK SEDGE (T. Thomas)

Hook: 12–14
Body: Black wool or chenille with a palmered black cock hackle
Wing: Black deerhair tied flat, spread out

and clipped with square ends
Hackle: Ginger cock tied in front of the wing

G&H SEDGE   Plate 26

A popular pattern devised by John Goddard and Cliff Henry (hence the G&H). It is an excellent floater because of the deerhair body, which also produces a good silhouette. John Goddard suggests that when used from the bank on a stillwater it should be tied to the point of a very long leader, in excess of 18 feet. It should be allowed to lie motionless unless trout are reluctant to take it, and then a little tweak may induce a favourable response. In rough water it should be retrieved fairly quickly across the surface. Fished as a top dropper from a drifting boat, 'it reigns supreme'. The smaller sizes are more suitable

for rivers. Dyed deerhair can be used for different species of sedge.

Hook: Longshank 8–12
Tying silk: Green
Body: Bunches of deerhair spun on and trimmed. All the body is covered and then trimmed, tapering towards the eye. All the underside hair is removed and partway along each side to give a sedge silhouette
Hackles: Two rusty-dun cock hackles trimmed at the top. The hackle-stems can be used for forward-pointing antennae
Lower body: Dark green seal's fur twisted in between the double length of green tying thread, tied in at the outset. This is pulled taut under the trimmed hair body and whipped in at the eye

168

GREEN SEDGE

A useful stillwater dry fly if you have the patience to watch it motionless on the surface. A long wait may be necessary, but the excitement of seeing a fish attack it with savage splash is great fun.

Hook: Longshank 10–12

Butt: Fluorescent-green wool
Body: Green polypropylene
Wing: A bunch of honey cock hackle fibres tied low over the back and extending to the butt
Hackle: Two honey cock hackles

KAHL SEDGE

A North American pattern highly praised by Donald Overfield.

Hook: 14
Tying silk: White
Tail: Grizzle cock fibres

Body: Stripped peacock quill
Wing: Rolled mallard flank-feather tied flat and clipped square
Hackle: Grizzle cock

LIGHT SEDGE (T. Thomas)

Hook: 12–14
Body: Light cock-pheasant tail fibres wound on thickly and palmered with a ginger cock hackle

Wing: Brown deerhair tied flat and spread out with the ends trimmed square
Hackle: Black cock

LITTLE RED SEDGE (G. E. M. Skues)   Plate 26

Although he did not greatly appreciate grayling, Skues said of this pattern that if he had just one fly with which to kill grayling (by which I assume he meant chalk-stream grayling), he would select this one. It kills trout and grayling on northern streams, too. In one twenty-minute spell on the Wharfe one November day, my friend, David Burnett, killed half a dozen grayling between 1 lb and 1¾ lb on the fly when there wasn't a sedge in sight. I know anglers who have fished that stretch of the Wharfe for many years, and I'm told that a grayling of 1½ lb is rare. I think the catch was viewed with some scepticism!

Hook: 12–14
Tying silk: Hot-orange
Body: Darkest hare's fur with a palmered short-fibred red cock hackle
Rib: Fine gold wire
Wing: Landrail wing, bunched and rolled and sloping well back over the tail
Hackle: Five or six turns of deep-red cock in front of the wings (longer-fibred than the body)

PALE SEDGE (David Jacques)

Smaller sizes are recommended for daytime use and larger for dusk. It is a useful imitation of any of the paler sedges and the grousewing and caperer.

Hook: 10–14
Body: Cinnamon turkey tail fibres

Rib: Gold twist
Wing: Natural hen-pheasant wing fibres, rolled and tied flat over the body
Hackles: Palmered ginger cock over the body with a second ginger cock at the head

RED SEDGE (Richard Walker) Plate 26

Hook: Standard or longshank 10
Tag: Orange fluorescent wool
Body: Clipped chestnut ostrich herl or chestnut pheasant-tail fibres
Wing: Natural red cock hackle fibres clipped level with the bend, or red cree, or cuckoo cock
Hackle: Two long-fibred natural red cock hackles

SAVILLE'S SUPER SEDGE (Tom Saville) Plate 22

Hook: 8–12
Tying silk: Well-waxed brown
Body: Ostrich herl dyed cinnamon with a palmered ginger cock hackle
Rib: Arc-chrome DRF nylon floss
Wing: Two hen pheasant or woodcock body fibres drawn through Cellire varnish between the thumb and finger; tied in a roof-shape extending beyond the bend

SEPIA DUN (*Leptophlebia marginata*)   See EPHEMEROPTERA

The distribution, habitat and general appearance of this fly are similar to those of the Claret dun, described elsewhere in greater detail. The most obvious difference is that the rarer sepia dun has a darker body and wings, appears between April and mid-May and is slightly larger. The female spinner has three dark-brown tails and a black patch on the leading edge of the wings. The heavily-built nymph, which swims in laboured fashion, has prominent gill filaments down the side of its body, three widely splayed-out tails and a sepia body. In April the nymphs move into shallower water in the margins before emerging by climbing up vegetation or waterside stones. It is during this move into the shallows that they are most profitably imitated. A Pheasant-Tail Spinner should be sufficient for those rare occasions that trout feed upon the female spinner. See also under MALLARD AND CLARET (*page 103*) and GROUSE AND CLARET (*page 80*).

SEPIA NYMPH (Richard Walker)

Hook: 12–16
Tying silk: Black
Tail: Very dark hen-pheasant fibres
Body: Natural black sheep's wool
Rib: Black floss or black plastic strip. The body fibres are extensively picked out between the ribbing and trimmed for the gills
Wing-case and legs: Dark hen-pheasant fibres dyed sepia
Thorax: Black floss tied fat

SEPIA NYMPH Plate 15

Hook: 12–14
Tying silk: Dark brown
Tail: Dark brown hen hackle fibres
Body: A 5:1 mixture of dark brown and ginger seal's fur, well picked out at each side; or dark brown floss or seal's fur with a silver wire rib
Thorax: Black seal's fur
Hackle: Dark brown hen or hen dyed sepia

SEPIA DUN (Oliver Kite)

Hook: 14
Tying silk: Dark brown
Tail: Dark-brown or black cock fibres
Body and thorax: Dark heron herls, doubled and redoubled at the thorax
Rib: Fine gold wire down the abdomen only
Hackle: Black cock with a brown tinge

170

SEPIA DUN (David Jacques)

Hook: 12
Tying silk: Maroon or claret
Tail: Pheasant tail fibres well spaced out
Body: Pheasant tail fibres

Rib: Fine gold wire
Wing: Mottled brown cock wing-slips
Hackle: Furnace cock

SHREDGE   Plate 13

Tony Knight devised this mixed-up Shrimp and Sedge dressing. So mixed-up is it that it kills as a shrimp pattern, as a hatching sedge or as a sedge-pupa imitation. Bob Carnill and Steve Parton, two excellent Rutland anglers, speak highly of the Shredge and its variants. Bob praises the hackled, wingless version when fished in a team of three. Steve ties the body with dark sienna seal's fur taken well round the hook-bend and tapering to the rear, with a sparse ginger cock hackle rear-sloping. This is called the **Emergent Tobacco Sedge**.

Hook: 10–12 standard or sedge hook
Tying silk: Primrose
Body: Light tobacco-coloured seal's fur produced by mixing 70 per cent cinnamon and 30 per cent yellow seal's fur
Rib: Fine gold wire
Wing: Short grey mallard flight feather. A variation is to tie two wings at the sides of the body rather than on top
Hackle: Pale ginger hen or cinnamon

SHRIMPS (*Gammarus pulex, G. lacustris*)

These crustaceans are widely distributed in rivers and stillwaters throughout the U.K. but they are of greater value to the river fisherman. They thrive in alkaline waters and are most abundant in chalk-streams, where they live in weed-beds or on the bottom. A deep-sunk artificial can be a killing pattern for trout and grayling. Both species feed upon shrimp in large quantities where they are readily available. Grayling are primarily bottom-feeders and a large proportion of their diet is shrimp because during those months of the year when grayling feed most avidly, there are fewer nymphs, duns and other flies.

The natural shrimp is unmistakable with its arched translucent-grey body which turns orangey-brown during the mid-summer mating season. Their length varies from 12–18 mm. They swim in a peculiar stop-start darting motion. Imparting some lift to the artificial often brings a response from a fish that refuses to look at a fly in a straight drift. See also KILLER BUG (*page 93*).

SHRIMP (Eric Horsfall Turner)

Hook: 10–12
Body: Orange DFM wool or floss silk
Rib: Silver wire through the hackle

Hackle: Palmered ginger cock
Back: Light-brown turkey fibres

SHRIMP (Richard Walker)

This leaded pattern fishes upside down and is less likely to catch on weeds than other dressings.

Hook: 10–12
Tying silk: Olive
Body: An underbody of fine strips of lead, built as a hump on the shank, overlaid with olive wool and varnished along the back
Hackle: Palmered ginger trimmed on the top and side to leave underside only

171

MATING SHRIMP (John Goddard and Brian Clarke)   Plate 14

Brian Clarke's version:

Hook: Wide-gape 8–12
Tying silk: Olive
Body: An underbody of lead wire with an overbody of mixed olive and amber seal's fur (4:1)
Rib: Fine gold wire
Back: Clear polythene or PVC

John Goddard's version:

Hook: Wide-gape 8–12
Tying silk: Olive
Body: An underbody of narrow lead strips built into a hump on top of the shank. An overbody of mixed seal's fur, 60 per cent olive, 30 per cent dark brown and 10 per cent DFM pink
Rib: Oval silver wire
Back: Clear PVC or polythene

RED SPOT SHRIMP (Neil Patterson)   Plate 14

Until recently I had not come across the phenomenon of shrimps with a red blob on their bellies. However, Neil Patterson has noted that some early-season shrimps have this feature, and he suggests that it is the early stages of the egg-sac. The highly-visible fluorescent red spot on the artificial makes it a useful pattern for slightly-coloured water.

Hook: Sedge hook 8–14
Tying silk: Waxed olive

Underbody: Fine lead wire
Body: A short length of red DFM wool tied in on the centre of the shank at right-angles to it; on an equal mixture of olive mohair and olive seal's fur dubbed on and wound to the head through the wool. The red wool is clipped to form two spots on the body sides
Back: Double layer of clear plastic sheet over the body and rib
Rib: Gold wire over the body
Legs: Olive body fibres picked out

SILVER MARCH BROWN   Plate 16

Although this is a variant of the March Brown, a river pattern, it has become a useful lake and sea-trout fly together with the **Gold March Brown**, which differs from this dressing only by the gold tinsel body and rib. Both are useful hatching-sedge patterns when fished near the surface at the appropriate time.

Hook: 10–12
Tail: Partridge tail fibres
Body: Flat silver tinsel
Rib: Oval silver tinsel or wire
Wing: Partridge tail or hen-pheasant wing
Hackle: Brown partridge
   An alternative dressing has a hare's ear fur body with a closely wound rib of silver Lurex.

SINFOIL'S FRY   Plate 9

This stillwater fry imitation is named after its creator, Ken Sinfoil, at the time a bailiff at Weir Wood reservoir. I believe Ken Sinfoil was the first U.K. fly-tyer to make use of polythene in fly bodies.

Hook: Longshank 8–12
Tying silk: Black

Underbody: Flat silver tinsel
Overbody: Thick clear polythene or PVC built up into a fry-shape
Collar: Fluorescent or ordinary scarlet floss
Back: Pale-brown mallard fibres tied in only at the head
Head: Varnished black silk with an eye painted either side

SMALL DARK OLIVE (*Baetis scambus*)
See EPHEMEROPTERA

Also known as the July Dun. The species is common and well distributed on rivers throughout the country and is most abundant on limestone streams. The nymph is a very small agile-darting type inhabiting weeds, moss and sometimes stones. The adult is also very small. Adults have been known to appear as early as February and as late as November, but they are most common between May and August and usually hatch during the afternoons. The female spinner crawls under the surface to deposit her eggs. Trout feed upon the spent spinners, which after laying their eggs are unable to break through the surface film and become trapped below or within it. The possibility of fish feeding on these should not be overlooked if floating duns and spinners are being refused by feeding fish.

The male dun has medium- to dark-grey wings. The abdomen is pale grey-green olive with the last two segments yellowish. The legs are pale yellow-olive and the two tails are grey. The female dun has similar wings and the abdomen is grey-olive with the last two segments yellowish. The legs and tails are as for the male.

The female spinner, also known as the small red spinner, has transparent wings with blackish veins. The abdomen varies between dark brown tinged with olive to mahogany-brown. The legs are olive-brown and the two tails greyish-white. The male spinner is of no interest.

See also DARK OLIVE (*page 48*) and LARGE DARK OLIVE (*page 96*) for the larger-sized imitations, which can be tied smaller, and GOLD-RIBBED HARE'S EAR (*page 72*), PHEASANT-TAIL SPINNER (*page 147*), LUNN'S PARTICULAR (*page 102*), SNIPE BLOA (*page 22*) and OLIVE BLOA (*page 21*).

JULY DUN (SDO) NYMPH (G. E. M. Skues)

Hook: 16
Tying silk: Yellow or primrose
Tail: Short dark-blue hen fibres
Body: Mixed olive seal's fur and dark brown bear's fur
Rib: Gold wire through the rear half
Hackle: Two turns of short-fibred rusty-dun hen

SMALL DARK OLIVE HATCHING SPECIAL

A pattern created by Terry Griffiths to represent the hatching dun in the surface film.

Hook: 16–18
Tail: Very short blue-dun fibres
Body: A short body of mole's fur
Rib: Fine gold thread
Hackles: Rhode Island Red with a blue-dun in front

JULY DUN (SDO) (John Veniard)

Hook: 14
Tail: Medium-olive cock fibres
Body: Yellow heron herl
Rib: Gold wire
Wing: Dark starling wing
Hackle: Medium-olive cock
A wingless version can be tied with a dark dun hackle replacing the olive one.

SMALL YELLOW SALLY (*Chloroperla terrentium*)
See STONEFLY

A different species from the yellow sally, but imitations of that will be sufficient. It is fairly common on rivers with a sandy or stony bottom, but has a preference for upland waters. The nymph is fairly small, measuring 5–8 mm long. The adults are 5–8 mm long and are slim and yellowish or yellowish-brown and appear between April and August.

SMUTS (*Similium*)   See DIPTERA

Known as reed smuts or the black curse, these are members of the Diptera Order of flat-winged flies. They inhabit rivers and stillwaters as long as there is some movement or current. The adults are very small, averaging no more than 3–4 mm in length, although there are a few larger species. The body colour varies from dark brown to black, and the wings are broad and transparent. The larvae cling to weeds and are avidly devoured by trout and grayling. The adult fly, emerging from its pupal case, rises to the surface in a gas bubble. The relatively dry adult spends little time on the surface before flying off. The rising adult in its gas bubble is difficult to imitate, but sub-surface patterns that incorporate a white wing or silver ribbing help the deception. Small versions of the Black Gnat also suitably represent the smuts.

TORP'S REED SMUTS   Plate 28

These two patterns are the creation of Preben Torp Jacobsen, of Denmark, who comments: 'Everyone sooner or later has the experience that they cannot get a rise to any of their flies. They have tried every pattern in the fly-box in vain. That also happened to me and my friends, and one day in spring my close friend, Ove Neilson, found out the reason: Hanging out over the bank of the stream with his nose only inches from the water surface, he could see the tiny black flies hanging in the film. They were *Similium* flies, either hanging just under the surface or on their way through it.

'In the following months I tried to find a solution to the problems. In the meantime I heard from England about a series of flies created by W. H. Lawrie called **Hairy Fairy** and sold by Hardy Bros. I got a tackle-shop in Copenhagen to procure them for me, and among them was a tiny black fly,

the **Black Imp**, nearly only a bubble of black wool with silver wire on a hook size 16. I discovered that silver wire in nearly all wet flies gives the impression of glittering air bubbles around the fly. In autumn 1971 I tied my first Reed Smut Nymph. The pattern is as follows:

Hook: Mustad 72500 size 14
Tying silk: Brown
Body: Blood-red cow's hair over a base of thin copper wire. The body material should be thoroughly soaked in silicone liquid to ensure the air-bubbles adhere to the body. Four or five turns of 0.15 mm silver wire are made in front and behind the body. The impregnated hair will take a lot of air down into the water and turns of silver wire in the front and rear will help create the impression that the ''fly'' is enveloped in a sac of air, just like the natural when its pupal stage rises to the surface. The body is only short, occupying the middle-third of the shank. One could tie the fly on a much smaller hook, but I want a good gape and the weight of the

bigger hook to help me to bring the fly down – the same reason for the heavier silver wire.

'The hatching smuts penetrate the surface very fast – you will never see them "standing" on the surface. Only those that can't penetrate the surface film will be hanging in it and will be caught by trout. This is the second situation, where a trout has the possibility to catch it.

'From earlier experiences I had great faith in small flies tied with a Parachute hackle. I had used a Parachute version of the Grey Duster during Caenis hatches with extraordinary results and christened it the **Parachuting Badger**. Likewise, I tied a similar fly to imitate the smuts hanging in the surface unable to hatch.'

SIMILIUM (P. T. Jacobsen)

Hook: 16–18
Tying silk: Black
Body: Black condor herl tied fairly short

Hackle: Long-stemmed short-fibred black cock tied in Parachute style in the middle of the short body

SMUT (J. C. Mottram)

This wet pattern was devised by J. C. Mottram, author of *Fly Fishing: Some New Arts and Mysteries*, published about 1920. I can boast of catching smutting grayling on this fly. That difficult task should be proof enough of its value.

Hook: 14–16
Thorax: Black floss silk at the thorax only. I tie in a small tip of silver tinsel behind the thorax
Hackle: One turn of a small starling breast feather

SMUT (Taff Price)

An adult imitation.

Hook: 18–20
Tying silk: Grey

Body: Two fibres of oak-turkey feather
Hackle: Badger cock clipped small

SNAILS

Snails provide a major contribution to the diet of stillwater trout, and to a lesser extent river trout and grayling. For the most part they live on the lake- or river-bed or on weeds, and they are therefore difficult to imitate successfully. There is a period in mid-summer when snails migrate to the surface and hang beneath the surface film. They do this probably because of the de-oxygenation of the water. During July and August it is not uncommon to catch trout full of snails, and the imitation fished slowly just below the surface can have great effect. The Black and Peacock Spider is a useful pattern on such an occasion.

FLOATING SNAIL (Cliff Henry)

Hook: Wide-gape 10–14
Tying silk: Black
Body: Shaped cork or Plastazote tapering to the rear and covered in stripped

peacock eye quill except for the front two turns, which should be of bronze peacock herl

FLOATING SNAIL (Bob Church)   Plate 12

I doubt whether there is an easier dressing to tie.

Hook: 10–12

Body: Black or brown chenille in a ball-shape

FLOATING SNAIL (D. Barker)

Hook: Wide-gape 8–10
Body: A large dome-shaped body of cork with a shallow groove cut out for the hook-shank to slot into. A small hole is made at the top of the dome and a lead shot is glued in. The body is coloured with indelible felt-pen (dark green or black) and glued to the shank. The artificial floats dome downwards imitating the natural

SNIPE AND GOLD Plate 20

This is a fly I use for early-season trout on the Yorkshire Dales and moorland rivers. I suspect that the flash of the gold body puts the fly in the "attractor" category. It has done well for me as a point fly on a three-fly leader.

Hook: 14
Body: Flat gold tinsel
Rib: Fine gold wire
Hackle: Dark snipe

SNIPE AND PURPLE Plate 21

An old North Country iron blue imitation and an exceptional pattern for both trout and grayling. It is useful early in the season and again from September to November. That expert grayling fisher, Reg Righyni, places this as his favourite top dropper on a three-fly leader. He also incorporates a fine copper rib on some of his patterns. The soft snipe hackle can be worked in the current when the fly is fished upstream and this would seem to be a major factor in the pattern's representation of the nymph or dun struggling to emerge.

Hook: 12–16
Body: Purple silk
Hackle: Dark snipe tied sparsely

SNIPE AND YELLOW

This used to be known as the **Light Snipe** and it is similar to the Snipe Bloa, listed under BLOAS (*page 20*). It is an old North Country fly usually fished early- and late-season.

Hook: 14
Body: Yellow silk
Hackle: Dark snipe sparsely tied

SOMETHING AND NOTHING Plate 14

This is a nondescript sub-surface pattern devised by Roger Fogg. Some twenty years ago he was fishing with a well-chewed and well-worn Coachman, and the more tatty it became, the more fish it caught. As a result he tied a fly with a well-worn look, and the origin of its name is obvious.

Roger says: 'It is perhaps my favourite pattern, the nearest I have got to the philosopher's stone, but by accident rather than alchemy – it seems to be all things to all fish. It may not look much, but it catches fish unleaded, leaded, on small hooks, on lure hooks, on rivers and on stillwaters. Further, it succeeds throughout the season. Although I prefer the imitative approach, it is a good pattern with which to catch your first fish on an alien water. Then the fish may be spooned.'

There are two versions, the second of which is best fished sink-and-draw, perhaps on a leader with midge-pupa imitations. The small, unleaded version fishes well retrieved gently just below the surface.

Hook: Any size, but size 12 is recommended
Tying silk: Brown
Body: Optional lead underbody covered with peacock herl with much of the flue clipped off
Hackle: Any brownish hackle clipped short as a rough collar
Wing: White hen feather or similar tied in the usual manner and clipped to a short stub

A second version is dressed as above, but with a body of fine dark copper wire of the type found in a small electric motor.

SPIDERS

Plate 16

The wingless, hackled wet flies used on rivers particularly in the north of the country are certainly suggestive of the natural spider, but this is not what they are intended to represent. The imitation of the stillwater spiders has been largely overlooked by angler-entomologists. This is surprising in view of the potential food source they represent. They live close to weed-beds and carry with them a single large air-bubble or trap smaller bubbles in their body hairs. They seem to prefer lake margins where the journey to replenish their air is not great. Many terrestrial spiders find their way on to the water and are often seen struggling on the surface.

Hook: 12–14
Body: Brown seal's fur
Rib: Silver tinsel with a tip at the rear
Hackle: Brown partridge

WINDBORNE SPIDER (Taff Price)

A pattern to represent the terrestrial spiders.
Hook: 14–16
Body: A button of red, brown, yellow, grey or black polypropylene
Hackle: A cock hackle tied in Parachute style and coloured as for the body

Taff Price suggests that for added realism a single human hair should be tied in at the tail to represent the gossamer thread spun by the spider. I can't for a moment think that it makes the slightest difference!

SPRUCE FLY

A streamer-style lure.
Hook: Longshank 6–10
Tail: Peacock sword feather herl
Body: Rear half, red floss; front half, thin black chenille
Wing: Two cree hackle-points tied back-to-back
Hackle: Brown cock tied as a rear-facing collar

SPUDDLER

Plate 4

This hybrid lure was created by crossing a Muddler with a Spruce Fly.
Hook: Longshank 6–10
Tail: Brown calf-tail or Canadian fox squirrel-hair
Body: Cream wool
Thorax: Orange floss
Wing: Two cree hackle points tied in at the rear of the thorax
Neck: Canadian fox squirrel-hair
Head: Spun deerhair clipped in an oval shape with a flat bottom
Variations include a hot-orange goat-hair tail, or a silver rib to aid its attractiveness.

SPURWINGS *(Centroptilum luteolum, C.pennulatum)*
See EPHEMEROPTERA

The small spurwing (*C. luteolum*) and large spurwing (*C. pennulatum*) used to be classed with the pale wateries, but now they are better known in their own right. The small spurwing is small to medium-sized and similar in its dun stage to the pale watery or small dark olive, the main difference being the small spur-shaped hind-wing which is detectable only with the aid of a magnifying glass.

Distribution is widespread except in Wales. It is found in rivers and sometimes on lakes and it has a preference for alkaline water. The nymph is an agile-darting type inhabiting weed-beds.

The adults appear from early May to October, their most prolific month being June. Their presence is often spread throughout the day, particularly during the early months, but as the season progresses the hatches become restricted to late afternoons.

C. luteolum

The male dun has pale grey or blue-grey wings. The abdomen is pale olive-grey with a brown-olive underside. The legs are watery-grey or olive-brown and the two tails are pale grey. The female dun has wings similar to the male's. The abdomen is pale watery-olive or green-olive with pale olive under. The legs are very pale olive and the two tails grey.

The male spinner has colourless wings and a translucent white abdomen of which the last three segments are reddish-brown. The underside is grey-white. The legs are pale olive and the two tails grey-white. The female spinner, known also as the little amber spinner, has transparent colourless wings. The abdomen is yellow-brown which becomes amber in the spent fly. The underside is creamy-yellow. The legs are pale olive and the two tails pale olive-white.

The large spurwing is a medium-to-large-sized adult. Distribution is localised in the south and north and in the Usk area of Wales. One distinguishing feature of the duns is that the wings are spread well apart when at rest, whereas most duns hold their wings more or less vertically. The nymph is an agile-darting type, preferring to live on weeds or moss in slower-moving water. The adults emerge from late May to September. Like the small spurwing, it has a small spur-shaped hind-wing.

The male dun has dark blue-grey wings and a pale olive-brown or greyish abdomen, of which the upperside of the last three segments is amber. The legs are pale olive-brown and the two tails grey. The female dun also has blue-grey wings. The abdomen is pale olive-grey. The legs are olive on the upper sections and grey-white lower down and the two tails grey. The male spinner has transparent wings. The abdomen is translucent white with pale red rings, with the last three segments dark amber. The legs are pale grey and the two tails grey-white.

The female spinner, also known as the large amber spinner, has transparent wings with pale olive veins. The abdomen is olive with amber flecks, or all amber with greyish wings. The underside is olive-white. The legs are olive-grey and the two tails pale grey.

For other artificials see GREY DUSTER *(page 79)*, LUNN'S YELLOW BOY (*page 102*), PINK SPINNER (*page 149*), POULT BLOA (*page 21*), TUP'S INDISPENSABLE (*page 188*), LAST HOPE (*page 71*), PHEASANT-TAIL SPINNER (*page 147*) and GREY GOOSE NYMPH (*page 79*).

SPURWING NYMPH (Tony Waites)   Plate 19

A pattern belonging to Tony Waites, head-keeper for the Driffield Anglers' Club. Donald Overfield suggests that a wing-case of heron herl could be added.

Hook: 14–18

Tying silk: Grey
Body: An underbody of fine silver fuse-wire covered with three natural heron herls tapering to the rear
Rib: Fine silver fuse-wire

LARGE SPURWING (G. E. M. Skues)

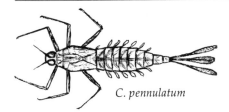

C. pennulatum

Hook: 14
Tying silk: Waxed orange
Body: Spun white lamb's wool
Hackle: Dark-blue hen

LARGE SPURWING DUN (John Goddard)

Hook: 14
Tying silk: Cream
Tail: Pale blue-dun cock fibres

Body: Cream seal's fur
Wing: Pale starling in a V-shape
Hackle: Pale-olive cock

SQUIRREL AND SILVER   Plate 3

A useful fry-imitation best fished in the late season when coarse-fish fry appear in the larger reservoirs. I have seen a number of variations on the squirrel-tail wing and silver body. That given below was devised by John McLellan.

Hook: Longshank 6–10

Tying silk: Black
Tail: Tuft of red wool
Body: Flat silver tinsel
Rib (optional): Oval silver tinsel
Wing: Natural grey squirrel-tail (brownish roots and grey tips)
Throat hackle: Silver mallard breast fibres

S.S. or SAWYER'S SWEDISH NYMPH   Plate 15

This is a Frank Sawyer imitation of the pond olive and claret dun nymphs and is of most use between June and August.

Hook: 10–14
Tying silk: None

Tail: Tips of the body fibres
Body: Dark-grey goose herls and red copper wire wound and tied in the same manner as for the GREY GOOSE NYMPH (*page 79*).

THE STALKING FLY

This method and style of tying a floating fly was devised by H. Jans-sen, of the United States. The fly was so named because it is used for selective fish. The USD series of Goddard and Clarke is similar, but Janssen offered alternative designs. Many dun and spinner imitations can be tied in these styles.

The basic fly used a down-eyed hook with a Parachute hackle tied on top of the shank with split hackle-tip wings tied on the underside. The Parachute hackle is wound round the stalks of the wings. The fly floats upside down with the point and wings uppermost and the hackle below the body. One alternative and more durable method of winging is to use hackle-fibre wings. The second option is a no-hackle dressing which uses three bunches of hackle fibres. One bunch acts as an upright wing; the other two are divided as legs on either side of the body in a V-shape.

STANK HEN SPIDER

A Scottish Border wet fly. Taff Price suggests that it is a pale watery copy.
Hook: 14

Body: Well-waxed yellow silk
Hackle: Light blue-dun hen

STICKFLY

Caddis larvae imitations (see under SEDGE) which should be fished slowly along lake and reservoir beds. In addition to those in the SEDGE section and under WORMFLY, I have included two dressings which are representative of the many similar dressings available.

STICK FLY (Brian Harris)   Plate 11

Hook: Longshank 10–12
Tying silk: Buff
Body: An underbody of lead wire (0.037 mm) wound over a varnished shank, coated with varnish and allowed to dry
Overbody: Natural brown condor herl or a substitute of dyed turkey-tail

Rib: Fine oval gold tinsel
Head: Amber poly-dubbing or chopped wool or dyed rabbit fur
Hackle: Two turns of short-fibred medium red cock

Brian Harris suggests that it should also be fished unleaded, especially in the smaller sizes.

STICKFLY (Dave Collyer)

Hook: Longshank 8–10
Tying silk: Black or dark olive
Body: Dark cock-pheasant tail fibres and a few olive swan herls wound together over a varnished shank.
Rib: Copper, silver or gold tinsel, on their own or in combination, wound the opposite way to the body herls and then ribbed with green peacock herl
Thorax: Yellow or off-white floss silk
Hackle: Sparsely-tied pale ginger cock
Head: Varnished tying silk

STONEFLIES (*Plecoptera*)

Of the thirty or more members of the Plecoptera Order, the following stoneflies of interest to trout and grayling fishers: Large and medium stonefly, February Red, yellow sally, small yellow sally, willow fly, early brown, small brown and needle-flies.

As their name implies, these species prefer rivers with a stony or gravel bed and many of these are upland rather than lowland rivers. As stillwater flies their value is minimal, but of their great importance as a source of river trout and grayling food there is no doubt. On some rivers stonefly nymphs and adults take upon the same significance as the upwinged flies on other rivers. The nymph or creeper is so-called because the nymphs actually crawl out of the river before the adult fly emerges. The natural nymph is found only close to the river-bed, never rising to the surface to hatch as do the Ephemeroptera nymphs. The imitation should therefore be fished deep, where it gets the best results.

Nymphs crawling to the shore to emerge may well be caught up by the current and find themselves in midwater. When the adults are about one is much more likely to catch a fish on a nymph imitation fished nearer the surface. The nymphs are both carniverous and herbivorous and will often eat Ephemeroptera nymphs, which are generally smaller than stonefly nymphs. In addition to the difference in size, the stonefly nymphs have only two tails, whereas the Ephemeropterans have three.

The length of the adult stage varies from species to species, but it can extend from two or three days to a similar number of weeks. The adults have four hard, shiny wings which are long and narrow and which lie flat over the body at rest. The wings are frequently longer than the body in the females; the wings of the males are usually much shorter. The female adult returns to the water after mating to lay her eggs. With the exception of those detailed below, members of the Order are considered under their own names elsewhere.

LARGE STONEFLY (*Perlodes microcepala*)

The adults appear in April and May and are fairly common throughout the country. They are large, with the female adults 16–23 mm and the male 12–18 mm. They have mottled brown wings with a wingspan of about 50 mm (2-inches). The nymphs are correspondingly large, up to 28 mm.

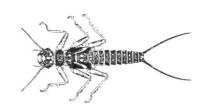

LARGE STONEFLY (*Perla bipuncta*)

The largest of the stoneflies, this is common except in the south and east. The adults appear between May and June and range in size between 16 mm and 24 mm, with a wingspan often in excess of 35 mm. The nymph reaches 33 mm in length.

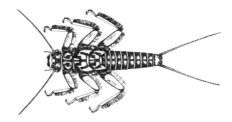

LARGE STONEFLY (*Perla cephalotes*)

A species similar to the one above. Together they are the largest stoneflies. Distribution is wide- spread. The adults are the same mottled brown colour and they appear in May and June.

MEDIUM STONEFLY (*Diura bicaudata*)

This is common in the localised areas of its distribution i.e. the Lake District, West Wales and Scotland. Small stony streams and stony lake margins are its habitat. The adults are between 10 and 14 mm and are mottled brown and appear from April until June. The nymphs vary between 9 and 17 mm.

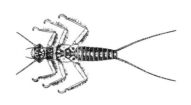

SMALL BROWNS (*Nemoura cinerea, Nemurella picteti*)

Similar to the early browns, but slightly slimmer and darker. The small browns prefer slow moving water. They appear from February to September.

In addition to the patterns below, see also under PARTRIDGE AND ORANGE (*page 141*), LIGHT WOOD-COCK (*page 100*), WINTER BROWN (*page 200*) and individual members of the Order.

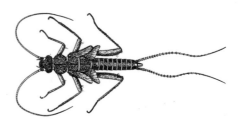

DARK CREEPER (Taff Price)

A nymph imitation.

Hook: Longshank 14
Tying silk: Brown
Body: Brown seal's fur
Rib: Yellow silk

Thorax: Dark hare's ear fur
Wing-case: Dark turkey fibres
Legs: Wing-case fibres turned beneath the body and trimmed

STONEFLY NYMPH (Dave Whitlock)

A North American pattern comes from one of that country's leading fly-tyers.

Hook: 10–14
Tying silk: Orange
Tail: Dark-brown or black horsehair
Abdomen: A mixture of 25 per cent dark brown seal's fur, 25 per cent golden-brown rabbit or beaver fur, 25 per cent burnt-orange seal's fur, 25 per cent dark amber seal's fur
Rib: Fine gold wire
Thorax: As for the abdomen, but more pronounced over a lead-wire underbody
Wing-case: Dark brown turkey fibres
Throat hackle: Grizzle-fibres dyed light brown

BROWN STONEFLY NYMPH (Roger Fogg)   Plate 15

This is a pattern weighted so that it fishes with the point facing upwards. It is excellent for getting down deep in those pools and runs where trout keep near the bottom.

Hook: 8–14
Tying silk: Brown
Body: Lead-foil strips tied on top of the shank. The remainder of the fly is dressed upside-down because of the way it is

presented in the water. The body is one of various shades of brown seal's fur (from amber to chocolate-brown) building up at the thorax.

Hackle: Palmered brown hen to match the body colour. The upper and lower fibres are trimmed away, leaving only the sides as legs. The top of the thorax is varnished to represent the wing-cases and to give added strength.

Rib: Nylon monofilament (about 4 lb b/s) over the body and hackle, or one strand of amber marabou floss silk

STONEFLY NYMPH   Plate 15

I have found this pattern extremely useful on rivers where natural stoneflies abound. It is so broadly impressionist that it represents most of the different nymph species. Different natural nymphs can be imitated by varying the size of the artificial.

Hook: 10–14
Tying silk: Dark brown

Tail: Stiff light-brown feather-fibres
Body: Hackle-stalk dyed brown, tapering to the rear
Thorax: An optional underbody of lead or copper wire covered with bronze peacock herl
Wing-case: Any brown feather-fibres
Leg hackle: Dark-brown partridge hackle tied fairly generously on the underside only

ADULT STONEFLY (John Veniard)   Plate 24

Hook: 14
Tying silk: Yellow
Body: Mixed hare's ear and yellow seal's fur
Rib: Yellow silk
Wing: Dark blue-dun hackle tip tied flat over the back
Hackle: Dark grizzle cock

I have resisted including the elaborate stonefly nymph patterns developed across the Atlantic. Fortunately, their use has not caught on here. They look realistic, but they are relatively difficult and time consuming to construct (I hesitate to say 'tie'). Some of them are fairly rigid and are more like models than fishing flies. One U.K. fly-tyer told me that he tied up one of these complex creations right down to the accurately-tinted latex wing-cases. It took so long to tie that he didn't dare use it in case he lost it!

STREAKER

The attractive combination of orange and black is used to good effect in this Syd Brock lure. The Streaker should be fished close to the bottom with a long, steady retrieve. Later in the season, when orange flies are generally more popular, it takes at all depths.

Hook: Longshank 6–10

Tying silk: Black
Tail: Black squirrel
Body: Black wool or black plastic strip wound on
Rib: Silver or stiff white plastic tape
Wing: Black squirrel with an overwing or orange cock fibres tied as long as the squirrel fibres
Throat hackle: Orange cock tied about half the body-length

STREAMERS

These lures of North American origin became popular with the steady growth of reservoir trout fishing in the U.K. The winging material is the saddle hackle of domestic and game-cocks, both natural and (more frequently) dyed. Some patterns have herl or hair overwings in addition to the whole feather-wings. The wing sometimes becomes caught up under the hook-bend during casting, so the lure is not fished effectively. This is one reason for the development of bucktail and marabou as winging materials.

Two feathers are tied back-to-back at the shoulder to extend beyond the bend of the hook. Four feather-wings are often an improvement on two.

They are tied by stripping away the soft flue at the base and doubling back the stalk over itself to form the head. This makes a much more durable wing. In addition the stalk can be varnished or glued for greater strength.

STURDY'S FANCY

This Yorkshire grayling fly is best fished dry. Reg Righyni, author of *Grayling*, includes this as one of his favourite flies, although he ties it with a close rib of crimson silk. He has suggested that Sturdy evolved the pattern for evening fishing when spinners were on the water, and therefore the red glint suggested by

the rib is not out of place. I rate this as my first-choice fancy dry fly for when no naturals are on the water. I have also caught dozens of trout with it.

Hook: 14–16
Tag: Red wool
Body: Peacock herl
Hackle: White cock or hen

SUNK SPINNER

The medium olive, large and small dark olives and iron blue female spinners all return to lay their eggs under the surface. Trout often feed upon these even when duns or the spinners of other species are on the surface. If fish are feeding and the usual floating patterns and nymphs fail, then a more specialised imitation may be required. This imitation, which should be fished upstream in a straight drift, was devised by Neil Patterson.

Hook: 12–16

Tying silk: Crimson
Tail and rib: Two hare's whiskers or white horsehair
Underbody: Dark-red enamel copper wire with a built-up thorax
Overbody: Flattened nylon monofilament (6 lb b/s) ribbed with one hare's whisker
Thorax: Cock-pheasant tail fibres
Wing: Two turns of badger hackle trimmed above and below the hook to represent the spent wing. The thorax fibres are doubled and redoubled over the hackle to build up the thorax. A dab of varnish at the base of the tail keeps the two hairs well apart

SWEENEY TODD

This successful and popular lure was devised by Richard Walker and Peter Thomas. The former wrote that if he had to be limited to just one stillwater fly, this would be it. An extra-long wing about twice the hook-length is one variation. This is not a hindrance to hooking, as Richard Walker points out that the fluorescent wool at the shoulder seems to be the trouts' aiming point. Other variations have

been devised. See under NOBBLERS (*page 127*).

Hook: Longshank 6–14
Tying silk: Black
Body: Black floss
Rib: Flat silver tinsel
Throat: Two or three turns of DF neon-magenta wool tied behind the wing roots
Wing: Black squirrel-tail for the smaller sizes, black bucktail for the larger
Beard hackle: Crimson hackle-fibres

TADPOLES

In May many lake margins and shallows are black with newly-hatched tadpoles. What a banquet they represent! I have caught trout as fat as pigs, bulging with tadpoles after feeding on them to the exclusion of all else.

Tadpoles rarely venture into deep water, and the artificial is best employed in the margins. See also BLACK AND PEACOCK SPIDER (*page 15*) and DAWN-AND-DUSK LURE (*page 49*) for other patterns.

TADPOLE   Plate 5

A lure devised by John Wadham but popularised by Gordon Fraser. The black version looks like a tadpole. In Gordon Fraser's words, it is 'A gentleman's version of the Dog Nobbler'. Black or white versions are best early in the season, with orange or yellow dressings more useful as the season progresses. Other colours and fluorescent versions should not be ruled out. Leaded patterns will catch most fish during the early season.

Hook: Wide-gape 6–8
Tying silk: Waxed black
Tail: Generous plume of black marabou or Arctic fox
Body: Black chenille, with optional underbody of fine lead wire
Hackle (optional): Three turns of black hen

TADPOLE STREAMER (Taff Price)

Hook: Longshank 12
Tying silk: Black
Body: Black chenille tied fat, or spun and clipped black dyed deerhair over a copper-wire underbody

Wing: Two black hen hackles tied in at the tail back-to-back
Hackle: Sparse black hen tied in at the rear of the body

TADPOLLY   Plate 12

This is a John Goddard pattern. A buoyant version is tied with an Ethafoam ball which is slit to the centre, glued to the shank, coloured with black indelible felt-pen and covered with peacock herl. It should be fished with a fast-sinking line and retrieved with a long draw with a pause which will cause the fly to dive to the bottom and rise slowly.

Hook: 10–12
Tying silk: Black
Body: A ball of black seal's fur tied towards the front of the shank and covered with bronze peacock herl
Tail: Black marabou or three black hackle points

TEAL SERIES

A series of lake and sea-trout flies. The combination of colours is broadly similar to those in the Mallard, Grouse and Woodcock series, all of which differ in the main only in their wing material. Most of the patterns are listed in the MALLARD SERIES (*page 102*), but the exceptions are given below. The wing material is the black and white barred teal flank or breast-feather. See also PETER ROSS (*page 145*).

TEAL, BLUE AND SILVER Plate 16

This enjoys greater visibility than the others in the series, and for this reason is more effective in slightly-coloured water. It succeeds as a small fry-imitation and should be fished fast on the point.

Hook: 8–14
Tail: Golden-pheasant tippets
Body: Flat silver tinsel
Rib: Fine silver wire
Wing: Teal flank feather
Hackle: Bright-blue cock

TEAL AND CLARET

Tail: Golden-pheasant tippets
Body: Claret seal's fur or dubbed wool
Rib: Gold tinsel

Wing: Teal breast feather
Hackle: Claret cock or hen

TEAL AND GREEN

Probably of early nineteenth-century Scottish origin, developed for the lochs. It is very likely taken for a sedge or shrimp, depending upon how it is fished. I have caught only two trout on this pattern. It seems to be one of those I pass over in favour of a more imitative dressing.

Tail: Golden-pheasant tippets
Body: Green seal's fur or dubbed wool
Rib: Oval silver tinsel
Wing: Teal breast feather
Hackle: Light red hen

TEAL AND MIXED

Tail: Golden-pheasant tippets
Body: One-third each of yellow, red and blue seal's fur. Other combinations should as a rule have the darkest colour at the front and the lightest at the tail
Rib: Silver or gold tinsel
Wing: Teal breast
Hackle: Black cock or hen

TERRY'S TERROR

Devised by Dr Cecil Terry and Ernest Lock. It is said to represent all the olive duns, in its smaller sizes the iron blue dun, and in its larger sizes a sedge. Dave Collyer writes in *Fly Dressing II* that it is a useful dry fly on big reservoirs when fished on the edge of a ripple. Peter Deane rates it highly as a wet fly.

Hook: 10–16
Tag: Mixed orange and yellow goathair trimmed short
Body: One strand of peacock herl
Rib: Flat copper tinsel
Hackle: Fox-red cock

TERRORS

Two tandem lures. The **Blue Terror** has a wing of two blue cock hackles flanked by strips of grey drake fibres.

RED TERROR

Rear hook
Tail: Red fluorescent wool
Body: Flat silver tinsel

Rib: Silver wire

Front hook
Body and rib: As for the rear
Wing: Two dyed red hackles tied back-to- back and flanked by swan herls dyed red with strands of green peacock herl over

TOM'S TERROR
Plate 9

This pattern was devised by Tom Saville. He describes it as an excellent lure for rainbow trout when they are fry-feeding. He also comments that the lure is selling well – a sure sign that it is catching fish!

Hook: 8 (Mustad 9672 is recommended)

Body: Silver Mylar tubing
Wing: Black bucktail with orange over
Throat hackle: White bucktail
Eyes: Thin slice of white electric flex with the wire removed, stuck on to the wet varnish.

TRAFFIC LIGHTS
Plate 1

A number of tandem lures have been devised to be fished deep behind a boat on some of the Midlands reservoirs. This one is recommended for Rutland. It was developed by Tom Saville. The reason for its name is self-evident.

Hooks: Longshank 6 (Mustad 9672 recommended)

Front hook

Tail: Arc-chrome DRF wool
Body and rib: As for the rear
Wing: As for the rear
Cheeks: Neon-magenta DRF wool
Throat hackle: Black

Rear hook

Tail: Signal-green DRF wool
Body: Medium black chenille
Rib: Oval silver tinsel
Wing: Black marabou

TRAIN'S TERRORS

Two tandem lures devised by David Train. The **Olive Terror** is a useful perch-fry imitation. Its dressing is as below but with black hackle wings substituted for olive.

Rear hook

Tail: Golden-pheasant tippets in a fan-shape
Body: Silver tinsel
Rib: Silver wire

Front hook

Body and rib: As for rear
Hackle: Hen dyed red
Wing: Three or four peacock sword herls flanked by two black cock hackles extending to the rear of the rear hook

TREACLE PARKIN
Plate 27

A northern variation of the Red Tag. It is fished both wet and dry, but is probably better as a dry fly than a wet. It is a good trout fly but it is as a grayling fly that it excels. Norman Roose, president of the Grayling Society, tied it with a tag of DRF arc-chrome wool. An afternoon's fishing with it on the Test resulted in sixteen grayling being caught.

Hook: 14–16
Rag: Orange or yellow wool
Body: Peacock herl
Hackle: Natural red-game

TUBE FLIES

Tube flies traditionally have belonged to the salmon-fisher, but reservoir boat anglers have been using them with heavy lines to fish deep down. Treble hooks are always used, so these flies may be prohibited on some waters.

The tube may be brass, aluminium, polythene or hard nylon according to the weight needed. The length of tube can be varied to offer different sizes of fly (and different weights). The tube is given a layer of black tying silk, finishing about 3 mm (⅛-inch) from the tube end. This is covered with the body floss and the tinsel rib is wound on. Bunches of the hairwing material are tied-in in sufficient quantity to go 360 degrees round the body. The wing should extend well beyond the end of the tube so that the treble hook is almost covered. Finally, a hackle (optional) is tied-in at the front of the tube. The leader is threaded through the front of the tube and tied on to a treble hook which is pulled up to the rear end of the tube body.

The treble may be given a matching long-fibred collar hackle.

Virtually any reservoir fly can be adapted to a tube dressing, but colour combinations recommended by Freddie Rice are:

Body	Rib	Wing	Head hackle
Black floss	Oval gold	Orange bucktail	Hot-orange
Black floss	Oval gold	Brown bucktail	Blue gallena
Yellow floss	Flat silver	Brown bucktail	Black
Teal blue floss	Flat silver	Black squirrel	Badger
Scarlet floss	Oval gold	Natural squirrel	Hot-orange

TUP'S INDISPENSABLE   Plate 28

R. S. Austin tied this classic fly in 1900, but it was left to G. E. M. Skues to put a name to the dressing. The dubbing material was kept a secret until 1934, twenty years after Austin's death, so that he, and later his daughter, had the monopoly in the supply of the correct dressing. Many imitations and substitutes have been used in the absence of the original material, some hideously corrupting the fly.

The unlikely dubbing material was first used by Alexander Mackintosh and publicised in his book, *The Driffield Angler*, 1806. Mackintosh's Greendrake pattern had this instruction: 'Take a little fine wool from the ram's testicles, which is a beautiful dusty yellow.' Austin tied the Tup's to represent the Red Spinner, the female spinner of some of the olives. Today it is probably fished as a copy of a pale watery spinner and a small spurwing spinner. Nymph patterns and many variations have been developed. The original dressing is:

Hook: 16
Tying silk: Yellow
Tail: Yellow-spangled lightish blue cock hackle fibres
Body: Mixed white fur from a ram's testicle, lemon-coloured fur from a spaniel, cream seal's fur and a small amount of yellow mohair. The last item was later replaced by crimson seal's fur on Skues' suggestion. A small tip of tying silk is exposed at the rear
Hackle: Yellow-spangled lightish-blue cock

TUP'S (Taff Price)

A dressing using modern substitutes.

Hook: 12–16
Tail: Honey-dun cock fibres
Body: Rear-half, yellow floss silk with a thorax of a mixture of yellow, red and honey-coloured seal's fur
Hackle: Honey-dun cock

TUP'S NYMPH (J. Leisenring)

Hook: 14
Tying silk: Claret or crimson
Body: Primrose marabou silk
Thorax: Mixed claret and yellow seal's fur
Hackle: Short-fibred light-blue or medium-dark honey-dun hen

DARK TUP'S (Dave Collyer)

Hook: 10–16
Tail: Fibres of the hackle used
Body: Rear two-thirds, lemon floss silk; front one-third, mole's fur
Hackle: Stiff honey-dun cock or light ginger cock
See also Tup's Pensioner under PEN-SIONERS (*page 143*).

TURKEY GREEN/YELLOW

These two patterns came to me with Steve Parton's comment that 'These flies could be described as reduced versions of an Invicta and Green Peter. Be that as it may, there is no doubt that they work.' I believe that it is because they do have the look of an Invicta or Green Peter that they do work so well. If any fly can match the trout-catching capability of these two, then it is a real winner. Both are hatching-sedge imitations and are best fished semi-submerged in the surface film or just below it. They represent a number of sedges, but Steve recommends that their time on Rutland comes in late June.

Hook: 10–14
Tying silk: Black
Body: Naples yellow or Green Highlander seal's fur with a palmered red-game hackle
Rib: Oval gold tinsel through the hackle
Wing: Oak turkey or owl substitute
Throat hackle: Red-game

THE TWITCHER   Plate 18

The deerhair Muddler head has in-spired many other patterns which have been evolved from the original minnow. This is one of the smaller non-lure offspring. It was created by Stan Headley to represent a range of insects in their vulnerable hatching-out phase. The Muddler head keeps the fly high in the water and produces that noticeable water-surface bulge which seems attractive to feeding fish.

Stan advises that it should not be fished in conjunction with large or heavy patterns as they sink the Twitcher from its best working area, the surface film. It seems unimportant that the colours do not match specific hatching species. Stan has had big baskets of fish during black and green midge hatches. I've had trout take it during a hatch of sedge. In calm conditions twitch the fly across the nose of a rising fish and prepare for action.

Hook: 12–14
Tying silk: Black
Body: White-phase blue mountain hare's ear fur well picked out (or rabbit's ear fur)
Rib: Fine gold wire

Hackle: Brown partridge hackle
Head: Deerhair spun and trimmed so that the hackle looks part of the head rather than separate, i.e. trim the head short at the eye, then steeply back to meet the hackle

TWITCHITT NYMPH

Plate 11

A variation of the Pheasant Tail Nymph devised by Alan Pearson. He advises that it should be fished 'as a single nymph to observed cruising trout; otherwise as a point fly on a team comprising two buzzer patterns in addition, or as a point fly on a team of wet flies for loch-style fishing'.

Hook: Longshank 12
Tail: Signal-green fluorescent wool or floss, teased out and not less than 6 mm (¼-inch) long
Body: Cock pheasant centre tail fibres
Rib (optional): Copper wire
Thorax: Fine lead or copper wire overlaid with pale grey rabbit's fur. This should be tied for about half the body-length, slim and barely thicker than the body
Hackle: Rear-sloping ginger cock as a collar

UNDERTAKER

Plate 8

This variation of the Baby Doll is successful when fished over a range of depths and at different rates of retrieve.

Hook: Longshank 6–8

Tying silk: Black
Body: Black wool, with an optional lead-foil underbody
Rib: Narrow silver tinsel
Back and tail: Black wool

USD PARADUNS

A series of upside-down floating patterns (together with the USD POLY-SPINNERS, *see below*) devised jointly by Brian Clarke and John Goddard. They are claimed as relatively new products of the continuing evolution of the British trout fly, but similar American and British dressings for duns had been around before Goddard and Clarke publicised their dressings. C. F. Walker's *Fly-Tying as an Art* of 1957 mentions and illustrates J. H. Stothert's **Upside-downer** which appears to be a USD Paradun by another name. Although the dressing is not given, the only variation seems to be that the wings are feather-slips and not the hackle-tips recommended by Goddard and Clarke. See also the STALKING FLY (*page 179*).

The design of the USD Paradun is such that it floats upside-down (hence the name) with the hook-point in the air. The Parachute hackle is wound on the top of the shank, which ultimately becomes the underside. The hackle-tip wings are cut slightly wider and longer than standard wings and are tied on the opposite side of the shank to the hackle and given a pronounced outward curve. Almost any dry fly can be tied in such a manner. The dressing is an improvement on the standard dressing of most flies, but it is difficult to tie and not as durable. Most fish do not need a USD pattern to tempt them, but it may just be the answer for the occasional difficult fish.

USD PARA-BLUE-WINGED OLIVE

Hook: 12–16
Tying silk: Orange
Tail: Three olive muskrat or mink whiskers; or a bunch of the hackle fibres

Body: Natural heron herl
Wing: Dark-grey or dark blue-dun hackle tips
Hackle: Rusty-dun cock

USD PARA-OLIVE

Hook: 12–16
Tying silk: Brown
Tail: Two olive muskrat or mink whiskers; or a bunch of the hackle fibres

Body: Olive heron herl
Wing: Pale blue-dun hackle tips
Hackle: Olive cock

USD PARA-PALE WATERY

Hook: 16
Tying silk: Yellow
Tail: Pale-honey hackle fibres

Body: Greyish goose primary herls
Wing: Cream or pale blue-dun hackle tips
Hackle: Rusty-dun cock

USD POLY-SPINNERS

These patterns are tied upside-down on keel hooks. The Parachute hackle is tied on top of the body on the bend nearest the eye and the wings are tied in the same position. Except on the larger Mayfly spinners, the wings are of fine-gauge clear polythene cut with a wing-cutter. The polythene should be lightly pierced many times with a thick but sharp needle. The wings are tied in the spent position.

USD MAYFLY SPINNER

Hook: Longshank keel 10
Tying silk: Yellow
Tail: Three dark pheasant tail fibres
Body: White polypropylene fibres
Rib: Black monocord or doubled silk

Hackle: Two turns of hot-orange cock on either side of the wings. This is a conventional hackle, not a Parachute one
Wing: Grizzle hackle-points tied spent

USD POLY-ORANGE SPINNER

Hook: Keel 14
Tying silk: Orange
Tail: Three muskrat or mink whiskers coloured brown

Body: Orange seal's fur
Rib: DFM orange floss
Wing: Polythene (see introduction)
Hackle: Bright ginger cock

USD POLY-PHEASANT TAIL SPINNER

Hook: Keel 12–14
Tying silk: Orange
Tail: Two muskrat or mink whiskers coloured pale brown

Body: Pheasant tail fibres
Wing: Polythene (see introduction)
Hackle: Rusty-dun cock

USD POLY-RED SPINNER

Hook: Keel 12–16
Tying silk: Brown
Tail: Two pale blue muskrat or mink whiskers

Body: Red seal's fur
Wing: Polythene (see introduction)
Hackle: Pale blue-dun cock

USD POLY-SHERRY SPINNER

Hook: Keel 14
Tying silk: Orange
Tail: Three pale brown muskrat or mink whiskers
Body: Orange and green seal's fur mixed with hare's poll fur

Rib: Fine gold wire
Wing: Polythene (see introduction)
Hackle: Pale-honey cock with a dark centre

Two terrestrial patterns are also tied in the USD style:

USD BLACK GNAT

Hook: Keel 16
Tying silk: Black
Body: Cock-pheasant tail fibres dyed black
Wing: A single wing cut from clear polythene. It should be longer than the hook. It is impaled on the hook-point and worked half-way down the bend to rest on top of the rear of the body. The other end is tied in at the head end of the body at the bend nearest the eye. The wing is doubly secured at each end

Hackle: Black tied in the normal manner, not Parachute

USD HAWTHORN

Hook: Keel 12
Tying silk: Black
Body: Five or six black ostrich herls
Rib: Nylon monofilament (4 lb b/s)
Legs: Two knotted pheasant-tail fibres dyed black and tied in front of the body at the rear of the short shank before the eye

Wing: Two clear polythene wings tied in on top of the body, a third of the way back from the eye, and set at a slight angle apart and slightly upwards
Hackle: Black cock tied in the normal manner, not Parachute

VARIANTS

This is the term applied to dry flies which have much longer-fibred hackles than the standard dressings. The flies may be existing named patterns or nondescript general floating flies. Dr Baigent, of Northallerton, brought them into prominence with his series of Variants around the turn of the century, and other patterns have been added since. Winged patterns have the wings tied fairly small and thin, and sloping forward slightly over the eye.

BAIGENT'S BROWN

Hook: 14
Body: Yellow floss

Wing: Hen-pheasant wing
Hackle: Long-fibred stiff furnace cock

BAIGENT'S BLACK

Hook: 14
Body: Black floss

Rib: Peacock herl
Hackle: Long-fibred stiff black cock

BAIGENT'S LIGHT

Hook: 14
Body: Stripped peacock quill

Hackle: Long-fibred stiff light blue-dun cock

192

BLUE VARIANT (E. C. Coombes)

Hook: 14
Tying silk: Pale yellow
Tail: Light-blue cock fibres

Body: Blue fur
Rib: Tying silk
Hackle: Long-fibred light blue-dun cock

GOLD VARIANT (John Veniard)

Hook: 14
Body: Flat gold tinsel
Wing: Starling wing

Hackle: Long-fibred medium blue-dun cock

VIVA   Plate 5

An excellent lure which works best in the marabou-winged version. It is particularly useful during the first two months of the season. On a number of occasions I have seen anglers using all-black lures without success when a Viva has been fished with great effect. The fluorescent green tag is vital. I fish a variation which has a large tip of fluorescent pink Dollybody which replaces the green on the standard Viva. Both patterns are best fished fairly slowly.

Hook: Longshank 6–10
Tying silk: Black
Tag: Green fluorescent wool (tied as a tag or as a large tip)
Body: Black chenille
Rib: Silver tinsel
Wing: Four black cock hackles or black marabou plume
Throat hackle: Black cock

WASP

Dame Juliana Berners tied an imitation of this insect in the fifteenth century. I suspect it is rarely used today as a dry fly for trout, but it is a chub fly of some repute. The natural grub of the wasp is an excellent chub bait, and I imagine that where the wasp grub becomes available to trout, they, too, will take it eagerly.

WASP GRUB

Hook: 8
Body: Lead or copper-wire underbody covered with dirty off-white wool or cream seal's fur, tapering at each end
Head: Peacock herl

WASP FLY

Hook: 10–12
Body: Dark-brown hair and black rabbit's fur mixed with a little mohair
Rib: Thick yellow thread

Wing: Grey mallard tied flat across the back
Hackle: Black cock, or the body fibres well picked out

WATCHETS

These old and reliable northern wet flies are typical of the soft-hackled spider-type of flies associated with this part of the country. They imitate mainly the emerging nymphs and drowned duns and spinners of the iron blue. Most traditional wet flies used by northern anglers are more than a hundred years old, even two hundred, and modern materials and fly-tying styles have failed to improve these most basic imitations. Any of the variations below will prove a dependable pattern for trout and grayling on northern streams.

DARK WATCHET (T. E. Pritt)   Plate 20

Hook: 14–16
Body: Orange tying silk dubbed with mole's fur
Hackle: Waterhen breast feather
Head: Peacock herl

DARK WATCHET (Edmonds and Lee)

Hook: 14
Body: Orange and purple tying silks twisted together and thinly dubbed with mole's fur
Hackle: Jackdaw throat feather

LIGHT WATCHET   Plate 20

Hook: 12–16
Body: Straw-coloured silk
Hackle: Golden plover or starling

LITTLE DARK WATCHET

Hook: 14–16
Body: Orange and purple tying silks twisted together and dubbed with water-rat's fur
Hackle: A feather from the outside of a coot's wing
Head: Orange tying silk

WATER CRICKET   Plate 12

This small aquatic beetle is more common on lakes than on rivers. The adult has a dark brown body with two orange stripes down the back. The underside is orange.

Hook: 12–14
Body: Orange floss
Back: Any dark brown feather-fibres
Hackle: Brown partridge

WATERHEN AND RED

A Scottish wet fly. The first version is from W. H. Lawrie, who sums up the pattern as 'reliable'; the second pattern is listed by Taff Price in *Rough Stream Trout Flies*.

Hook: 14
Tail: Golden-pheasant tippets

Body: Red wool
Rib: Gold or silver fine tinsel or wire
Wing: Waterhen wing
Hackle: Natural red hen
Or
Body: Red silk
Hackle: The spoon-shaped feather of a waterhen (moorhen) wing

WATER-LOUSE

The water-louse is prolific throughout the country on stillwaters and to a lesser extent on rivers. It is usually found on decaying vegetable matter in shallow water, always near the bottom, or on stakes going into the water. The adults reach about 15 mm in length and move slowly. The artificial should be fished near the bottom in a similar fashion. The water-louse is also known as the hog-louse or water slater. A March Brown is a suitable imitation.

WATER-LOUSE (Peter Gathercole)

Hook: 10–12
Body: Grey rabbit's fur with a short-fibred brown partridge hackle laid over the back and ribbed with silver wire
Back: Grey-brown feather-fibres
Tail: A few back fibres sticking out as a tail
Antennae (optional): Two brown feather-fibres

WATER-LOUSE (Geoffrey Bucknall)

A variant on a dressing from C. F. Walker.

Hook: 14
Legs: Grey partridge hackles tied in two bunches in the spent position at the rear of the body
Body: Pale-olive or any neutral shade of seal's fur or wool
Rib: Very fine oval silver tinsel

WATER TIGER   Plate 11

A pattern devised by Dave Collyer to imitate the great diving beetle, a largish aquatic beetle up to 30 mm long which inhabits the shallower areas of lakes and reservoirs. It rises periodically to the surface to take air. It is sufficiently aggressive even to attack small fish. Aquatic beetles often feature in trout autopsies, but few patterns are tied specifically to represent them. Terrestrial beetle patterns often work when fished near the lake-bed. See also WATER CRICKET (*page 194*).

Hook: Longshank 8–10
Tail: Speckled turkey-tail fibres or condor herl dyed sepia
Body: As tail
Rib: Copper wire
Thorax: Yellowish-olive seal's fur or wool

Wing-case: Body fibres
Hackle: Two bunches of brown partridge feather-fibres, one either side of the head and rear-slanting just beyond the thorax

The second pattern of Water Tiger is that devised and tied by Sid Knight. It was tied originally on a longshank 10 hook, but most anglers prefer the standard length hook. Additional weight to enable the fly to be fished deep down is optional.

Hook: 10
Tying silk: Brown
Tail: Natural red cock hackle fibres
Body: Green peacock herl tapering to the rear
Rib: Brown silk
Thorax: Green peacock herl built up
Wing-case: Mottled-brown feather-fibres
Hackle: Natural red cock

WATSON'S FANCY   Plate 17

An old Scottish loch and sea-trout pattern that is still popular in its home country.

Hook: 8–14
Tail: Small golden-pheasant crest feather
Body: Rear half, red seal's fur; front half, black seal's fur
Rib: Silver tinsel
Wing: Crow wing with a small jungle-cock eye at either side
Hackle: Black hen

WELSHMAN'S BUTTON

The name Welshman's Button has been applied to a species of sedge and to a beetle. The beetle was the first to take the name in a book *The Angler's Museum* by Thomas Shirley in 1784, but because Halford and Lunn

195

applied the name to two species of sedge, with much greater publicity, the name has become more associated with the sedge. Patterns for the sedge are given under SEDGE-FLIES (*pages 157–170*).

WELSH PARTRIDGE

A fancy pattern by this name is listed by Courtney Williams, but I suspect that its use is now somewhat infrequent. However, I include a variation of the pattern as suggested by Roger Fogg, who has found it eagerly taken by stillwater rainbows when fished as a top dropper at the beginning and end of the trout season.

Hook: 12–14
Tying silk: Claret
Tail: Pheasant tippets
Body: Purple seal's fur roughly dubbed
Rib: Fine oval gold tinsel
Hackle: Mixed hackle of dark brown partridge back feather and dark crimson hen

WESTWARD BUG

Devised specifically to take the large Avington trout, this pattern has done well also on other small, well-stocked fisheries. The weighted underbody is important as it allows the bug to sink rapidly. Takes often come on the drop.

Hook: Standard or longshank 8–12

Tying silk: Black
Body: Brown marabou fibres tied fat and wound over lead strips or wire underbody
Rib: Orange floss
Back: Shellback-brown or grey feather-fibres
Throat hackle: Honey-coloured cock

WHISKERS   Plate 6

There are scores of variations on the marabou-winged or marabou-tailed lure. The colour permutations are endless. Because the marabou action is so effective, it doesn't take much skill either to devise or to tie these lures. Whiskers is my variation on the theme, the whiskers being the addition of a fluorescent cat's whisker style head of wool or Dollybody. The lures may be unleaded or may incorporate a small underbody of lead wire towards the front of the shank. My most successful versions are black or white with fluorescent-pink whiskers. The method of tying in the

whiskers is to take a length or wool or Dollybody after the body and rib are finished and to push this over the eye of the hook so that the latter sticks through the middle of the fibres. The material is then bound on so that the two ends stick out sideways and can be trimmed to the appropriate length.

Hook: Longshank 8–12
Tying silk: To match the body colour
Tail: White or black marabou plumes
Body: White or black chenille
Rib: Silver wire or oval tinsel
Whiskers: Pink Dollybody or fluorescent wool
Head: Black or white, varnished

WHISKY FLY   Plates 9 & 18

This excellent lure was devised by Albert Willock for Hanningfield reservoir, but it has subsequently caught many big rainbow trout across the country. It is best fished fast near the surface during the second half of the season, although it seems to catch fish at a variety of speeds and depths.

It is a useful pattern for water affected by algae or when daphnia are in evidence. The original pattern had a Sellotape body, but this is not very durable when wet.

Hook: Longshank 6–10
Tying silk: Red or scarlet fluorescent floss
Body: Flat silver or gold Mylar or Lurex with a butt of scarlet or red fluorescent floss
Rib: Scarlet or red fluorescent floss. The whole body is clear varnished
Wing: Hot-orange calf-tail tied as long as the body

Throat hackle: Hot-orange cock
Head: Longish head of fluorescent tying silk

Various versions have been tied with one or more of the following combinations included: Jungle-cock cheeks; an orange floss body ribbed with gold tinsel and covered with polythene strip; or wings of four hot-orange cock hackles tied back-to-back. See also Whisky Muddler under MUDDLERS (*page 122*). It is a measure of the pattern's success that so many variations have developed.

WHITE AND ORANGE LURE

This is one of Steve Parton's lures.

Hook: Longshank 6–10
Body: White chenille
Rib: Oval silver tinsel
Wing: Arctic fox tail
Throat hackle: Orange cock

WHITE LURES

There are many different white lure dressings in addition to the white lures known by other names. Three of the better-known patterns are given.

See also under MARABOU-WINGED LURE (*page 104*) for Steve Parton's unnamed white lure.

WHITE MARABOU (Bob Carnill)   Plate 5

A useful all-season lure. Bob Carnill fishes it during spring on a fast-sink shooting-head and in the summer and autumn on a floating line. He suggests experiment with the rate of retrieve to determine what the trout prefer. Not all lures lend themselves to this approach, but the White Marabou is particularly suited, being both lightly built and highly mobile. Any retrieve from a figure-of-eight to a fast strip can be employed with confidence.

Hook: Longshank 4–10
Tying silk: Waxed red
Tail: Fluorescent white Bri-nylon baby wool
Body: Fluorescent white chenille
Rib: Flat silver tinsel
Beard hackle: Scarlet cock fibres
Wing: White marabou extending just beyond the tail

WHITE MARABOU TANDEM (Bob Church and M. Nicholls)

Hooks: Longshank 6–10
Tying silk: Black

Front hook

Body: As for rear
Wing: A large plume of white marabou
Head: Natural deerhair spun and clipped in Muddler-style and trimmed to a dome-shape

Rear hook

Tail and body: White Sirdar Baby wool

WHITE LURE (R. French)

Hooks: Longshank 8

Front hook

Body and rib: As for rear
Hackle: Scarlet cock
Wing: White bucktail tied at the shoulder and a middle wing tied in at the rear of the body of the front hook.
Head: Varnished black with painted eyes

Rear hook

Tail: White DFM wool
Body: Silver or gold Lurex
Rib: Fine silver or gold tinsel
Wing: White bucktail

WHITE NYMPHS

I have selected two of the four white nymph imitations. A fly-tyer with a little imagination could easily de-velop other variants. See also nymph patterns under CAENIS.

WHITE NYMPH (Roger Fogg)   Plate 15

Roger Fogg suggests that this pattern should be fished no more than a foot below the surface. Because of its translucency, it is also a suitable Phantom Midge pupa imitation. It seems to attract more brown trout than rainbows. Roger writes: 'This is an extremely killing pattern. I gave up using it in 1983 because it caught too many fish too easily!'

Hook: 10–14
Tying silk: White
Tail: White rabbit guard-hairs or white feather-fibres
Body: Underbody of silver Mylar or tinsel with an overbody of loosely-dubbed white rabbit's fur
Rib: Fine oval silver tinsel
Hackle: Two turns of small white hen

WHITE NYMPH (Wallace)   Plate 15

A Scottish pattern which originated on Loch Leven.

Hook: 10–12
Tying silk: White
Tail: White wool

Body: White wool
Rib: Silver tinsel
Thorax: Hen-pheasant centre tail fibres
Beard hackle: Hot-orange

WHITMORE'S FANCY   Plate 25

I doubt if this pattern is known beyond a few of the members of York Fly Fishers' Club. It is an excellent general dry fly tied by one of the club's members, Harry Whitmore, and it has killed scores of trout on the rivers of the Yorkshire Dales and moors. Its success justifies its in-clusion here.

Hook: 12–14
Tying silk: Red
Tail: Medium natural red cock fibres
Body: Bronze peacock herl
Rib: Red silk
Hackle: Medium natural red cock wound in Parachute style

WHOGSTOPPER

Plate 4

A Muddler variation devised by Steve Parton. The extra deerhair at the tail enables it to be stripped through the surface without the rear of the fly dropping down at the end of each pull. It fishes level in the water. There is no doubt that it is a lure, but Steve tells me that it can be fished in a totally different manner by greasing it and fishing it as a giant dry fly when sedges start mating. In these circumstances it works best as a static fly, but on occasions, particularly in calm water, it pays to twitch it along fairly steadily. Many Muddler variations are included elsewhere, so I have filed this one under its alternative use.

Hook: 4X longshank
Tail and butt: Spun deerhair trimmed to shape
Body: Copper-coloured Lurex
Rib: Copper wire
Underwing: Grey squirrel or timber wolf
Wing: Oak turkey or substitute
Head: Deerhair spun and trimmed to shape

WICKHAM'S FANCY

This fly, probably devised in the 1880s, has obscure origins, with at least two Wickhams claiming to have invented it. G. E. M. Skues knew Dr T. C. Wickham and regarded him as the originator. The pattern can be fished wet or dry, the latter more commonly on rivers and the former on stillwaters, where it is best fished slowly in the surface film and is probably taken for a sedge pupa. The dry pattern is good when trout and grayling are smutting and are refusing artificials of the natural smuts. Indeed, the Wickham's has always been considered a useful fly for just those circumstances.

Hook: 14–16
Tying silk: Brown
Tail: Guinea-fowl dyed reddish-brown, or ginger hackles
Body: Flat gold tinsel
Rib: Gold wire
Body hackle: Palmered ginger-red cock
Wing: Medium starling wings set upright and split for the floating dressing, or across the back in wet style for the wet fly
Hackle: Ginger-red cock

OLIVE WICKHAM'S

As for the Wickham's Fancy, but with an olive cock hackle for the body and head hackle and tail fibres.

PINK WICKHAM'S

Francis Francis's variant of the original. Courtney Williams describes it as 'A capital fly'. The starling wing is replaced by a landrail wing and modern dressings also include a pink floss body.

WIGGLE-NYMPH

John Goddard has suggested this unusual and effective nymph dressing for some of the larger stillwater nymphs. The second half of the body wiggles seductively as the fly is retrieved. Damsel nymph patterns are particularly suited to this dressing as the natural damsel nymph moves with a pronounced wiggle. The rear hook is dressed with the tail of the fly and the entire bend is clipped off and discarded. The two parts are connected by threading fine fuse wire through the eye of the rear section and whipping it on to the bare shank of the front hook before dressing it.

DAMSEL WIGGLE NYMPH (John Goddard) Plate 11

Hooks: Two straight-eyed standard 10–12
Tying silk: Brown
Tail: Three ginger-grizzle hackle tips
Body: Mixed golden-olive and brown seal's fur along the rear hook and on the rear half of the front hook.
Rib: Close rib of fine oval silver tinsel

Thorax: Rusty-brown seal's fur
Thorax cover: Mottled mid-brown feather-fibres
Hackle: Brown partridge feather.
 Other general nymph patterns can be imitated by altering the materials.

WILLOW FLY (*Leuctra geniculata*)

One of the few common chalk-stream stoneflies (see *page 180*). Elsewhere it is widely distributed, except in East Anglia. The nymphs prefer rivers with stony-bottoms over a sandy base. The adults are slim flies of 7–10 mm long with brownish wings and two long antennae. They appear between August and November. A few sources refer to them as appearing on stillwaters, but most list them exclusively as river flies.

 For other suitable imitations, see BROWN OWL (*page 28*), NEEDLE-FLY (*page 126*) and PARTRIDGE AND ORANGE (*page 141*).

WILLOW FLY (Taff Price)

Hook: 14
Tying silk: Orange
Body: Peacock herl dyed orange

Wing: Two small medium-grizzle hackles tied flat across the back
Hackle: Brown-dun cock

WILLOW FLY (W. H. Lawrie)

Hook: 12–14
Body: Brown rabbit's fur or peacock quill dyed brown

Hackle: Rusty-dun cock with a sharpe cock in front

WINTER BROWN Plate 21

A dressing to represent the needle flies. The first listed is a North Country wet version by T. E. Pritt that has changed little in a hundred years of use.

Hook: 14
Tying silk: Orange
Body: Orange silk
Hackle: Inside of a woodcock feather

Head: One turn of peacock herl
The following is a floating pattern:
Hook: 14
Tying silk: Brown
Body: Dark brown quill
Wing: Speckled hen wing or two dark-brown grizzle hackles tied low over the back
Hackle: Dark dun cock

WITCHES

A series of flies used mainly for grayling. They can be fished wet or dry. The original pattern was Rolt's Witch mentioned in H. A. Rolt's book *Grayling Fishing in South Country Streams* of 1901. Variants have been devised, all of which I can vouch for as grayling flies. Rolt was the first to weight flies with lead strips under the body material to get his patterns down to deep-lying grayling.

ROLT'S WITCH   Plate 20

Rolt described this as a 'glorified green insect'. He recommended a size 16 when grayling are smutting and difficult to catch.

Hook: 14–16
Tag: Red floss

Body: Green peacock herl
Rib: Gold wire
Hackle: Palmered honey-dun
The **White Witch** has a white floss tag and a palmered white cock over the body.

GRAYLING WITCH   Plate 20

A variant tied by Roger Woolley.

Hook: 14–16
Tag: Red floss

Body: Green peacock herl
Rib: Silver wire
Hackle: Palmered blue-dun cock

WOBBLE-WORM   Plate 12

This is Peter Lapsley's answer to the problem of imitating the bloodworm or midge larvae. It is effective because of the combination of weighted head and marabou herl tail which on the retrieve creates the wobble motion representative of the natural midge larva. It should be fished fairly close to the bottom and retrieved in short pulls.

Hook: 12–14 sedge hook

Tying silk: To match the body colour
Tail: Six strands of red, green or buff marabou betwen 12 mm and 25 mm (½ inch to 1-inch) long
Body: Underbody of Lurex (silver for the red version, gold for the green or buff) dubbed lightly with red, buff or green seal's fur
Rib: Silver or gold wire
Head: A split shot of appropriate size crimped on to the shank and painted or varnished red, green or buff as necessary

WONDERBUG   Plate 14

A series of stillwater leaded bugs developed by Alan Pearson. In one season he caught 1,000 lb of brown and rainbow trout between 4 lb and 9 lb on the Wonderbug. It is designed to be fished deep in waters holding big fish. Normal nymph colours are used, plus a black-and-white version, all with a touch of scarlet (*see below*). Alan Pearson suggests that hook-size should vary between a longshank 6 down to a longshank 16, with correspondingly less weight being used for the smaller sizes, or none at all.

The body material should be seal's fur or a coarse-fibred substitute, and 5 per cent scarlet seal's fur should be mixed in to represent veining. The body and thorax should be of equal length. The example given below is also a good dragonfly nymph imitation.

Hook: Longshank 6
Underbody: Fine lead wire at the thorax only
Body and thorax: Dark-olive seal's fur mixed with 5 per cent scarlet seal's fur
Hackle and wing-case: Black hackle
Tail: Black cock fibres

WOODCOCK SERIES

Two different series are known by this name. One is basically used for stillwater, the other for river fishing. The first is a series of lake and sea-trout flies used occasionally for brown or rainbow trout in rivers. The combination of colours is similar to those in the Mallard, Grouse and Teal series, all of which differ in the main only in their wing materials. Most of the patterns are listed under the MALLARD SERIES (*page 102*) but the exceptions are given below. The woodcock wing used is the wing quill.

WOODCOCK AND GREEN   Plate 17

Hook: 8–14
Tail: Golden-pheasant tippets
Body: Green seal's fur
Rib: Oval silver tinsel
Wing: Woodcock wing

Hackle: Ginger or green as the body colour
The **Woodcock and Red** is as above except that it has a dark red seal's fur body and a dark red hackle.

WOODCOCK AND HARE'S EAR

This pattern is most commonly used on rivers.

Hook: 8–14
Tip: Flat gold tinsel
Tail: Two brown mallard fibres
Body: Dark hare's ear fur with an optional pinch of green wool mixed in the dubbing
Rib (optional): Fine oval gold tinsel
Wing: Woodcock wing
Hackle: Body fibres picked out
The brown back and neck feathers of the woodcock have long been used for hackling North Country wet spider patterns. The dressings given may have two turns of the hackle at the shoulder or they may be thinly palmered down the front half of the body in Stewart-style. The **Woodcock and Brown**, **Woodcock and Orange**, **Woodcock and Yellow** are the same as the pattern given below apart from the colour of the seal's fur for the body. They are probably taken for an assortment of nymphs, emerging duns or sedge pupae.

WOODCOCK AND GREEN   Plate 19

Hook: 12–14
Body: Green seal's fur tied thinly

Hackle: Woodcock back or neck feather

WOOLLY WORM   Plate 11

This nondescript stillwater fly is generally suggestive of a variety of trout foods, depending on the method in which it is fished and the colour of the materials used. It could be taken for a caddis larva or, when tied with a green body, a damselfly. Similar dressings are popular in the United States, where the black-bodied versions are effective.

Hook: Standard or longshank 8–12
Tying silk: To match the body colour
Tag: A tuft or red wool (fluorescent green is useful for the damsel nymph)
Body: Coloured chenille over an optional underbody of lead wire
Hackle: Grizzle cock palmered down the body

WORMFLY

Plate 10

An old reservoir fly created in the 1870s by William Black. It is fished deep and slow along the bottom, where it is probably taken for a sedge larva in its case. It is also a useful top dropper in a wave. The dressing can be tied on a single longshank hook or on two standard hooks in tandem.

See also DAMBUSTER and FUZZY-WUZZY.

Tail: Red wool at the tail only or behind both bodies
Body: Bronze peacock herl in two bodies
Hackle: Natural red hen or coch-y-bondhu tied in front of each body

WULFFS

To devise a fly that gains worldwide recognition and continues in its popularity for more than fifty years must surely be the aspiration of all fly-tyers. Lee Wulff, the creator of this series, succeeded in doing just that. He comments: 'They represented a revolt against the typical dry flies of the time (I fished them first in the spring of 1930). Those dry flies had only the barest wrappings of silk or quill around the hook-shank. I didn't think they offered much meat to a hungry trout and wanted something that has as much body as a good greendrake or a terrestrial, so I beefed-up the bodies and, needing a better floating material for a heavier body than the feathered tails of the time, used bucktail for durability and strength in both tails and wings. They were durable and successful. There are myriad variations in colour and materials. Calf-tail is commonly used because it is easier to tie and tends to make a bushier wing. White goathair is sometimes used for small sizes. Essentially the Wulff series is a category of flies rather than a particular pattern or patterns.'

In the medium sizes they are useful rough-water flies, where their dressing makes them highly visible. In almost all reference books the dressing has the wing slanting forward, but Lee Wulff has emphasised that the wings should not slant forward. 'That,' he says 'is a sign of a fly-tyer who is either careless or unable to make them stand vertically'. You have been warned!

GREY WULFF

Plate 22

The larger sizes are useful Mayfly copies.

Hook: 8–14
Tail: Natural bucktail fibres

Body: Grey rabbit fur or angora wool
Wing: Brown bucktail tied upright or split in a V-shape
Hackle: Blue-dun cock

ROYAL WULFF

Plate 22

Hook: 8–12
Tail: Brown bucktail
Body: Peacock herl with a band of red floss silk in the centre

Wing: Two white bucktail bunches tied upright in a V-shape
Hackle: Two chocolate-brown cock hackles

A useful Mayfly copy.

Hook: 8–12
Tail: White bucktail
Body: Creamy-white wool

Wing: Two white bucktail bunches upright or in a V-shape
Hackle: One or two badger cock hackles

YELLOW BUCKTAIL

A stillwater lure most effective when fished fast fairly close to the surface during the summer.

Hook: Longshank 8–12
Tail: Small golden-pheasant crest feather

Body: Flat silver tinsel
Rib: Oval silver tinsel or wire
Wing: Yellow bucktail
Cheeks (optional): Jungle-cock
Throat hackle: Yellow cock fibres

YELLOW EVENING DUN (*Ephemerella notata*)
See EPHEMEROPTERA

A fairly localised species of upwinged dun found on rivers only in parts of the north-west, central Wales and southern Devon. The nymph is a moss-creeping type which avoids fast water. The medium- to large-sized adults appear during the late evenings and dusk of May and June and are similar to the Yellow May Dun, which is larger and has only two tails.

The male dun has pale grey wings with yellow veins. The abdomen is pale yellow with the last three segments pale amber. The legs are yellowish and the three tails are yellowish with brown rings. The female dun has pale yellow-grey wings with yellow veins. The abdomen is yellow and the legs are pale yellow to pale grey. The three tails are yellow with brown rings.

The female spinner has transparent wings with a yellowish leading edge. The abdomen is yellow-olive with the last three segments brown-olive. The legs are olive-yellow and the three tails yellow with red-brown rings. The male spinner is of no interest.

YELLOW EVENING DUN (J. R. Harris)

Hook: 14
Tying silk: Hot-orange
Tail: Ginger cock fibres
Body: Orange rayon floss

Rib: Gold wire
Wing: Cock fibres dyed pale yellow and tied sloping forward
Hackle: Ginger cock

YELLOW EVENING SPINNER (J. R. Harris)

The spinner is also well copied by Lunn's Yellow Boy.

Hook: 14
Tying silk: Hot-orange
Tail: Ginger cock fibres

Body: Orange seal's fur
Rib: Gold wire
Wing: Honey or ginger cock hackle fibres bunched and tied spent
Hackle: None

YELLOW HAMMER

This Syd Brock lure is a useful pattern to try on hot, windless mid-summer days. It takes at all depths of water, but it is probably best at a moderate depth on a slow-sink line.

Hook: Longshank 6–10

Tying silk: Black
Tail: Yellow cock fibres
Body: Yellow wool or yellow plastic tape
Rib: Stretched black plastic tape 1.5 mm

(¹⁄₁₆-inch) wide
Wing: Four yellow cock hackles or marabou with a black marabou overwing
Throat hackle: Yellow cock

YELLOW MAY DUN (*Heptagenia sulphurea*)
See EPHEMEROPTERA

A common river species, although it has a reputation for being unpopular with trout. It is not known on stillwaters on the U.K. mainland. The nymphs cling to stones on the river-bed, but they are also found in less stony rivers clinging to vegetation. The adults, which appear in the evenings of May to July, are medium- to large-sized with yellow bodies, pale yellow wings and two tails. The female spinner is a duller colour than the dun and the male has a dark olive-brown body. Both sexes have blue-black eyes which fade to become pale blue.

YELLOW DUN (John Veniard)

A wet fly.
Hook: 14
Tail: Light yellow-dun fibres

Body: Yellow mohair or floss or tying silk
Wing: Pale starling wing
Hackle: Light yellow-dun

YELLOW MAY DUN (Taff Price)

A floating pattern.
Hook: 12–14
Tying silk: Pre-waxed yellow
Tail: Yellow cock fibres
Body: Goose herl dyed yellow

Rib: Yellow Terylene thread
Wing: Two yellow hackle points tied upright
Hackle: Cock dyed yellow

YELLOW MAY DUN (John Roberts)   Plate 27

Hook: 14
Tying silk: Yellow
Tail: Badger or yellow cock hackle fibres

Body: Olive-yellow tying thread
Hackle: Cock dyed yellow

YELLOW OWL

A Scottish loch fly recommended for mid-summer evenings.
Hook: 12–14
Tying silk: Black
Tail: Brown partridge hackle fibres

Body: Straw-coloured rayon floss
Rib: Black silk
Wing: Hen-pheasant wing
Hackle: Brown partridge hackle

YELLOW SALLY (*Isoperla grammatica*)

A medium-sized stonefly (see *page 182*) which is easily recognisable by its yellow body and yellow-green wings. The length of the adult varies from 8–13 mm. The flies appear between April and August and are widely distributed on lowland rivers with

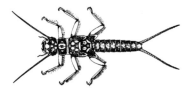

stony or sandy bottoms. They are absent from East Anglia and parts of the Midlands.

YELLOW SALLY (T. E. Pritt)

A wet pattern.

Hook: 14–16
Tying silk: Primrose

Body: Dubbed pale yellow wool
Hackle: White cock or hen dyed pale yellow

YELLOW SALLY

A southern dry fly.

Hook: 14
Tying silk: Primrose
Tail: Greenish-yellow cock fibres
Body: Drab light green dubbed wool

Hackle: Greenish-yellow cock
Another version is tied with a pale yellow dubbed wool body and a light ginger cock hackle and tail.

YORK'S FAVOURITE

A Welsh imitation of the Heather Fly.

Hook: 14
Tail: Swan fibres dyed red

Body: Black wool, floss or ostrich herl
Hackle: Coch-y-bondhu

ZERO

A bream-fry imitation from Steve Parton, and a useful pattern on waters such as Grafham, where bream occur. A roach-fry imitation can be tied by amending the tail and throat hackle fibres to crimson.

Hook: Fine-wire silvered 4
Tail: Hot-orange calf-tail

Body: Heavy white fluorescent chenille
Rib: Wide embossed flat silver tinsel
Throat hackle: White goathair
Wing: White goathair with silver baboon above and three white cock hackles on each side. The wing should be at 45 degrees to the body
Head: Black with a painted eye on each side

ZULUS

The Zulus have a worldwide reputation as killers of trout, sea-trout, grayling and chub, and it is used on rivers and stillwaters. I suspect that in this country it is more often used on stillwaters. The Black Zulu sometimes does well during a hatch of black midges. Some authorities suggest that it is taken as a beetle imitation, with the silver rib representing the air bubble common to aquatic beetles. It is popular as a general lake or loch pattern fished from a boat as a top dropper.

BLACK ZULU   Plate 18

Hook: 8–14
Tail: Red wool or ibis
Body: Black wool or seal's fur with a palmered black cock hackle
Rib: Fine flat silver tinsel

Head hackle (optional): Black cock or hen. The **Blue Zulu** is as above except that it has a bright blue hackle at the shoulder. The **Silver Zulu** is as for the black version, but has a silver tinsel body.

GOLD ZULU

Tail: Red wool or ibis
Body: Bronze peacock herl or flat gold tinsel with a palmered coch-y-bondhu hackle
Rib: Fine flat gold tinsel

ZULUKA

Plate 7

This dressing from Steve Parton is a cross between a Zulu and a matuka. Steve recommends it for 'anchor fishing' from a boat. The fluorescent version can be exceptionally good in the evening when fished by the 'sideswiping' method. A large green version tied in tandem catches trout lying deep in the difficult conditions of high summer. If the terms 'anchor fishing' and 'sideswiping' are alien to you, then I recommend Steve's book, *Boatfishing for Trout*, which tells all you need to know.

Hook: Longshank 6–8
Tying silk: Black
Tail: Red wool or neon-magenta DRF wool
Body: Black chenille
Rib: Oval gold or silver tinsel wound through the wing hackles
Wing: Six black cock hackles tied matuka-style
Hackle: Large black cock wound as a collar

Glossary

Abdomen: The larger rear part of an insect's body.

Andalusian: A type of hackle. The colour was originally jet-black, but now the name covers a range of blue-dun shades.

Anterior wings: The main forewings of an adult insect.

Back: A back referred to in a fly pattern should be tied in at the head and tail of the fly unless otherwise stated.

Bi-visible flies: Floating flies with an additional light-coloured hackle in front of the normal hackle as an aid to visibility. In theory any dry fly can be renamed with the bi-visible suffix by including an extra hackle. See BI-VISIBLES in the main text.

Blackbird: The wing feathers of both the cock and the hen bird are used as winging material.

Bucktail: See under this heading in the main text.

Cape: The skin and feathers from the head and neck of poultry or some other birds of which the hackle feathers are used for hackling flies and also for some types of wings. See under Hackles and Wings.

Cheeks: That part of a wet fly or lure at the base and on either side of the wings. Eyed jungle-cock feathers are commonly used.

Chenille: A fuzzy, fibrous material used in the making of bodies, particularly popular for lure bodies. It is available in a range of colours and fluorescent colours. There is also a thicker 'jumbo' chenille, a 'sparkle' chenille with a core of silver tinsel, 'speckle' chenille which is banded with two colours, and 'suede' chenille.

Condor: The wing herl is used in the natural colour or dyed for a body material.

Coot: The wing feather is used for winging wet and dry flies, mainly olive imitations.

Crow: The wing feather is used mainly in the winging of wet flies.

Dapping: A method of stillwater fishing practised mainly in Scotland and Ireland. A large well-hackled artificial fly is cast out or allowed to be blown out with the wind and lowered on to the surface. Longish rods with short floss lines are favoured so that only the fly touches the water. In addition to specialist patterns, densely hackled Crane-flies, Mayflies, the Pennell series and Palmers are also suitable.

Deerhair: Deer body-hair fibres are stiff and hollow and can be spun on to the hook-shank as a body or head material to make an extremely buoyant floating pattern. The most common use for the material is in the Muddler head. Deerhair fibres are laid on the shank where the head is to be formed. Strong thread is wrapped round and, as this is done, the fibres are moved completely to surround the shank. The thread is pulled tight and the fibres stand erect. This is repeated until sufficient hair is tied in. The hair is then trimmed to the cone-, dome- or ball-shape required. Some tyers prefer to leave a trailing hackle of some of the longer fibres. Whole bodies can be constructed by using some of the small hairs and trimming them much narrower. Such bodies are virtually unsinkable.

Detached body: Separate bodies tied on to the shank and not around the shank in the usual manner. They can be built up around a stiff piece of nylon monofilament, bristle, cork, feather quill, or be a specially-made plastic body. Detached bodies are often used in crane-fly and Mayfly artificials. See also under Hooks.

Dry fly: An artificial fly constructed so that it floats on the water surface. It represents the adult stage of the insect's life or a terrestrial.

DRF: Depth-ray-fire, see under Fluorescence.

Dubbing: The technique of twisting fur or wool fibres round the tying silk and winding it around the shank to build up a body. The fibres may be picked out with a dubbing needle to represent the legs or wings of the natural.

Duck: Whole wing quills are used for winging and are easily dyed.

Dun: The first winged state, known as the sub-imago, of the upwinged flies, the *Ephemeropterans*. Also used to describe a duller colour shade, e.g. blue-dun.

Ethafoam: A synthetic material used to make buoyant lures and dry flies. It is used in the Suspender patterns of midges and nymphs. Similar to Plastazote.

'Flexi-tail' lures: Also known as Waggy Lures, these are standard patterns (in a few instances, nymphs) that incorporate a flexible plastic tail tied in at the rear of the body. Many lures and nymphs can be adapted. The tails come in a variety of colours, some transparent, others fluorescent.

Floss: A natural or synthetic body material, also available in fluorescent colours.

Flybody fur: A synthetic seal's fur substitute.

Fluorescence: Fluorescent materials reflect their own colour under conditions of ultra-violet light, i.e. in the hours of daylight. Trout flies incorporating fluorescing materials sometimes prove especially attractive to trout. Even when fished fairly deep, patterns tied with fluorescing materials will reflect ultra-violet light and be more visible than normal materials. Thomas Clegg's book, *The Truth about Fluorescents*, is worth reading. Two terms applied to these materials are DRF and DFM which stand for depth-ray-fire and daylight-fluorescent material respectively. These materials can be mixed with fur, chenille, wool, herls, hackle-fibres for wings, and horsehair. Fluorescent hackles, seal's fur, chenille, wool, floss and marabou herls are available. One of the secrets of using these materials in imitating natural flies is not to over-use them but to use just sufficient to add interest to the pattern and not deter fish. Various dressings are given in the text that incorporate fluorescent materials.

French partridge: The breast-feathers are used for Mayfly hackles.

Fur: Many natural animal furs are used for the bodies of flies. Exotic and domestic animals and household pets are all used in the search for a particular colour shade. Seal's fur is probably the most commonly used material. It is bright and shiny and can be dyed any colour.

Gallina: Another name for guinea-fowl. See under this heading.

Gallows tool: An ingenious device clipped over the vice to hold the hackle-stalk when tying-in Parachute hackles.

Golden pheasant: The crest (head) feathers and the tippets (neck) are used mainly for the tails of lake trout flies.

Goose: The herls from the shoulder feathers are used as body materials and are easily dyed. The wing cossette feather is used for winging wet flies.

Grouse: The neck and under-covert feathers are used for hackling wet flies and are sometimes used on dry patterns. The tail feathers are used for winging e.g. the grouse series. The covert-wing feather is also used for winging.

Guinea-fowl: Also called gallina. The plain blue neck feathers have fibres which have small hairs on them. The fibres make excellent tails or legs of nymphs.

H&F: An abbreviation for hair-and-fur. This indicates that the fly has been tied with these materials only, omitting any feather materials.

Hackle: This has two meanings in fly-dressing terms. The first is that it describes that part of the artificial fly that represents the legs of the natural or sometimes the wings, or is a false, beard or throat hackle on a lure. This is usually a feather, or feather-fibres or animal hair in the case of an H&F pattern. The second meaning is the name given to the neck or cape feathers of poultry or game or any bird's neck feather used in fly-tying. The part of the artificial fly known as the hackle comes under these headings.

COLLAR HACKLE: A 360-degree hackle, often with a slight rearward tilt, and usually described as a collar on lures only to differentiate it from a beard or throat hackle.

Dry-fly hackle: Usually the hackle is tied to represent the legs of the floating insect. A cock hackle is preferred as it has the springiness to support the floating artificial. A hackle with points which are too stiff will penetrate the surface film; this is to be avoided, as the natural's legs rest on the surface. The hackle is normally wound in turns around the shank behind the eye. See also Parachute Fly. Hackles are occasionally tied-in reversed, i.e. at the bend end of the shank. If a springy hackle of the correct size is not available, two turns of a larger hackle can be used, trimmed to about 6 mm (¼-inch). The main, non-springy hackle can be tied-in in front. This adds the necessary support.

FALSE, BEARD OR THROAT HACKLE: Tied on wet flies and lures on the underside of the body only, and rear-facing. They may be poultry hackles, hackle fibres, hair or other feather-fibres.

FORE-AND-AFT HACKLES: A means of hackling a dry fly. See FORE-AND-AFT in the main text.

NYMPH HACKLES: These should be tied sparsely to represent the legs of the natural, and tied on the underside of the body. They are occasionally tied as a sparsely-wound full hackle. If there is a wing-case, the fibres are often tied in over the upper hackles, leaving only those below the body.

SADDLE HACKLES: The longish shiny feathers taken from the side of a bird.

STEWART-STYLE HACKLES: A style named after W. C. Stewart, who palmered the front half of the body of a wet fly to give it more life, the impression of an emerging dun.

WET-FLY HACKLE: A hen hackle is preferred on a spider-type wet fly because of its softness, which gives a look of mobility or lifelikeness. On a winged wet fly the upper hackle fibres are bunched below the body and are covered by the tying-in of the wing, or are tied as a throat hackle.

POULTRY HACKLE COLOURS (NATURAL):
    Badger: Black centre with a cream or white outer.
    Black: Black.
    Blue-dun: Blue-grey or smoky-grey.
    Brassy-dun: Similar to the blue-dun, but with a golden tinge.
    Buff: Buff.
    Cree: Alternate bars of black and red.
    Coch-y-bondhu: Black centre with a red outer and tips.
    Dun: Dingy-brown colour.
    Furnace: Black centre with a reddish outer.
    Greenwell: Black centre with a ginger outer.
    Ginger: Ginger.
    Grizzle: Plymouth Rock, alternate black and white bars.
    Honey-dun: Dun-coloured with honey-coloured tips.
    Honey blue-dun: A blue-dun centre with honey-coloured tips.
    Honey: Pale gingery buff.
    Iron blue dun: Ink-blue or dark slate-grey.
    Plymouth Rock: See grizzle.
    Red Game: Old English game.
    Rhode Island Red: Red-brown.
    Rusty-dun or rusty blue-dun: Dun or blue-dun centres with deep honey tips.
    White: White.

Good-quality hackles are both scarce and they are expensive. Dyed capes are much cheaper and probably quite as good for all but the most exacting of fly-dressers. Barred hackles can be made by using a stubby felt-pen. Other markings can be achieved in the same way with moderate success.

Hair: Animal hair is used as wing material in many lures in addition to being used for bodies and Muddler heads. The main animal hairs used for the winging of bucktail lures are: squirrel, stoat, goat, bucktail (deer), calf, badger, moose, marten, mink, monkey, fox. Horsehair is used as a body material. Among the more unusual body-hair used was a seventeenth-century dressing using abortive colt and calf hair.

Head: Lures of all types should be finished off with a head built up of tying silk and varnished black or an appropriate colour. A painted eye can be added. A small head of varnished tying silk makes a winged wet fly look neater.

Heron: The grey breast-feather and wing quill herls are used for herl bodies.

Hooks: A variety of hook designs exhibit differing lengths of shank, shapes of bend, sizes of gape and styles of eyes. Each has a role to play. Whatever hook is chosen for a particular pattern of fly, be sure that the hook is strong (you can test it by placing it in the tying vice and gently trying to bend the shank), that the point is sharp, that the metal of the bend or shank has no flaws, and that the eye is fully closed. Any failure of the hook will represent time wasted and fish lost, so discard any hook that is suspect.

The two popular designs in the eye of the hook are up-eyed and down-eyed. Few flies are tied on ball-eyed hooks, i.e. hooks in which the eye is horizontal. Most dry flies are tied on up-eyed hooks. This is assumed in the text, and exceptions are detailed. Most wet flies, nymphs, pupae, buzzers and lures are tied on down-eyed hooks. Again, exceptions are mentioned in the dressings.

The weight of a hook is important. Lightness is a desirable feature for a dry-fly pattern, while a wider shank or heavier metal is preferred for wet flies and lures. Strength is an important attribute for the stillwater fly, which hopefully will have to cope with much larger fish than are generally caught on rivers. For this reason, some of the lighter, fine-wire hooks are unsuitable for big fish.

Shanks vary in length. The shortest hooks are half the standard length and the longest are three times the standard length. Most common dry and wet flies imitating *ephemeropteran* duns, spinners and nymphs and many other flies are tied on standard-length hooks. Imitations of larger natural insects and lures are tied on longer-shanked hooks. Shorter-than-normal lengths are less commonly used, but they are sometimes employed in the tying of spider patterns and small dry flies.

In addition to a variety of hooks with different bend shapes, other specialist hooks are worthy of consideration.

Barbless hook: The barb has been under attack for the possible damage it does to fish in catch-and-release fisheries. Whether more fish are lost as a result of using barbless hooks is a matter of debate. Many lure-type hooks are not available in barbless form, but the barb can be flattened with a pair of pliers.

Detached-body hook: See under Yorkshire Flybody hook.

Double hook: A hook with two bends and points available in lure sizes or in tiny wet-fly sizes. An aid to hooking and giving extra weight to a pattern that has to be fished deep.

Flat-bodied nymph hook: This has a wide shank on which a nymph body can be tied. The extra weight improves the sinking rate.

Grub-shrimp, Caddis or Yorkshire Sedge hook: A wide-gape hook with a short shank and a long bend. The body of a sedge-pupa or other grub pattern can be tied-in around the bend, helping to represent the shape of the natural.

Keel hook: Turn a long-shanked hook upside down and imagine that two-thirds along the shank it is bent up at a steep angle and then straightened out again level with the hook-point. This is the design of the keel hook, which fishes with the point uppermost. It does not snag the bottom. Hairwinged lures hide the point well. Dry flies can be tied on this type of hook.

Midge hook: A tiny hook, down to size 28, for floating midge and caenis patterns. It has a relatively wide gape and short body of lightweight wire. Specially fine tying thread is needed to tie patterns on them.

Parachute-fly hook: A small vertical shank around which the hackle can be tied is attached at right angles to the top of the shank.

Swedish/Danish Dry Fly hook: This has a special kink in the shank behind the eye which provides a base for a Parachute hackle.

Yorkshire Flybody hook: A novel design of dry-fly hook that has a small detached body extending beyond the bend. A disadvantage is the extra weight of the detached body.

Horsehair: Used as a body material or for ribbing.

Horns: The forward-projecting antennae of some species.

Ibis: Red ibis feathers are used for tail fibres. Substitutes are now used, i.e. feathers dyed red.

Jay: The blue-barred lesser wing coverts are used for throat hackles and sometimes in tails. The dark grey quills are used for winging and the brown elbow wing feather is used for hackling wet flies.

Jungle cock: The hackles of the jungle cock are unique and highly prized by the fly-dresser for their cream eyes which, incorporated as cheeks or shoulders on many flies and bucktail and streamer lures, seem to provide an added attraction. Because the species is protected in its home country, India, substitutes have been made. Eyes can be painted on black hackles or specially prepared substitutes can be bought. These are probably as good as the real thing so far as the trout is concerned. The whole jungle-cock feather is used for the wings of some streamer flies.

Landrail: The wings are used as a winging material. Starling is a suitable substitute.

Lapwing: The brown rump feather is used for hackling.

Legs: The legs of an adult fly are represented by the hackle. Legs on nymph patterns are copied with a short hackle or hackle fibres.

Lurex: A type of plastic material which in its metallic colours looks like tinsel. It is not as strong as tinsel and should be ribbed for extra durability. A wide variety of colours is available.

Latex dental dam: The use of this material in fly-tying was developed in the U.S.A., largely by Raleigh Boaze, jr. Almost any nymph body can be constructed from it if dyed or marked the appropriate colour. The material is translucent and highly durable, and excellent segmentation is possible. Various thicknesses are available, the thicker ones being the most suitable.

Mallard: The grey breast and flank feathers are used for wings and hackles. The following feathers are also used for winging: white-tipped blue wing quill, grey wing quill, brown shoulder feather and white underwing coverts. The brown shoulder feathers are used in the mallard series.

Mandarin duck: Similar to the wood-duck. The brown flank feathers are used for wings and the white breast feather is used for fan-wings.

Marabou: Turkey fibres which have been extensively employed in fly-dressing only in recent years. Their value as wings and tails in lures and nymphs is because the long fluffy fibres, which can be dyed any colour, are extremely lifelike and give the artificials the appearance of mobility when wet. Fluorescent colours are available.

Micro-web: A translucent sheeting which can be cut to form natural-looking wings.

Mohair: Similar to angora wool. Used as a body material.

Mylar: A metallic-looking plastic tinsel available in tube or sheet form. The sheet can be cut to form strips for a flashy body material, or the tube with the centre core removed can be pushed over a hook-shank to make a complete body. The tubing gives an excellent scale-effect and is useful in fry-imitations.

Ostrich: Wing and tail herls are used as body materials.

Palmer: A style of dressing a fly with a hackle wound along the body from shoulder to tail. Such flies may be known as Palmers. It is the oldest style of hackling a fly.

Parachute fly: A fly with a hackle wound horizontally rather than vertically round the shank. If a winged pattern is needed, the hook is turned upside down and the hackle wound on the underside. A couple of turns of the hackle are all that are necessary as all the fibres touch the water. Special Parachute hooks are available with a vertical stem on the shank around which the hackle can be wound, but most tyers wrap the hackle around its own hackle stalk, which is tied to stick up vertically.

Partridge: The brown back and grey breast feathers are used for hackling wet flies. The wing and tail feather are used for winging.

Peacock: The eyed tail feather is used for quill and herl bodies. The bronze herl comes from the stem of the eye tail; the green herl comes from the sword feathers at the base of the tail. The blue neck feathers are occasionally used.

Pheasant: The centre-tail feather herls of the cock bird are used for the bodies and tails of nymphs and dry flies; and the copper neck feathers are occasionally used for hackles. The secondary wing feathers of the hen are used for winging. The centre-tail feathers are similarly used.

Plastazote: A polythene foam used to make the bodies of dry flies or buoyant wet flies and lures. Similar to Ethafoam.

Polypropylene: A synthetic material, the fibres of which are suitable for dubbing and are sometimes used for winging. It is excellent for floating flies as it has a specific gravity of less than 1. It is available in a range of colours.

Poultry: The neck hackles of hen birds are used for hackling. They are used mainly in wet flies, as these need a soft, mobile feather. The saddle hackles are used for the wings of streamer lures. The cock bird's neck hackles are used for hackling dry flies and are often used for the tails of artificial flies. The lesser coverts and wing quills are used for wings.

PVC: Transparent colourless or semi-transparent coloured PVC used as a body material. Because it is transparent, an overbody of PVC helps give the impression of translucency.

Raffene: A manufactured substitute for raffia and available in many colours.

Raffia: A natural body material which has largely been superseded by Raffene.

Rib: Turns of tying silk, wire, tinsel, herl or other materials to represent the natural segmentation of a natural insect or to add strength to the body.

Rook: The wings, similar to, but smaller than, the crow's are used for winging.

Seal's fur: Fur from a young seal. It is creamy-coloured and easily dyed. The fibres are bright and shiny even when wet and make excellent dubbed bodies for dry flies, wet flies, nymphs and lures.

Snipe: The back feathers are used for hackling flies such as the Snipe and Purple. The wing feathers are used in winging.

Sparkle bodies: Bodies of lures covered in silver or gold glitter of the type used for Christmas decorations. The body wool is soaked in varnish and rolled in the glitter.

Sparkle yarn: Also known as Antron. It is a synthetic translucent yarn to which air-bubbles cling when it is wet. It is an excellent body material for imitations of those insects that carry air bubbles. It is suitable for hatching nymph or pupa patterns.

Spinner: The adult stage (imago) of the *ephemeropterans.*

Starling: The wing quills are popular for winging. The back and breast feathers are used for hackling.

Streamer: See under this heading in the list of flies. Long saddle hackles are normally used for the wings of streamer lures.

Summer duck: Also known as wood-duck. Similar to the mandarin duck. See under the latter heading for details.

Swan: The shoulder feather herl is used as a body material. It dyes well. Goose or turkey are suitable substitutes.

Tag: A short tail of feather-fibres, wool or floss.

Tail: Sometimes called whisk. Usually feather-fibres to imitate the tails of a natural insect. Lures and attractor-type flies also have tails, but these are only to enhance the attraction of the pattern.

Tandem hooks: Almost any lure, and many attractor-type lake flies, can be tied in tandem, either on a single longshank hook on which are tied two flies (the front fly usually omitting any tail appendages), or on two hooks tied in tandem and linked by strong nylon monofilament whipped and glued on to each shank. Various hook combinations can be used. Sometimes the front hook is two sizes larger than the rear. In some three-hook combinations, the middle hook faces upwards. On other two-hook lures, the rear hook may be a double or treble.

Teal: The barred breast and flank feathers are used for winging lake flies and sometimes for the fan-wings of dry flies. The green and the grey wing quills are also used for wings.

Thorax: The part of the insect's body between the abdomen and neck to which the legs and wings are attached.

Tinsel: A thin metallic material used for ribbing or making complete bodies. Gold, silver or copper colours are available. Flat, oval, round or embossed tinsels are all used in various widths.

Tip: Sometimes referred to as a tag, which is misleading, as a tag is detached from the shank rather than wrapped round. The tip is usually tinsel, silk or floss in a few turns at the rear of the body.

Tippet: See golden pheasant.

Topping: The long crest feather of a golden pheasant.

Turkey: The cinnamon tail herls are used for bodies. The white-tip rump feather is used for winging and the mottled-brown tail feather is similarly used. See also Marabou.

Twist: A ribbing material, usually a tinsel thread or strands of round tinsel twisted together.

Tying silk: The binding agent by which all the other materials are attached to the hook (although glue or varnish may assist). Real silk was originally used and still is to some extent, but nylon and rayon are more commonly used. Gossamer silk is suitable for all but the large lures, when stronger Naples silk is better. Floss and other multi-strand or heavier gauge threads are also used. Marabou floss has the advantage of splitting into separate strands. Waxing the silk is an aid to binding the materials and holds dubbed fur better than unwaxed silk. If the colour of the tying silk is not specified in a dressing, choose one that matches the colour of the dubbing. If there is no dubbing, choose one to match the hackle colour.

Underbody: That part of the body which is wound on first, over the tying silk, before being covered by another material. The underbody is frequently used to give the fly extra weight.

Underwing: A wing, usually of a whole hackle, hackle-tip or fibres, that is tied in under the body.

Varnish: Applied to the whip-finish to secure the tying silk. Clear varnish is best used on dry flies, but coloured varnish is used for lures and wet flies. The backs of some fly bodies are occasionally coated with clear varnish.

Waterhen: Also known as moorhen. The wings are used for wings and hackles.

Wax: Solid or liquid wax is rubbed on the tying silk to help bind the materials firmly.

Wet fly: An artificial fly tied to fish below the surface.

Whip-finish: All flies should be finished with this method of sealing the tying silk. Two or three turns of tying silk are wrapped round the end of the silk and the shank before the end is passed through and pulled tight.

Whisks: See under Tail.

Wings: The style and set of the wings varies with the type of fly. The styles most commonly tied are:

Advance wing: A single or split-wing tied forward-slanting over the eye of the hook. Floating patterns only.

Bunch wing: A wing made from a bunch of feather-fibres and tied in the manner required.

Double split-wing: Two sets of wings made by taking two sections from a pair of matched wing quills and tying them with the tips pointing outwards. The second set of wings is less than half the size of the main forewings.

Down wing: Tied low over the back, usually to imitate sedges and stoneflies.

Fan-wing: Two small breast feathers tied curving outwards. Popular on Mayfly patterns.

Hackle-fibre wing: The same as a bunch wing.

Hackle-point wing: The tips of cock hackles used as the wings of adult flies.

Hairwing: Natural or dyed animal hair is used for wings on lures, dry and wet flies. Lures with hair wings are known as bucktails.

Herl wing: The herl from some feathers occasionally used for winging. Peacock herl is the commonest.

Loopwing: A dry-fly style of winging devised by Andre Puyans in the early 1970s. Six long mallard shoulder or flank fibres are tied in on the bare shank at the wing position. The ends are tied in as the tail. The wing fibres are looped over in a wing-shape to the appropriate size, divided in two with a dubbing needle, and tied in with figure-of-eight turns of the tying silk. The body is tied-in and the hackle wound on either side of the wing.

Marabou wing: A number of lures have a spray of a marabou plume as a wing. It gives a lot of mobility in the water.

Polywing: Transparent or coloured polythene sheet cut to a wing-shape and tied in the manner required.

Rolled wing: Feather-fibres rolled in two or three and are used on sedge and stonefly imitations. The wing is made from a single feather.

Streamer wing: Whole saddle hackles extending beyond the hook-bend. See streamers in the main text.

Spent wing: Tied horizontally at right-angles to the body to imitate the spent spinner.

Shaving-brush wing: A bunch of hair or feather-fibres tied forward over the eye in a single or split bunch.

Split-wing: Any wing which is divided without the tips meeting.

Upright wing: Any style of wing that stands at 90 degrees to the shank.

Wet-fly wing: A wing sloping back over the body, not quite flat but at a slight angle.

Whole-feather wing: See streamers.

Wing-cutter: The tool with which wing-shaped hackles are cut out for use as hackle wings. Different sizes of cutter are available.

Wing-cases: The humps on the back of the thorax of the mature nymph from which the wings of the adults emerge. Beetle and other terrestrials also have wing-cases, and on these imitations the wing-case is represented by feather-fibres or other material tied in as a back over the length of the body. Wing-cases on nymph patterns are usually feather-fibres tied-in over the thorax only unless otherwise stated. The wing-cases on nymph patterns cover the top of the hackle, so that this is on the underside only.

Wire: Usually fine gold- or silver-coloured wire for ribbing small flies.

Woodcock: The breast, back and neck feathers are used for hackling and the lesser covert wing feathers are used for winging the Woodcock series.

Wood-duck: The feathers are similar to those of the mandarin duck. The wood-duck is also known as the summer duck.

Wool: Dubbed or wound wool is the oldest fly-body material known, but it has been improved upon by furs. Nylon-based wools, such as baby wool, are popular in lure dressings and are available in fluorescent colours.

Bibliography

Bainbridge, W. G., *The Fly-Fisher's Guide of Aquatic Flies*, 1936
Bridgett, R. C., *Dry Fly Fishing*, 1922
Bridgett, R. C., *Loch Fishing*, 1925
Bucknall, G., *Fly Fishing Tactics on Stillwater*, 1966
Burrard, Sir G., *Fly-tying: Principles and Practice*, 1940
Chinery, M., *Insects of Britain and Northern Europe*, 1972
Clarke, B., *The Pursuit of Stillwater Trout*, 1975
Clegg, J., *Pond and Stream Life*, 1963
Clegg, T., *The Truth about Fluorescents*, 1967
Colyer and Hammond, *Flies of the British Isles*, 1951
Collyer, D., *Fly Dressing*, 1975
Collyer, D., *Fly Dressing II*
Dunne, J. W., *Sunshine and the Dry Fly*, 1924
Dyson, C., *Bob Church Reservoir Trout Fishing*, 1977
Edmonds and Lee, *Brook and River Trouting*, 1916
Fogg, R. W. S., *The Art of the Wet Fly*, 1979
Francis, F., *A Book on Angling*, 1897
Goddard, J., *Trout Fly Recognition*, 1966
Goddard, J., *Stillwater Trout Flies*, 1969
Goddard, J., *Superflies of Stillwater*, 1977
Goddard, J., *Stillwater Flies; How and When to fish them*, 1982
Goddard, J. and Clarke B., *The Trout and the Fly*, 1980
Halford, F. M., *Floating Flies and How to Dress them*, 1886
Halford, F. M., *Dry-Fly Fishing in Theory and Practice*, 1889
Harris, J. R., *An Angler's Entomology*, 1952
Ivens, T. C., *Still Water Fly-fishing*, 1952
Jacques, D., *Fisherman's Fly and other studies*, 1965
Jacques, D., *The Development of Modern Stillwater Fishing*, 1974
Jorgensen, P., *Modern Trout Flies*, 1979
Kite, O., *Nymph Fishing in Practice*, 1963
Lake, R., *The Grayling*, 1946
Lane, Colonel J., *Lake and Loch Fishing*, 1955
Lapsley, P., *The Bankside Book of Reservoir Trout Flies*, 1978
Lawrie, W. H., *Border River Angling*, 1943
Lawrie, W. H., *The Book of the Rough Stream Nymph*, 1947
Lawrie, W. H., *Scottish Trout Flies*, 1966
Lawrie, W. H., *English and Welsh Trout Flies*, 1967
Lawrie, W. H., *A Reference Book of English Trout Flies*, 1967
Mosely M. E. *Dry-Fly Fisherman's Entomology*, 1921
Overfield D., *Famous Flies and their Originators*, 1972
Overfield, D., *50 Favourite Nymphs*, 1978
Overfield, D., *50 Favourite Dry Flies*
Parton, S., *Boat Fishing for Trout*, 1983
Price, S. D., *Lures for Game, Coarse and Sea Fishing* 1972
Price, S. D., *Rough Stream Trout Flies*, 1976
Price, S. D., *Stillwater Flies I, II, III*
Platts, W. Carter, *Grayling Fishing*, 1939
Pritt, T. E., *Yorkshire Trout Flies*, 1885

Quigley, M., *Invertebrates of Streams and Rivers*, 1977
Rice, F. A., *Fly-Tying Illustrated for Nymphs and Lures*, 1976
Rice, F. A., *Fly-Tying Illustrated – Wet and Dry Patterns*, 1981
Righyni, R., *Grayling*, 1968
Roberts, J., *The Grayling Angler*, 1982
Robson, K., *Robson's Guide*, 1985
Rolt, H. A., *Grayling Fishing in South Country Streams*, 1901
Ronalds, A., *The Fly-Fisher's Entomology*, 1836
Sawyer, F., *Nymphs and the Trout*, 1958
Skues, G. E. M., *Nymph Fishing for Chalk Stream Trout*, 1939
Stewart, T., *200 Popular Flies*, 1979
Stewart, W. C., *The Practical Angler*, 1857
Veniard, J., *Fly Dresser's Guide*, 1979
Veniard, J., *Further Guide to Fly Dressing*, 1964
Veniard, J., *Reservoir and Lake Flies*, 1974
Veniard, J., *Fly Dressing Materials*, 1977
Wakeford, J., *Flytying Techniques*, 1980
Walker, C. F., *The Art of Chalk Stream Fishing*, 1968
Walker, C. F., *Lake Flies and their Imitation*, 1969
Walker, R., *Fly Dressing Innovations*, 1974
Walker, R., *Modern Fly Dressings*, 1980
West, L., *The Natural Trout Fly and Its Imitation*, 1912
Williams, A. Courtney, *Dictionary of Trout Flies*, 1949, 1973
Woolley, R., *Modern Trout Fly Dressing*, 1932

Scientific publications published by the Freshwater Biological Association:

Elliott and Humpesch, *A Key to the Adults of the British Ephemeroptera*, 1983
Hynes, H. B. N., *A Key to the Adults and Nymphs of the British Stoneflies*, 1977
Macan, T. T., *A Key to the Nymphs of the British Ephemeroptera*, 1979
Macan, T. T., *A Key to the Adults of the British Tricoptera*, 1973

Indexes

NATURAL AND ARTIFICIAL FLIES

Note: numbers in bold denote plates

NAMES OF PEOPLE MENTIONED IN THE TEXT